Cassandra: The Definitive Guide

Cassandra: The Definitive Guide

Eben Hewitt

O'REILLY®

Beijing · Cambridge · Farnham · Köln · Sebastopol · Tokyo

Cassandra: The Definitive Guide

by Eben Hewitt

Published by O'Reilly Media, Inc., 1005 Gravenstein Highway North, Sebastopol, CA 95472.

O'Reilly books may be purchased for educational, business, or sales promotional use. Online editions are also available for most titles (*http://my.safaribooksonline.com*). For more information, contact our corporate/institutional sales department: (800) 998-9938 or *corporate@oreilly.com*.

Editor: Mike Loukides
Production Editor: Holly Bauer
Copyeditor: Genevieve d'Entremont
Proofreader: Emily Quill

Indexer: Ellen Troutman Zaig
Cover Designer: Karen Montgomery
Interior Designer: David Futato
Illustrator: Robert Romano

Printing History:

November 2010: First Edition.

This book uses RepKover™, a durable and flexible lay-flat binding.

ISBN: 978-1-449-39041-9

[M]

1289489010

*This book is dedicated to my sweetheart,
Alison Brown. I can hear the sound of violins,
long before it begins.*

Table of Contents

Foreword

Cassandra was open-sourced by Facebook in July 2008. This original version of Cassandra was written primarily by an ex-employee from Amazon and one from Microsoft. It was strongly influenced by Dynamo, Amazon's pioneering distributed key/value database. Cassandra implements a Dynamo-style replication model with no single point of failure, but adds a more powerful "column family" data model.

I became involved in December of that year, when Rackspace asked me to build them a scalable database. This was good timing, because all of today's important open source scalable databases were available for evaluation. Despite initially having only a single major use case, Cassandra's underlying architecture was the strongest, and I directed my efforts toward improving the code and building a community.

Cassandra was accepted into the Apache Incubator, and by the time it graduated in March 2010, it had become a true open source success story, with committers from Rackspace, Digg, Twitter, and other companies that wouldn't have written their own database from scratch, but together built something important.

Today's Cassandra is much more than the early system that powered (and still powers) Facebook's inbox search; it has become "the hands down winner for transaction processing performance," to quote Tony Bain, with a deserved reputation for reliability and performance at scale.

As Cassandra matured and began attracting more mainstream users, it became clear that there was a need for commercial support; thus, Matt Pfeil and I cofounded Riptano in April 2010. Helping drive Cassandra adoption has been very rewarding, especially seeing the uses that don't get discussed in public.

Another need has been a book like this one. Like many open source projects, Cassandra's documentation has historically been weak. And even when the documentation ultimately improves, a book-length treatment like this will remain useful.

Thanks to Eben for tackling the difficult task of distilling the art and science of developing against and deploying Cassandra. You, the reader, have the opportunity to learn these new concepts in an organized fashion.

—Jonathan Ellis
Project Chair, Apache Cassandra, and Cofounder, Riptano

Preface

Why Apache Cassandra?

Apache Cassandra is a free, open source, distributed data storage system that differs sharply from relational database management systems.

Cassandra first started as an incubation project at Apache in January of 2009. Shortly thereafter, the committers, led by Apache Cassandra Project Chair Jonathan Ellis, released version 0.3 of Cassandra, and have steadily made minor releases since that time. Though as of this writing it has not yet reached a 1.0 release, Cassandra is being used in production by some of the biggest properties on the Web, including Facebook, Twitter, Cisco, Rackspace, Digg, Cloudkick, Reddit, and more.

Cassandra has become so popular because of its outstanding technical features. It is durable, seamlessly scalable, and tuneably consistent. It performs blazingly fast writes, can store hundreds of terabytes of data, and is decentralized and symmetrical so there's no single point of failure. It is highly available and offers a schema-free data model.

Is This Book for You?

This book is intended for a variety of audiences. It should be useful to you if you are:

- A developer working with large-scale, high-volume websites, such as Web 2.0 social applications
- An application architect or data architect who needs to understand the available options for high-performance, decentralized, elastic data stores
- A database administrator or database developer currently working with standard relational database systems who needs to understand how to implement a fault-tolerant, eventually consistent data store

- A manager who wants to understand the advantages (and disadvantages) of Cassandra and related columnar databases to help make decisions about technology strategy
- A student, analyst, or researcher who is designing a project related to Cassandra or other non-relational data store options

This book is a technical guide. In many ways, Cassandra represents a new way of thinking about data. Many developers who gained their professional chops in the last 15–20 years have become well-versed in thinking about data in purely relational or object-oriented terms. Cassandra's data model is very different and can be difficult to wrap your mind around at first, especially for those of us with entrenched ideas about what a database is (and should be).

Using Cassandra does not mean that you have to be a Java developer. However, Cassandra is written in Java, so if you're going to dive into the source code, a solid understanding of Java is crucial. Although it's not strictly necessary to know Java, it can help you to better understand exceptions, how to build the source code, and how to use some of the popular clients. Many of the examples in this book are in Java. But because of the interface used to access Cassandra, you can use Cassandra from a wide variety of languages, including C#, Scala, Python, and Ruby.

Finally, it is assumed that you have a good understanding of how the Web works, can use an integrated development environment (IDE), and are somewhat familiar with the typical concerns of data-driven applications. You might be a well-seasoned developer or administrator but still, on occasion, encounter tools used in the Cassandra world that you're not familiar with. For example, Apache Ivy is used to build Cassandra, and a popular client (Hector) is available via Git. In cases where I speculate that you'll need to do a little setup of your own in order to work with the examples, I try to support that.

What's in This Book?

This book is designed with the chapters acting, to a reasonable extent, as standalone guides. This is important for a book on Cassandra, which has a variety of audiences and is changing rapidly. To borrow from the software world, I wanted the book to be "modular"—sort of. If you're new to Cassandra, it makes sense to read the book in order; if you've passed the introductory stages, you will still find value in later chapters, which you can read as standalone guides.

Here is how the book is organized:

Chapter 1, Introducing Cassandra
    This chapter introduces Cassandra and discusses what's exciting and different about it, who is using it, and what its advantages are.

Chapter 2, Installing Cassandra
    This chapter walks you through installing Cassandra on a variety of platforms.

Chapter 3, The Cassandra Data Model

Here we look at Cassandra's data model to understand what columns, super columns, and rows are. Special care is taken to bridge the gap between the relational database world and Cassandra's world.

Chapter 4, Sample Application

This chapter presents a complete working application that translates from a relational model in a well-understood domain to Cassandra's data model.

Chapter 5, The Cassandra Architecture

This chapter helps you understand what happens during read and write operations and how the database accomplishes some of its notable aspects, such as durability and high availability. We go under the hood to understand some of the more complex inner workings, such as the gossip protocol, hinted handoffs, read repairs, Merkle trees, and more.

Chapter 6, Configuring Cassandra

This chapter shows you how to specify partitioners, replica placement strategies, and snitches. We set up a cluster and see the implications of different configuration choices.

Chapter 7, Reading and Writing Data

This is the moment we've been waiting for. We present an overview of what's different about Cassandra's model for querying and updating data, and then get to work using the API.

Chapter 8, Clients

There are a variety of clients that third-party developers have created for many different languages, including Java, C#, Ruby, and Python, in order to abstract Cassandra's lower-level API. We help you understand this landscape so you can choose one that's right for you.

Chapter 9, Monitoring

Once your cluster is up and running, you'll want to monitor its usage, memory patterns, and thread patterns, and understand its general activity. Cassandra has a rich Java Management Extensions (JMX) interface baked in, which we put to use to monitor all of these and more.

Chapter 10, Maintenance

The ongoing maintenance of a Cassandra cluster is made somewhat easier by some tools that ship with the server. We see how to decommission a node, load-balance the cluster, get statistics, and perform other routine operational tasks.

Chapter 11, Performance Tuning

One of Cassandra's most notable features is its speed—it's very fast. But there are a number of things, including memory settings, data storage, hardware choices, caching, and buffer sizes, that you can tune to squeeze out even more performance.

Chapter 12, Integrating Hadoop

In this chapter, written by Jeremy Hanna, we put Cassandra in a larger context and see how to integrate it with the popular implementation of Google's Map/Reduce algorithm, Hadoop.

Appendix

Many new databases have cropped up in response to the need to scale at Big Data levels, or to take advantage of a "schema-free" model, or to support more recent initiatives such as the Semantic Web. Here we contextualize Cassandra against a variety of the more popular nonrelational databases, examining document-oriented databases, distributed hashtables, and graph databases, to better understand Cassandra's offerings.

Glossary

It can be difficult to understand something that's really new, and Cassandra has many terms that might be unfamiliar to developers or DBAs coming from the relational application development world, so I've included this glossary to make it easier to read the rest of the book. If you're stuck on a certain concept, you can flip to the glossary to help clarify things such as Merkle trees, vector clocks, hinted handoffs, read repairs, and other exotic terms.

 This book is developed against Cassandra 0.6 and 0.7. The project team is working hard on Cassandra, and new minor releases and bug fix releases come out frequently. Where possible, I have tried to call out relevant differences, but you might be using a different version by the time you read this, and the implementation may have changed.

Finding Out More

If you'd like to find out more about Cassandra, and to get the latest updates, visit this book's companion website at *http://www.cassandraguide.com*.

It's also an excellent idea to follow me on Twitter at @ebenhewitt.

Conventions Used in This Book

The following typographical conventions are used in this book:

Italic

Indicates new terms, URLs, email addresses, filenames, and file extensions.

`Constant width`

Used for program listings, as well as within paragraphs to refer to program elements such as variable or function names, databases, data types, environment variables, statements, and keywords.

Constant width bold

    Shows commands or other text that should be typed literally by the user.

Constant width italic

    Shows text that should be replaced with user-supplied values or by values determined by context.

    This icon signifies a tip, suggestion, or general note.

    This icon indicates a warning or caution.

Using Code Examples

This book is here to help you get your job done. In general, you may use the code in this book in your programs and documentation. You do not need to contact us for permission unless you're reproducing a significant portion of the code. For example, writing a program that uses several chunks of code from this book does not require permission. Selling or distributing a CD-ROM of examples from O'Reilly books does require permission. Answering a question by citing this book and quoting example code does not require permission. Incorporating a significant amount of example code from this book into your product's documentation does require permission.

We appreciate, but do not require, attribution. An attribution usually includes the title, author, publisher, and ISBN. For example: "*Cassandra: The Definitive Guide* by Eben Hewitt. Copyright 2011 Eben Hewitt, 978-1-449-39041-9."

If you feel your use of code examples falls outside fair use or the permission given here, feel free to contact us at *permissions@oreilly.com*.

Safari® Enabled

Safari Books Online is an on-demand digital library that lets you easily search over 7,500 technology and creative reference books and videos to find the answers you need quickly.

With a subscription, you can read any page and watch any video from our library online. Read books on your cell phone and mobile devices. Access new titles before they are available for print, and get exclusive access to manuscripts in development and post feedback for the authors. Copy and paste code samples, organize your favorites, download chapters, bookmark key sections, create notes, print out pages, and benefit from tons of other time-saving features.

O'Reilly Media has uploaded this book to the Safari Books Online service. To have full digital access to this book and others on similar topics from O'Reilly and other publishers, sign up for free at *http://my.safaribooksonline.com*

How to Contact Us

Please address comments and questions concerning this book to the publisher:

O'Reilly Media, Inc.
1005 Gravenstein Highway North
Sebastopol, CA 95472
800-998-9938 (in the United States or Canada)
707-829-0515 (international or local)
707 829-0104 (fax)

We have a web page for this book, where we list errata, examples, and any additional information. You can access this page at:

http://oreilly.com/catalog/0636920010852/

To comment or ask technical questions about this book, send email to:

bookquestions@oreilly.com

For more information about our books, conferences, Resource Centers, and the O'Reilly Network, see our website at:

http://www.oreilly.com

Acknowledgments

There are many wonderful people to whom I am grateful for helping bring this book to life.

Thanks to Jeremy Hanna, for writing the Hadoop chapter, and for being so easy to work with.

Thank you to my technical reviewers. Stu Hood's insightful comments in particular really improved the book. Robert Schneider and Gary Dusbabek contributed thoughtful reviews.

Thank you to Jonathan Ellis for writing the foreword.

Thanks to my editor, Mike Loukides, for being a charming conversationalist at dinner in San Francisco.

Thank you to Rain Fletcher for supporting and encouraging this book.

I'm inspired by the many terrific developers who have contributed to Cassandra. Hats off for making such a pretty and powerful database.

As always, thank you to Alison Brown, who read drafts, gave me notes, and made sure that I had time to work; this book would not have happened without you.

## CHAPTER 1

Introducing Cassandra

If at first the idea is not absurd,
then there is no hope for it.

—Albert Einstein

Welcome to *Cassandra: The Definitive Guide*. The aim of this book is to help developers and database administrators understand this important new database, explore how it compares to the relational database management systems we're used to, and help you put it to work in your own environment.

What's Wrong with Relational Databases?

If I had asked people what they wanted, they
would have said faster horses.

—Henry Ford

I ask you to consider a certain model for data, invented by a small team at a company with thousands of employees. It is accessible over a TCP/IP interface and is available from a variety of languages, including Java and web services. This model was difficult at first for all but the most advanced computer scientists to understand, until broader adoption helped make the concepts clearer. Using the database built around this model required learning new terms and thinking about data storage in a different way. But as products sprang up around it, more businesses and government agencies put it to use, in no small part because it was fast—capable of processing thousands of operations a second. The revenue it generated was tremendous.

And then a new model came along.

The new model was threatening, chiefly for two reasons. First, the new model was very different from the old model, which it pointedly controverted. It was threatening because it can be hard to understand something different and new. Ensuing debates can help entrench people stubbornly further in their views—views that might have been largely inherited from the climate in which they learned their craft and the circumstances in which they work. Second, and perhaps more importantly, as a barrier, the new model was threatening because businesses had made considerable investments in the old model and were making lots of money with it. Changing course seemed ridiculous, even impossible.

Of course I'm talking about the Information Management System (IMS) hierarchical database, invented in 1966 at IBM.

IMS was built for use in the Saturn V moon rocket. Its architect was Vern Watts, who dedicated his career to it. Many of us are familiar with IBM's database DB2. IBM's wildly popular DB2 database gets its name as the successor to DB1—the product built around the hierarchical data model IMS. IMS was released in 1968, and subsequently enjoyed success in Customer Information Control System (CICS) and other applications. It is still used today.

But in the years following the invention of IMS, the new model, the disruptive model, the threatening model, was the relational database.

In his 1970 paper "A Relational Model of Data for Large Shared Data Banks," Dr. Edgar F. Codd, also at IBM, advanced his theory of the relational model for data while working at IBM's San Jose research laboratory. This paper, still available at *http://www .seas.upenn.edu/~zives/03f/cis550/codd.pdf*, became the foundational work for relational database management systems.

Codd's work was antithetical to the hierarchical structure of IMS. Understanding and working with a relational database required learning new terms that must have sounded very strange indeed to users of IMS. It presented certain advantages over its predecessor, in part because giants are almost always standing on the shoulders of other giants.

While these ideas and their application have evolved in four decades, the relational database still is clearly one of the most successful software applications in history. It's used in the form of Microsoft Access in sole proprietorships, and in giant multinational corporations with clusters of hundreds of finely tuned instances representing multi-terabyte data warehouses. Relational databases store invoices, customer records, product catalogues, accounting ledgers, user authentication schemes—the very world, it might appear. There is no question that the relational database is a key facet of the modern technology and business landscape, and one that will be with us in its various forms for many years to come, as will IMS in its various forms. The relational model presented an alternative to IMS, and each has its uses.

So the short answer to the question, "What's wrong with relational databases?" is "Nothing."

There is, however, a rather longer answer that I gently encourage you to consider. This answer takes the long view, which says that every once in a while an idea is born that ostensibly changes things, and engenders a revolution of sorts. And yet, in another way, such revolutions, viewed structurally, are simply history's business as usual. IMS,

RDBMS, NoSQL. The horse, the car, the plane. They each build on prior art, they each attempt to solve certain problems, and so they're each good at certain things—and less good at others. They each coexist, even now.

So let's examine for a moment why, at this point, we might consider an alternative to the relational database, just as Codd himself four decades ago looked at the Information Management System and thought that maybe it wasn't the only legitimate way of organizing information and solving data problems, and that maybe, for certain problems, it might prove fruitful to consider an alternative.

We encounter scalability problems when our relational applications become successful and usage goes up. Joins are inherent in any relatively normalized relational database of even modest size, and joins can be slow. The way that databases gain consistency is typically through the use of transactions, which require locking some portion of the database so it's not available to other clients. This can become untenable under very heavy loads, as the locks mean that competing users start queuing up, waiting for their turn to read or write the data.

We typically address these problems in one or more of the following ways, sometimes in this order:

- Throw hardware at the problem by adding more memory, adding faster processors, and upgrading disks. This is known as *vertical scaling*. This can relieve you for a time.

- When the problems arise again, the answer appears to be similar: now that one box is maxed out, you add hardware in the form of additional boxes in a database cluster. Now you have the problem of data replication and consistency during regular usage and in failover scenarios. You didn't have that problem before.

- Now we need to update the configuration of the database management system. This might mean optimizing the channels the database uses to write to the underlying filesystem. We turn off logging or journaling, which frequently is not a desirable (or, depending on your situation, legal) option.

- Having put what attention we could into the database system, we turn to our application. We try to improve our indexes. We optimize the queries. But presumably at this scale we weren't wholly ignorant of index and query optimization, and already had them in pretty good shape. So this becomes a painful process of picking through the data access code to find any opportunities for fine tuning. This might include reducing or reorganizing joins, throwing out resource-intensive features such as XML processing within a stored procedure, and so forth. Of course, presumably we were doing that XML processing for a reason, so if we have to do it somewhere, we move that problem to the application layer, hoping to solve it there and crossing our fingers that we don't break something else in the meantime.

- We employ a caching layer. For larger systems, this might include distributed caches such as memcached, EHCache, Oracle Coherence, or other related products. Now we have a consistency problem between updates in the cache and updates in the database, which is exacerbated over a cluster.

- We turn our attention to the database again and decide that, now that the application is built and we understand the primary query paths, we can duplicate some of the data to make it look more like the queries that access it. This process, called denormalization, is antithetical to the five normal forms that characterize the relational model, and violate Codd's 12 Commandments for relational data. We remind ourselves that we live in this world, and not in some theoretical cloud, and then undertake to do what we must to make the application start responding at acceptable levels again, even if it's no longer "pure."

I imagine that this sounds familiar to you. At web scale, engineers have started to wonder whether this situation isn't similar to Henry Ford's assertion that at a certain point, it's not simply a faster horse that you want. And they've done some impressive, interesting work.

We must therefore begin here in recognition that the relational model is simply a model. That is, it's intended to be a useful way of looking at the world, applicable to certain problems. It does not purport to be exhaustive, closing the case on all other ways of representing data, never again to be examined, leaving no room for alternatives. If we take the long view of history, Dr. Codd's model was a rather disruptive one in its time. It was new, with strange new vocabulary and terms such as "tuples"—familiar words used in a new and different manner. The relational model was held up to suspicion, and doubtless suffered its vehement detractors. It encountered opposition even in the form of Dr. Codd's own employer, IBM, which had a very lucrative product set around IMS and didn't need a young upstart cutting into its pie.

But the relational model now arguably enjoys the best seat in the house within the data world. SQL is widely supported and well understood. It is taught in introductory university courses. There are free databases that come installed and ready to use with a $4.95 monthly web hosting plan. Often the database we end up using is dictated to us by architectural standards within our organization. Even absent such standards, it's prudent to learn whatever your organization already has for a database platform. Our colleagues in development and infrastructure have considerable hard-won knowledge.

If by nothing more than osmosis—or inertia—we have learned over the years that a relational database is a one-size-fits-all solution.

So perhaps the real question is not, "What's wrong with relational databases?" but rather, "What problem do you have?"

That is, you want to ensure that your solution matches the problem that you have. There are certain problems that relational databases solve very well.

If massive, elastic scalability is not an issue for you, the trade-offs in relative complexity of a system such as Cassandra may simply not be worth it. No proponent of Cassandra that I know of is asking anyone to throw out everything they've learned about relational databases, surrender their years of hard-won knowledge around such systems, and unnecessarily jeopardize their employer's carefully constructed systems in favor of the flavor of the month.

Relational data has served all of us developers and DBAs well. But the explosion of the Web, and in particular social networks, means a corresponding explosion in the sheer volume of data we must deal with. When Tim Berners-Lee first worked on the Web in the early 1990s, it was for the purpose of exchanging scientific documents between PhDs at a physics laboratory. Now, of course, the Web has become so ubiquitous that it's used by everyone, from those same scientists to legions of five-year-olds exchanging emoticons about kittens. That means in part that it must support enormous volumes of data; the fact that it does stands as a monument to the ingenious architecture of the Web.

But some of this infrastructure is starting to bend under the weight.

In 1966, a company like IBM was in a position to really make people listen to their innovations. They had the problems, and they had the brain power to solve them. As we enter the second decade of the 21st century, we're starting to see similar innovations, even from young companies such as Facebook and Twitter.

So perhaps the real question, then, is not "What problem do I have?" but rather, "What kinds of things would I do with data if it wasn't a problem?" What if you could easily achieve fault tolerance, availability across multiple data centers, consistency that you tune, and massive scalability even to the hundreds of terabytes, all from a client language of your choosing? Perhaps, you say, you don't need that kind of availability or that level of scalability. And you know best. You're certainly right, in fact, because if your current database didn't suit your current database needs, you'd have a nonfunctioning system.

It is not my intention to convince you by clever argument to adopt a non-relational database such as Apache Cassandra. It is only my intention to present what Cassandra can do and how it does it so that you can make an informed decision and get started working with it in practical ways if you find it applies. Only you know what your data needs are. I do not ask you to reconsider your database—unless you're miserable with your current database, or you can't scale how you need to already, or your data model isn't mapping to your application in a way that's flexible enough for you. I don't ask you to consider your database, but rather to consider your organization, its dreams for the future, and its emerging problems. Would you collect more information about your business objects if you could?

Don't ask how to make Cassandra fit into your existing environment. Ask what kinds of data problems you'd like to have instead of the ones you have today. Ask what new kinds of data you would like. What understanding of your organization would you like to have, if only you could enable it?

A Quick Review of Relational Databases

Though you are likely familiar with them, let's briefly turn our attention to some of the foundational concepts in relational databases. This will give us a basis on which to consider more recent advances in thought around the trade-offs inherent in distributed data systems, especially very large distributed data systems, such as those that are required at web scale.

RDBMS: The Awesome and the Not-So-Much

There are many reasons that the relational database has become so overwhelmingly popular over the last four decades. An important one is the Structured Query Language (SQL), which is feature-rich and uses a simple, declarative syntax. SQL was first officially adopted as an ANSI standard in 1986; since that time it's gone through several revisions and has also been extended with vendor proprietary syntax such as Microsoft's T-SQL and Oracle's PL/SQL to provide additional implementation-specific features.

SQL is powerful for a variety of reasons. It allows the user to represent complex relationships with the data, using statements that form the Data Manipulation Language (DML) to insert, select, update, delete, truncate, and merge data. You can perform a rich variety of operations using functions based on relational algebra to find a maximum or minimum value in a set, for example, or to filter and order results. SQL statements support grouping aggregate values and executing summary functions. SQL provides a means of directly creating, altering, and dropping schema structures at runtime using Data Definition Language (DDL). SQL also allows you to grant and revoke rights for users and groups of users using the same syntax.

SQL is easy to use. The basic syntax can be learned quickly, and conceptually SQL and RDBMS offer a low barrier to entry. Junior developers can become proficient readily, and as is often the case in an industry beset by rapid changes, tight deadlines, and exploding budgets, ease of use can be very important. And it's not just the syntax that's easy to use; there are many robust tools that include intuitive graphical interfaces for viewing and working with your database.

In part because it's a standard, SQL allows you to easily integrate your RDBMS with a wide variety of systems. All you need is a driver for your application language, and you're off to the races in a very portable way. If you decide to change your application implementation language (or your RDBMS vendor), you can often do that painlessly, assuming you haven't backed yourself into a corner using lots of proprietary extensions.

Transactions, ACID-ity, and two-phase commit

In addition to the features mentioned already, RDBMS and SQL also support transactions. A database *transaction* is, as Jim Gray puts it, "a transformation of state" that has the ACID properties (see *http://research.microsoft.com/en-us/um/people/gray/papers/theTransactionConcept.pdf*). A key feature of transactions is that they execute virtually at first, allowing the programmer to undo (using ROLLBACK) any changes that may have gone awry during execution; if all has gone well, the transaction can be reliably committed. The debate about support for transactions comes up very quickly as a sore spot in conversations around non-relational data stores, so let's take a moment to revisit what this really means.

ACID is an acronym for Atomic, Consistent, Isolated, Durable, which are the gauges we can use to assess that a transaction has executed properly and that it was successful:

Atomic
> Atomic means "all or nothing"; that is, when a statement is executed, every update within the transaction must succeed in order to be called successful. There is no partial failure where one update was successful and another related update failed. The common example here is with monetary transfers at an ATM: the transfer requires subtracting money from one account and adding it to another account. This operation cannot be subdivided; they must both succeed.

Consistent
> Consistent means that data moves from one correct state to another correct state, with no possibility that readers could view different values that don't make sense together. For example, if a transaction attempts to delete a Customer and her Order history, it cannot leave Order rows that reference the deleted customer's primary key; this is an inconsistent state that would cause errors if someone tried to read those Order records.

Isolated
> Isolated means that transactions executing concurrently will not become entangled with each other; they each execute in their own space. That is, if two different transactions attempt to modify the same data at the same time, then one of them will have to wait for the other to complete.

Durable
> Once a transaction has succeeded, the changes will not be lost. This doesn't imply another transaction won't later modify the same data; it just means that writers can be confident that the changes are available for the next transaction to work with as necessary.

On the surface, these properties seem so obviously desirable as to not even merit conversation. Presumably no one who runs a database would suggest that data updates don't have to endure for some length of time; that's the very point of making updates—that they're there for others to read. However, a more subtle examination might lead us to want to find a way to tune these properties a bit and control them slightly. There is, as they say, no free lunch on the Internet, and once we see how we're paying for our transactions, we may start to wonder whether there's an alternative.

Transactions become difficult under heavy load. When you first attempt to horizontally scale a relational database, making it distributed, you must now account for *distributed transactions*, where the transaction isn't simply operating inside a single table or a single database, but is spread across multiple systems. In order to continue to honor the ACID properties of transactions, you now need a transaction manager to orchestrate across the multiple nodes.

In order to account for successful completion across multiple hosts, the idea of a two-phase commit (sometimes referred to as "2PC") is introduced. But then, because two-phase commit locks all associate resources, it is useful only for operations that can complete very quickly. Although it may often be the case that your distributed operations can complete in sub-second time, it is certainly not always the case. Some use cases require coordination between multiple hosts that you may not control yourself. Operations coordinating several different but related activities can take hours to update.

Two-phase commit *blocks*; that is, clients ("competing consumers") must wait for a prior transaction to finish before they can access the blocked resource. The protocol will wait for a node to respond, even if it has died. It's possible to avoid waiting forever in this event, because a timeout can be set that allows the transaction coordinator node to decide that the node isn't going to respond and that it should abort the transaction. However, an infinite loop is still possible with 2PC; that's because a node can send a message to the transaction coordinator node agreeing that it's OK for the coordinator to commit the entire transaction. The node will then wait for the coordinator to send a commit response (or a rollback response if, say, a different node can't commit); if the coordinator is down in this scenario, that node conceivably will wait forever.

So in order to account for these shortcomings in two-phase commit of distributed transactions, the database world turned to the idea of *compensation*. Compensation, often used in web services, means in simple terms that the operation is immediately committed, and then in the event that some error is reported, a new operation is invoked to restore proper state.

There are a few basic, well-known patterns for compensatory action that architects frequently have to consider as an alternative to two-phase commit. These include writing off the transaction if it fails, deciding to discard erroneous transactions and reconciling later. Another alternative is to retry failed operations later on notification. In a reservation system or a stock sales ticker, these are not likely to meet your requirements. For other kinds of applications, such as billing or ticketing applications, this can be acceptable.

 Gregor Hohpe, a Google architect, wrote a wonderful and often-cited blog entry called "Starbucks Does Not Use Two-Phase Commit." It shows in real-world terms how difficult it is to scale two-phase commit and highlights some of the alternatives that are mentioned here. Check it out at *http://www.eaipatterns.com/ramblings/18_starbucks.html*. It's an easy, fun, and enlightening read.

The problems that 2PC introduces for application developers include loss of availability and higher latency during partial failures. Neither of these is desirable. So once you've had the good fortune of being successful enough to necessitate scaling your database past a single machine, you now have to figure out how to handle transactions across multiple machines and still make the ACID properties apply. Whether you have 10 or 100 or 1,000 database machines, atomicity is still required in transactions as if you were working on a single node. But it's now a much, much bigger pill to swallow.

Schema

One often-lauded feature of relational database systems is the rich schemas they afford. You can represent your domain objects in a relational model. A whole industry has sprung up around (expensive) tools such as the CA ERWin Data Modeler to support this effort. In order to create a properly normalized schema, however, you are forced to create tables that don't exist as business objects in your domain. For example, a schema for a university database might require a Student table and a Course table. But because of the "many-to-many" relationship here (one student can take many courses at the same time, and one course has many students at the same time), you have to create a join table. This pollutes a pristine data model, where we'd prefer to just have students and courses. It also forces us to create more complex SQL statements to join these tables together. The join statements, in turn, can be slow.

Again, in a system of modest size, this isn't much of a problem. But complex queries and multiple joins can become burdensomely slow once you have a large number of rows in many tables to handle.

Finally, not all schemas map well to the relational model. One type of system that has risen in popularity in the last decade is the complex event processing system, which represents state changes in a very fast stream. It's often useful to contextualize events at runtime against other events that might be related in order to infer some conclusion to support business decision making. Although event streams could be represented in terms of a relational database, it is an uncomfortable stretch.

And if you're an application developer, you'll no doubt be familiar with the many object-relational mapping (ORM) frameworks that have sprung up in recent years to help ease the difficulty in mapping application objects to a relational model. Again, for small systems, ORM can be a relief. But it also introduces new problems of its own, such as extended memory requirements, and it often pollutes the application code with increasingly unwieldy mapping code. Here's an example of a Java method using Hibernate to "ease the burden" of having to write the SQL code:

```
@CollectionOfElements
@JoinTable(name="store_description",
  joinColumns = @JoinColumn(name="store_code"))
@MapKey(columns={@Column(name="for_store",length=3)})
@Column(name="description")
private Map<String, String> getMap() {
  return this.map;
}
//... etc.
```

Is it certain that we've done anything but move the problem here? Of course, with some systems, such as those that make extensive use of document exchange, as with services or XML-based applications, there are not always clear mappings to a relational database. This exacerbates the problem.

Sharding and shared-nothing architecture

> *If you can't split it, you can't scale it.*
>
> —Randy Shoup, Distinguished Architect, eBay

Another way to attempt to scale a relational database is to introduce *sharding* to your architecture. This has been used to good effect at large websites such as eBay, which supports billions of SQL queries a day, and in other Web 2.0 applications. The idea here is that you split the data so that instead of hosting all of it on a single server or replicating all of the data on all of the servers in a cluster, you divide up portions of the data horizontally and host them each separately.

For example, consider a large customer table in a relational database. The least disruptive thing (for the programming staff, anyway) is to vertically scale by adding CPU, adding memory, and getting faster hard drives, but if you continue to be successful and add more customers, at some point (perhaps into the tens of millions of rows), you'll likely have to start thinking about how you can add more machines. When you do so, do you just copy the data so that all of the machines have it? Or do you instead divide up that single customer table so that each database has only some of the records, with their order preserved? Then, when clients execute queries, they put load only on the machine that has the record they're looking for, with no load on the other machines.

It seems clear that in order to shard, you need to find a good key by which to order your records. For example, you could divide your customer records across 26 machines, one for each letter of the alphabet, with each hosting only the records for customers whose last names start with that particular letter. It's likely this is not a good strategy, however—there probably aren't many last names that begin with "Q" or "Z," so those machines will sit idle while the "J," "M," and "S" machines spike. You could shard according to something numeric, like phone number, "member since" date, or the name of the customer's state. It all depends on how your specific data is likely to be distributed.

There are three basic strategies for determining shard structure:

Feature-based shard or functional segmentation
> This is the approach taken by Randy Shoup, Distinguished Architect at eBay, who in 2006 helped bring their architecture into maturity to support many billions of queries per day. Using this strategy, the data is split not by dividing records in a single table (as in the customer example discussed earlier), but rather by splitting into separate databases the features that don't overlap with each other very much. For example, at eBay, the users are in one shard, and the items for sale are in another. At Flixster, movie ratings are in one shard and comments are in another. This approach depends on understanding your domain so that you can segment data cleanly.

Key-based sharding
> In this approach, you find a key in your data that will evenly distribute it across shards. So instead of simply storing one letter of the alphabet for each server as in the (naive and improper) earlier example, you use a one-way hash on a key data element and distribute data across machines according to the hash. It is common in this strategy to find time-based or numeric keys to hash on.

Lookup table
> In this approach, one of the nodes in the cluster acts as a "yellow pages" directory and looks up which node has the data you're trying to access. This has two obvious disadvantages. The first is that you'll take a performance hit every time you have to go through the lookup table as an additional hop. The second is that the lookup table not only becomes a bottleneck, but a single point of failure.

 To read about how they used data sharding strategies to improve performance at Flixster, see *http://lsvp.wordpress.com/2008/06/20*.

Sharding can minimize contention depending on your strategy and allows you not just to scale horizontally, but then to scale more precisely, as you can add power to the particular shards that need it.

Sharding could be termed a kind of "shared-nothing" architecture that's specific to databases. A *shared-nothing* architecture is one in which there is no centralized (shared) state, but each node in a distributed system is independent, so there is no client contention for shared resources. The term was first coined by Michael Stonebraker at University of California at Berkeley in his 1986 paper "The Case for Shared Nothing."

Shared Nothing was more recently popularized by Google, which has written systems such as its Bigtable database and its MapReduce implementation that do not share state, and are therefore capable of near-infinite scaling. The Cassandra database is a shared-nothing architecture, as it has no central controller and no notion of master/slave; all of its nodes are the same.

You can read the 1986 paper "The Case for Shared Nothing" online at *http://db.cs.berkeley.edu/papers/hpts85-nothing.pdf*. It's only a few pages. If you take a look, you'll see that many of the features of shared-nothing distributed data architecture, such as ease of high availability and the ability to scale to a very large number of machines, are the very things that Cassandra excels at.

MongoDB also provides auto-sharding capabilities to manage failover and node balancing. That many nonrelational databases offer this automatically and out of the box is very handy; creating and maintaining custom data shards by hand is a wicked proposition. It's good to understand sharding in terms of data architecture in general, but especially in terms of Cassandra more specifically, as it can take an approach similar to key-based sharding to distribute data across nodes, but does so automatically.

Summary

In summary, relational databases are very good at solving certain data storage problems, but because of their focus, they also can create problems of their own when it's time to scale. Then, you often need to find a way to get rid of your joins, which means denormalizing the data, which means maintaining multiple copies of data and seriously disrupting your design, both in the database and in your application. Further, you almost certainly need to find a way around distributed transactions, which will quickly become a bottleneck. These compensatory actions are not directly supported in any but the most expensive RDBMS. And even if you can write such a huge check, you still need to carefully choose partitioning keys to the point where you can never entirely ignore the limitation.

Perhaps more importantly, as we see some of the limitations of RDBMS and consequently some of the strategies that architects have used to mitigate their scaling issues, a picture slowly starts to emerge. It's a picture that makes some NoSQL solutions seem perhaps less radical and less scary than we may have thought at first, and more like a natural expression and encapsulation of some of the work that was already being done to manage very large databases.

Web Scale

> *An invention has to make sense in the world in which it is finished, not the world in which it is started.*
>
> —Ray Kurzweil

Because of some of the inherent design decisions in RDBMS, it is not always as easy to scale as some other, more recent possibilities that take the structure of the Web into consideration. But it's not only the structure of the Web we need to consider, but also its phenomenal growth, because as more and more data becomes available, we need

---

architecture that allow our organizations to take advantage of this data in near-time to support decision making and to offer new and more powerful features and capabilities to our customers.

 It has been said, though it is hard to verify, that the 17th-century English poet John Milton had actually read every published book on the face of the earth. Milton knew many languages (he was even learning Navajo at the time of his death), and given that the total number of published books at that time was in the thousands, this would have been possible. The size of the world's data stores have grown somewhat since then.

We all know the Web is growing. But let's take a moment to consider some numbers from the IDC research paper "The Expanding Digital Universe." (The complete paper is available at *http://www.emc.com/collateral/analyst-reports/expanding-digital-idc-white-paper.pdf*.)

- YouTube serves 100 million videos every day.
- Chevron accumulates 2TB of data every day.
- In 2006, the amount of data on the Internet was approximately 166 exabytes (166EB). In 2010, that number reached nearly 1,000 exabytes. An exabyte is one quintillion bytes, or 1.1 million terabytes. To put this statistic in perspective, 1EB is roughly the equivalent of 50,000 years of DVD-quality video. 166EB is approximately three million times the amount of information contained in all the books ever written.
- Wal-Mart's database of customer transactions is reputed to have stored 110 terabytes in 2000, recording tens of millions of transactions per day. By 2004, it had grown to half a petabyte.
- The movie *Avatar* required 1PB storage space, or the equivalent of a single MP3 song—if that MP3 were 32 years long (source: *http://bit.ly/736XCz*).
- As of May 2010, Google was provisioning 100,000 Android phones every day, all of which have Internet access as a foundational service.
- In 1998, the number of email accounts was approximately 253 million. By 2010, that number is closer to 2 billion.

As you can see, there is great variety to the kinds of data that need to be stored, processed, and queried, and some variety to the businesses that use such data. Consider not only customer data at familiar retailers or suppliers, and not only digital video content, but also the required move to digital television and the explosive growth of email, messaging, mobile phones, RFID, Voice Over IP (VoIP) usage, and more. We now have Blu-ray players that stream movies and music. As we begin departing from physical consumer media storage, the companies that provide that content—and the third-party value-add businesses built around them—will require very scalable data solutions. Consider too that as a typical business application developer or database administrator, we may be used to thinking of relational databases as the center of our universe. You might then be surprised to learn that within corporations, around 80% of data is unstructured.

Or perhaps you think the kind of scale afforded by NoSQL solutions such as Cassandra don't apply to you. And maybe they don't. It's very possible that you simply don't have a problem that Cassandra can help you with. But I'm not asking you to envision your database and its data as they exist today and figure out ways to migrate to Cassandra. That would be a very difficult exercise, with a payoff that might be hard to see. It's almost analytic that the database you have today is exactly the right one for your application of today. But if you could incorporate a wider array of rich data sets to help improve your applications, what kinds of qualities would you then be looking for in a database? The question becomes what kind of application would you want to have if durability, elastic scalability, vast storage, and blazing-fast writes weren't a problem?

In a world now working at web scale and looking to the future, Apache Cassandra might be one part of the answer.

The Cassandra Elevator Pitch

Hollywood screenwriters and software startups are often advised to have their "elevator pitch" ready. This is a summary of exactly what their product is all about—concise, clear, and brief enough to deliver in just a minute or two, in the lucky event that they find themselves sharing an elevator with an executive or agent or investor who might consider funding their project. Cassandra has a compelling story, so let's boil it down to an elevator pitch that you can present to your manager or colleagues should the occasion arise.

Cassandra in 50 Words or Less

"Apache Cassandra is an open source, distributed, decentralized, elastically scalable, highly available, fault-tolerant, tuneably consistent, column-oriented database that bases its distribution design on Amazon's Dynamo and its data model on Google's Bigtable. Created at Facebook, it is now used at some of the most popular sites on the Web." That's exactly 50 words.

Of course, if you were to recite that to your boss in the elevator, you'd probably get a blank look in return. So let's break down the key points in the following sections.

Distributed and Decentralized

Cassandra is *distributed*, which means that it is capable of running on multiple machines while appearing to users as a unified whole. In fact, there is little point in running a single Cassandra node. Although you can do it, and that's acceptable for getting up to speed on how it works, you quickly realize that you'll need multiple machines to really realize any benefit from running Cassandra. Much of its design and code base is specifically engineered toward not only making it work across many different machines, but also for optimizing performance across multiple data center racks, and even for a single Cassandra cluster running across geographically dispersed data centers. You can confidently write data to anywhere in the cluster and Cassandra will get it.

Once you start to scale many other data stores (MySQL, Bigtable), some nodes need to be set up as masters in order to organize other nodes, which are set up as slaves. Cassandra, however, is decentralized, meaning that every node is identical; no Cassandra node performs certain organizing operations distinct from any other node. Instead, Cassandra features a peer-to-peer protocol and uses gossip to maintain and keep in sync a list of nodes that are alive or dead.

The fact that Cassandra is *decentralized* means that there is no single point of failure. All of the nodes in a Cassandra cluster function exactly the same. This is sometimes referred to as "server symmetry." Because they are all doing the same thing, by definition there can't be a special host that is coordinating activities, as with the master/slave setup that you see in MySQL, Bigtable, and so many others.

In many distributed data solutions (such as RDBMS clusters), you set up multiple copies of data on different servers in a process called replication, which copies the data to multiple machines so that they can all serve simultaneous requests and improve performance. Typically this process is not decentralized, as in Cassandra, but is rather performed by defining a *master/slave relationship*. That is, all of the servers in this kind of cluster don't function in the same way. You configure your cluster by designating one server as the master and others as slaves. The master acts as the authoritative source of the data, and operates in a unidirectional relationship with the slave nodes, which must synchronize their copies. If the master node fails, the whole database is in jeopardy. The decentralized design is therefore one of the keys to Cassandra's high availability. Note that while we frequently understand master/slave replication in the RDBMS world, there are NoSQL databases such as MongoDB that follow the master/slave scheme as well.

Decentralization, therefore, has two key advantages: it's simpler to use than master/slave, and it helps you avoid outages. It can be easier to operate and maintain a decentralized store than a master/slave store because all nodes are the same. That means that you don't need any special knowledge to scale; setting up 50 nodes isn't much different from setting up one. There's next to no configuration required to support it. Moreover, in a master/slave setup, the master can become a single point of failure (SPOF). To avoid this, you often need to add some complexity to the environment in the form of multiple masters. Because all of the replicas in Cassandra are identical, failures of a node won't disrupt service.

In short, because Cassandra is distributed and decentralized, there is no single point of failure, which supports high availability.

Elastic Scalability

Scalability is an architectural feature of a system that can continue serving a greater number of requests with little degradation in performance. Vertical scaling—simply adding more hardware capacity and memory to your existing machine—is the easiest way to achieve this. Horizontal scaling means adding more machines that have all or some of the data on them so that no one machine has to bear the entire burden of serving requests. But then the software itself must have an internal mechanism for keeping its data in sync with the other nodes in the cluster.

Elastic scalability refers to a special property of horizontal scalability. It means that your cluster can seamlessly scale up and scale back down. To do this, the cluster must be able to accept new nodes that can begin participating by getting a copy of some or all of the data and start serving new user requests without major disruption or reconfiguration of the entire cluster. You don't have to restart your process. You don't have to change your application queries. You don't have to manually rebalance the data yourself. Just add another machine—Cassandra will find it and start sending it work.

Scaling down, of course, means removing some of the processing capacity from your cluster. You might have to do this if you move parts of your application to another platform, or if your application loses users and you need to start selling off hardware. Let's hope that doesn't happen. But if it does, you won't need to upset the entire apple cart to scale back.

High Availability and Fault Tolerance

In general architecture terms, the availability of a system is measured according to its ability to fulfill requests. But computers can experience all manner of failure, from hardware component failure to network disruption to corruption. Any computer is susceptible to these kinds of failure. There are of course very sophisticated (and often prohibitively expensive) computers that can themselves mitigate many of these circumstances, as they include internal hardware redundancies and facilities to send notification of failure events and hot swap components. But anyone can accidentally break an Ethernet cable, and catastrophic events can beset a single data center. So for a system to be highly available, it must typically include multiple networked computers, and the software they're running must then be capable of operating in a cluster and have some facility for recognizing node failures and failing over requests to another part of the system.

Cassandra is highly available. You can replace failed nodes in the cluster with no downtime, and you can replicate data to multiple data centers to offer improved local performance and prevent downtime if one data center experiences a catastrophe such as fire or flood.

Tuneable Consistency

Consistency essentially means that a read always returns the most recently written value. Consider two customers are attempting to put the same item into their shopping carts on an ecommerce site. If I place the last item in stock into my cart an instant after you do, you should get the item added to your cart, and I should be informed that the item is no longer available for purchase. This is guaranteed to happen when the state of a write is consistent among all nodes that have that data.

But there's no free lunch, and as we'll see later, scaling data stores means making certain trade-offs between data consistency, node availability, and partition tolerance. Cassandra is frequently called "eventually consistent," which is a bit misleading. Out of the box, Cassandra trades some consistency in order to achieve total availability. But Cassandra is more accurately termed "tuneably consistent," which means it allows you to easily decide the level of consistency you require, in balance with the level of availability.

Let's take a moment to unpack this, as the term "eventual consistency" has caused some uproar in the industry. Some practitioners hesitate to use a system that is described as "eventually consistent."

For detractors of eventual consistency, the broad argument goes something like this: eventual consistency is maybe OK for social web applications where data doesn't *really* matter. After all, you're just posting to mom what little Billy ate for breakfast, and if it gets lost, it doesn't really matter. But the data *I* have is actually really important, and it's ridiculous to think that I could allow eventual consistency in my model.

Set aside the fact that all of the most popular web applications (Amazon, Facebook, Google, Twitter) are using this model, and that perhaps there's something to it. Presumably such data is very important indeed to the companies running these applications, because that data is their primary product, and they are multibillion-dollar companies with billions of users to satisfy in a sharply competitive world. It may be possible to gain guaranteed, immediate, and perfect consistency throughout a highly trafficked system running in parallel on a variety of networks, but if you want clients to get their results sometime this year, it's a very tricky proposition.

The detractors claim that some Big Data databases such as Cassandra have merely eventual consistency, and that all other distributed systems have *strict* consistency. As with so many things in the world, however, the reality is not so black and white, and the binary opposition between consistent and not-consistent is not truly reflected in practice. There are instead *degrees* of consistency, and in the real world they are very susceptible to external circumstance.

Eventual consistency is one of several consistency models available to architects. Let's take a look at these models so we can understand the trade-offs:

Strict consistency
> This is sometimes called sequential consistency, and is the most stringent level of consistency. It requires that any read will always return the most recently written value. That sounds perfect, and it's exactly what I'm looking for. I'll take it! However, upon closer examination, what do we find? What precisely is meant by "most recently written"? Most recently to whom? In one single-processor machine, this is no problem to observe, as the sequence of operations is known to the one clock. But in a system executing across a variety of geographically dispersed data centers, it becomes much more slippery. Achieving this implies some sort of global clock that is capable of timestamping all operations, regardless of the location of the data or the user requesting it or how many (possibly disparate) services are required to determine the response.

Causal consistency
> This is a slightly weaker form of strict consistency. It does away with the fantasy of the single global clock that can magically synchronize all operations without creating an unbearable bottleneck. Instead of relying on timestamps, causal consistency instead takes a more semantic approach, attempting to determine the cause of events to create some consistency in their order. It means that writes that are potentially related must be read in sequence. If two different, unrelated operations suddenly write to the same field, then those writes are inferred not to be causally related. But if one write occurs after another, we might infer that they are causally related. Causal consistency dictates that causal writes must be read in sequence.

Weak (eventual) consistency
> Eventual consistency means on the surface that all updates will propagate throughout all of the replicas in a distributed system, but that this may take some time. Eventually, all replicas will be consistent.

Eventual consistency becomes suddenly very attractive when you consider what is required to achieve stronger forms of consistency.

When considering consistency, availability, and partition tolerance, we can achieve only two of these goals in a given distributed system (we explore the CAP Theorem in the section "Brewer's CAP Theorem" on page 19). At the center of the problem is data update replication. To achieve a strict consistency, all update operations will be performed synchronously, meaning that they must block, locking all replicas until the operation is complete, and forcing competing clients to wait. A side effect of such a design is that during a failure, some of the data will be entirely unavailable. As Amazon CTO Werner Vogels puts it, "rather than dealing with the uncertainty of the correctness of an answer, the data is made unavailable until it is absolutely certain that it is correct" ("Dynamo: Amazon's Highly Distributed Key-Value Store": [*http://www .allthingsdistributed.com/2007/10/amazons_dynamo.html*], 207).

We could alternatively take an optimistic approach to replication, propagating updates to all replicas in the background in order to avoid blowing up on the client. The difficulty this approach presents is that now we are forced into the situation of detecting and resolving conflicts. A design approach must decide whether to resolve these conflicts at one of two possible times: during reads or during writes. That is, a distributed database designer must choose to make the system either always readable or always writable.

Dynamo and Cassandra choose to be always writable, opting to defer the complexity of reconciliation to read operations, and realize tremendous performance gains. The alternative is to reject updates amidst network and server failures.

In Cassandra, consistency is not an all-or-nothing proposition, so we might more accurately term it "tuneable consistency" because the client can control the number of replicas to block on for all updates. This is done by setting the consistency level against the replication factor.

The *replication factor* lets you decide how much you want to pay in performance to gain more consistency. You set the replication factor to the number of nodes in the cluster you want the updates to propagate to (remember that an update means any add, update, or delete operation).

The *consistency level* is a setting that clients must specify on every operation and that allows you to decide how many replicas in the cluster must acknowledge a write operation or respond to a read operation in order to be considered successful. That's the part where Cassandra has pushed the decision for determining consistency out to the client.

So if you like, you could set the consistency level to a number equal to the replication factor, and gain stronger consistency at the cost of synchronous blocking operations that wait for all nodes to be updated and declare success before returning. This is not often done in practice with Cassandra, however, for reasons that should be clear (it defeats the availability goal, would impact performance, and generally goes against the grain of why you'd want to use Cassandra in the first place). So if the client sets the consistency level to a value less than the replication factor, the update is considered successful even if some nodes are down.

Brewer's CAP Theorem

In order to understand Cassandra's design and its label as an "eventually consistent" database, we need to understand the CAP theorem. The CAP theorem is sometimes called Brewer's theorem after its author, Eric Brewer.

While working at University of California at Berkeley, Eric Brewer posited his CAP theorem in 2000 at the ACM Symposium on the Principles of Distributed Computing. The theorem states that within a large-scale distributed data system, there are three requirements that have a relationship of sliding dependency: Consistency, Availability, and Partition Tolerance.

Consistency
> All database clients will read the same value for the same query, even given concurrent updates.

Availability
> All database clients will always be able to read and write data.

Partition Tolerance
> The database can be split into multiple machines; it can continue functioning in the face of network segmentation breaks.

Brewer's theorem is that in any given system, you can strongly support only two of the three. This is analogous to the saying you may have heard in software development: "You can have it good, you can have it fast, you can have it cheap: pick two."

We have to choose between them because of this sliding mutual dependency. The more consistency you demand from your system, for example, the less partition-tolerant you're likely to be able to make it, unless you make some concessions around availability.

The CAP theorem was formally proved to be true by Seth Gilbert and Nancy Lynch of MIT in 2002. In distributed systems, however, it is very likely that you will have network partitioning, and that at some point, machines will fail and cause others to become unreachable. Packet loss, too, is nearly inevitable. This leads us to the conclusion that a distributed system must do its best to continue operating in the face of network partitions (to be Partition-Tolerant), leaving us with only two real options to choose from: Availability and Consistency.

Figure 1-1 illustrates visually that there is no overlapping segment where all three are obtainable.

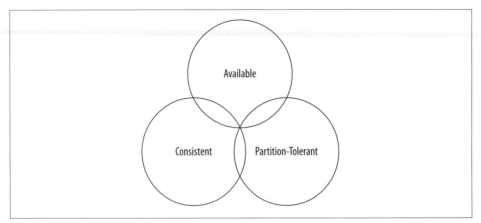

Figure 1-1. CAP Theorem indicates that you can realize only two of these properties at once

It might prove useful at this point to see a graphical depiction of where each of the nonrelational data stores we'll look at falls within the CAP spectrum. The graphic in Figure 1-2 was inspired by a slide in a 2009 talk given by Dwight Merriman, CEO and founder of MongoDB, to the MySQL User Group in New York City (you can watch it online at *http://bit.ly/7r6kRg*). However, I have modified the placement of some systems based on my research.

Figure 1-2 shows the general focus of some of the different databases we discuss in this chapter. Note that placement of the databases in this chart could change based on configuration. As Stu Hood points out, a distributed MySQL database can count as a consistent system only if you're using Google's synchronous replication patches; otherwise, it can only be Available and Partition-Tolerant (AP).

It's interesting to note that the design of the system around CAP placement is independent of the orientation of the data storage mechanism; for example, the CP edge is populated by graph databases and document-oriented databases alike.

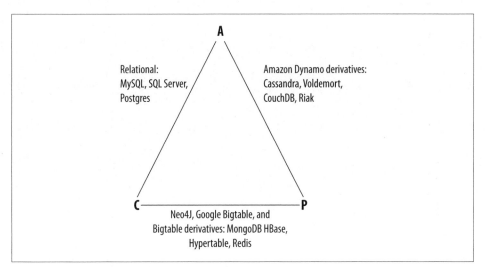

Figure 1-2. Where different databases appear on the CAP continuum

In this depiction, relational databases are on the line between Consistency and Availability, which means that they can fail in the event of a network failure (including a cable breaking). This is typically achieved by defining a single master server, which could itself go down, or an array of servers that simply don't have sufficient mechanisms built in to continue functioning in the case of network partitions.

Graph databases such as Neo4J and the set of databases derived at least in part from the design of Google's Bigtable database (such as MongoDB, HBase, Hypertable, and Redis) all are focused slightly less on Availability and more on ensuring Consistency and Partition Tolerance.

If you're interested in the properties of other Big Data or NoSQL databases, see this book's Appendix.

Finally, the databases derived from Amazon's Dynamo design include Cassandra, Project Voldemort, CouchDB, and Riak. These are more focused on Availability and Partition-Tolerance. However, this does not mean that they dismiss Consistency as unimportant, any more than Bigtable dismisses Availability. According to the Bigtable paper, the average percentage of server hours that "some data" was unavailable is 0.0047% (section 4), so this is relative, as we're talking about very robust systems already. If you think of each of these letters (C, A, P) as knobs you can tune to arrive at the system you want, Dynamo derivatives are intended for employment in the many use cases where "eventual consistency" is tolerable and where "eventual" is a matter of milliseconds, read repairs mean that reads will return consistent values, and you can achieve strong consistency if you want to.

So what does it mean in practical terms to support only two of the three facets of CAP?

CA

To primarily support Consistency and Availability means that you're likely using two-phase commit for distributed transactions. It means that the system will block when a network partition occurs, so it may be that your system is limited to a single data center cluster in an attempt to mitigate this. If your application needs only this level of scale, this is easy to manage and allows you to rely on familiar, simple structures.

CP

To primarily support Consistency and Partition Tolerance, you may try to advance your architecture by setting up data shards in order to scale. Your data will be consistent, but you still run the risk of some data becoming unavailable if nodes fail.

AP

To primarily support Availability and Partition Tolerance, your system may return inaccurate data, but the system will always be available, even in the face of network partitioning. DNS is perhaps the most popular example of a system that is massively scalable, highly available, and partition-tolerant.

Note that this depiction is intended to offer an overview that helps draw distinctions between the broader contours in these systems; it is not strictly precise. For example, it's not entirely clear where Google's Bigtable should be placed on such a continuum. The Google paper describes Bigtable as "highly available," but later goes on to say that if Chubby (the Bigtable persistent lock service) "becomes unavailable for an extended period of time [caused by Chubby outages or network issues], Bigtable becomes unavailable" (section 4). On the matter of data reads, the paper says that "we do not consider the possibility of multiple copies of the same data, possibly in alternate forms due to views or indices." Finally, the paper indicates that "centralized control and Byzantine fault tolerance are not Bigtable goals" (section 10). Given such variable information, you can see that determining where a database falls on this sliding scale is not an exact science.

Row-Oriented

Cassandra is frequently referred to as a "column-oriented" database, which is not incorrect. It's not relational, and it does represent its data structures in sparse multidimensional hashtables. "Sparse" means that for any given row you can have one or more columns, but each row doesn't need to have all the same columns as other rows like it (as in a relational model). Each row has a unique key, which makes its data accessible. So although it's not wrong to say that Cassandra is columnar or column-oriented, it might be more helpful to think of it as an indexed, row-oriented store, as we examine more thoroughly in Chapter 3. I list the data orientation as a feature, because there are several data models that are easy to visualize and use in a nonrelational model; it's a weird mixture of laziness and possibly inviting far more work than necessary to just assume that the relational model is always best, regardless of your application.

Cassandra stores data in what can be thought of for now as a multidimensional hash table. That means you don't have to decide ahead of time precisely what your data structure must look like, or what fields your records will need. This can be useful if you're in startup mode and are adding or changing features with some frequency. It is also attractive if you need to support an Agile development methodology and aren't free to take months for up-front analysis. If your business changes and you later need to add or remove new fields on the fly without disrupting service, go ahead; Cassandra lets you.

That's not to say that you don't have to think about your data, though. On the contrary, Cassandra requires a shift in how you think about it. Instead of designing a pristine data model and then designing queries around the model as in RDBMS, you are free to think of your queries first, and then provide the data that answers them.

Schema-Free

Cassandra requires you to define an outer container, called a keyspace, that contains column families. The keyspace is essentially just a logical namespace to hold column families and certain configuration properties. The column families are names for associated data and a sort order. Beyond that, the data tables are sparse, so you can just start adding data to it, using the columns that you want; there's no need to define your columns ahead of time. Instead of modeling data up front using expensive data modeling tools and then writing queries with complex join statements, Cassandra asks you to model the queries you want, and then provide the data around them.

High Performance

Cassandra was designed specifically from the ground up to take full advantage of multiprocessor/multicore machines, and to run across many dozens of these machines housed in multiple data centers. It scales consistently and seamlessly to hundreds of terabytes. Cassandra has been shown to perform exceptionally well under heavy load. It consistently can show very fast throughput for writes per second on a basic commodity workstation. As you add more servers, you can maintain all of Cassandra's desirable properties without sacrificing performance.

Where Did Cassandra Come From?

The Cassandra data store is an open source Apache project available at *http://cassandra .apache.org*. Cassandra originated at Facebook in 2007 to solve that company's inbox search problem, in which they had to deal with large volumes of data in a way that was difficult to scale with traditional methods. Specifically, the team had requirements to handle huge volumes of data in the form of message copies, reverse indices of messages, and many random reads and many simultaneous random writes.

The team was led by Jeff Hammerbacher, with Avinash Lakshman, Karthik Ranganathan, and Facebook engineer on the Search Team Prashant Malik as key engineers. The code was released as an open source Google Code project in July 2008. During its tenure as a Google Code project in 2008, the code was updateable only by Facebook engineers, and little community was built around it as a result. So in March 2009 it was moved to an Apache Incubator project, and on February 17, 2010 it was voted into a top-level project.

 A central paper on Cassandra by Facebook's Lakshman and Malik called "A Decentralized Structured Storage System" is available at: *http: //www.cs.cornell.edu/projects/ladis2009/papers/lakshman-ladis2009 .pdf*.

Cassandra today presents a kind of paradox: it feels new and radical, and yet it's solidly rooted in many standard, traditional computer science concepts and maxims that successful predecessors have already institutionalized. Cassandra is a realist's kind of database; it doesn't depart from the relational model to be a fun art project or experiment for smart developers. It was created specifically to solve a real-world problem that existing tools weren't able to solve. It acknowledges the limitations of prior methods and faces our new world of big data head-on.

How Did Cassandra Get Its Name?

I'm a little surprised how often people ask me where the database got its name. It's not the first thing I think of when I hear about a project. But it is interesting, and in the case of this database, it's felicitously meaningful.

In Greek mythology, Cassandra was the daughter of King Priam and Queen Hecuba of Troy. Cassandra was so beautiful that the god Apollo gave her the ability to see the future. But when she refused his amorous advances, he cursed her such that she would still be able to accurately predict everything that would happen—but no one would believe her. Cassandra foresaw the destruction of her city of Troy, but was powerless to stop it. The Cassandra distributed database is named for her. I speculate that it is also named as kind of a joke on the Oracle at Delphi, another seer for whom a database is named.

Use Cases for Cassandra

We have now unpacked the elevator pitch and have an understanding of Cassandra's advantages. Despite Cassandra's sophisticated design and smart features, it is not the right tool for every job. So in this section let's take a quick look at what kind of projects Cassandra is a good fit for.

Large Deployments

You probably don't drive a semi truck to pick up your dry cleaning; semis aren't well suited for that sort of task. Lots of careful engineering has gone into Cassandra's high availability, tuneable consistency, peer-to-peer protocol, and seamless scaling, which are its main selling points. None of these qualities is even meaningful in a single-node deployment, let alone allowed to realize its full potential.

There are, however, a wide variety of situations where a single-node relational database is all we may need. So do some measuring. Consider your expected traffic, throughput needs, and SLAs. There are no hard and fast rules here, but if you expect that you can reliably serve traffic with an acceptable level of performance with just a few relational databases, it might be a better choice to do so, simply because RDBMS are easier to run on a single machine and are more familiar.

If you think you'll need at least several nodes to support your efforts, however, Cassandra might be a good fit. If your application is expected to require dozens of nodes, Cassandra might be a great fit.

Lots of Writes, Statistics, and Analysis

Consider your application from the perspective of the ratio of reads to writes. Cassandra is optimized for excellent throughput on writes.

Many of the early production deployments of Cassandra involve storing user activity updates, social network usage, recommendations/reviews, and application statistics. These are strong use cases for Cassandra because they involve lots of writing with less predictable read operations, and because updates can occur unevenly with sudden spikes. In fact, the ability to handle application workloads that require high performance at significant write volumes with many concurrent client threads is one of the primary features of Cassandra.

According to the project wiki, Cassandra has been used to create a variety of applications, including a windowed time-series store, an inverted index for document searching, and a distributed job priority queue.

Geographical Distribution

Cassandra has out-of-the-box support for geographical distribution of data. You can easily configure Cassandra to replicate data across multiple data centers. If you have a globally deployed application that could see a performance benefit from putting the data near the user, Cassandra could be a great fit.

Evolving Applications

If your application is evolving rapidly and you're in "startup mode," Cassandra might be a good fit given its schema-free data model. This makes it easy to keep your database in step with application changes as you rapidly deploy.

Who Is Using Cassandra?

Cassandra is still in its early stages in many ways, not yet seeing its 1.0 release at the time of this writing. There are few easy, graphical tools to help manage it, and the community has not settled on certain key internal and external design questions that have been revisited. But what does it say about the promise, usefulness, and stability of a data store that even in its early stages is being used in production by many large, well-known companies?

It is a logical fallacy, informally called the Bandwagon Fallacy, to argue that just because something is growing in popularity means that it is "true." Cassandra is without a doubt enjoying skyrocketing growth in popularity, especially over the past year or so. Still, my point here is that the many successful production deployments at a variety of companies for a variety of purposes is sufficient to suggest its usefulness and readiness.

The list of companies using Cassandra is growing. These companies include:

- Twitter is using Cassandra for analytics. In a much-publicized blog post (at *http://engineering.twitter.com/2010/07/cassandra-at-twitter-today.html*), Twitter's primary Cassandra engineer, Ryan King, explained that Twitter had decided against using Cassandra as its primary store for tweets, as originally planned, but would instead use it in production for several different things: for real-time analytics, for geolocation and places of interest data, and for data mining over the entire user store.

- Mahalo uses it for its primary near-time data store.

- Facebook still uses it for inbox search, though they are using a proprietary fork.

- Digg uses it for its primary near-time data store.

- Rackspace uses it for its cloud service, monitoring, and logging.

- Reddit uses it as a persistent cache.

- Cloudkick uses it for monitoring statistics and analytics.

- Ooyala uses it to store and serve near real-time video analytics data.

- SimpleGeo uses it as the main data store for its real-time location infrastructure.

- Onespot uses it for a subset of its main data store.

Cassandra is also being used by Cisco and Platform64, and is starting to see use at Comcast and bee.tv for personalized television streaming to the Web and to mobile devices. There are others. The bottom line is that the uses are real. A wide variety of companies are finding use cases for Cassandra and seeing success with it. As of this writing, the largest known Cassandra installation is at Facebook, where they have more than 150TB of data on more than 100 machines.

Many more companies are currently evaluating Cassandra for production use in different projects, and a services company called Riptano, cofounded by Jonathan Ellis, the Apache Project Chair for Cassandra, was started in April of 2010. As more features are added and better tooling and support options are rolled out, anticipate even broader adoption.

Summary

In this chapter, we've taken an introductory look at Cassandra's defining characteristics, history, and major features. We have seen which major companies are using it and what they're using it for. We also examined a bit of history of the evolution of important contributions to the database field in order to gain a historical view of Cassandra's value proposition.

## CHAPTER 2

Installing Cassandra

For those among us who like instant gratification, we'll start by installing Cassandra. Because Cassandra introduces a lot of new vocabulary, there might be some unfamiliar terms as we walk through this. That's OK; the idea here is to get set up quickly in a simple configuration to make sure everything is running properly. This will serve as an orientation. Then, we'll take a step back and understand Cassandra in its larger context.

Installing the Binary

Cassandra is available for download from the Web at *http://cassandra.apache.org*. Just click the link on the home page to download the latest release version as a gzipped tarball. The prebuilt binary is named *apache-cassandra-x.x.x-bin.tar.gz*, where *x.x.x* represents the version number. The download is around 10MB.

Extracting the Download

The simplest way to get started is to download the prebuilt binary. You can unpack the compressed file using any regular ZIP utility. On Linux, GZip extraction utilities should be preinstalled; on Windows, you'll need to get a program such as WinZip, which is commercial, or something like 7-Zip, which is freeware. You can download the freeware program 7-Zip from *http://www.7-zip.org*.

Open your extracting program. You might have to extract the ZIP file and the TAR file in separate steps. Once you have a folder on your filesystem called *apache-cassandra-x.x.x*, you're ready to run Cassandra.

What's In There?

Once you decompress the tarball, you'll see that the Cassandra binary distribution includes several directories. Let's take a moment to look around and see what we have.

bin

> This directory contains the executables to run Cassandra and the command-line interface (CLI) client. It also has scripts to run the `nodetool`, which is a utility for inspecting a cluster to determine whether it is properly configured, and to perform a variety of maintenance operations. We look at `nodetool` in depth later. It also has scripts for converting SSTables (the datafiles) to JSON and back.

conf

> This directory, which is present in the source version at this location under the package root, contains the files for configuring your Cassandra instance. There are three basic functions: the *storage-conf.xml* file allows you to create your data store by configuring your keyspace and column families; there are files related to setting up authentication; and finally, the log4j properties let you change the logging levels to suit your needs. We see how to use all of these when we discuss configuration in Chapter 6.

interface

> For versions 0.6 and earlier, this directory contains a single file, called *cassandra.thrift*. This file represents the Remote Procedure Call (RPC) client API that Cassandra makes available. The interface is defined using the Thrift syntax and provides an easy means to generate clients. For a quick way to see all of the operations that Cassandra supports, open this file in a regular text editor. You can see that Cassandra supports clients for Java, C++, PHP, Ruby, Python, Perl, and C# through this interface.

javadoc

> This directory contains a documentation website generated using Java's JavaDoc tool. Note that JavaDoc reflects only the comments that are stored directly in the Java code, and as such does not represent comprehensive documentation. It's helpful if you want to see how the code is laid out. Moreover, Cassandra is a wonderful project, but the code contains precious few comments, so you might find the JavaDoc's usefulness limited. It may be more fruitful to simply read the class files directly if you're familiar with Java. Nonetheless, to read the JavaDoc, open the *javadoc/index.html* file in a browser.

lib

> This directory contains all of the external libraries that Cassandra needs to run. For example, it uses two different JSON serialization libraries, the Google collections project, and several Apache Commons libraries. This directory includes the Thrift and Avro RPC libraries for interacting with Cassandra.

Building from Source

Cassandra uses Apache Ant for its build scripting language and the Ivy plug-in for dependency management.

You can download Ant from *http://ant.apache.org*. You don't need to download Ivy separately just to build Cassandra.

Ivy requires Ant, and building from source requires the complete JDK, version 1.6.0_20 or better, not just the JRE. If you see a message about how Ant is missing *tools.jar*, either you don't have the full JDK or you're pointing to the wrong path in your environment variables.

If you want to download the most cutting-edge builds, you can get the source from Hudson, which the Cassandra project uses as its Continuous Integration tool. See *http://hudson.zones.apache.org/hudson/job/Cassandra/* for the latest builds and test coverage information.

If you are a Git fan, you can get a read-only trunk version of the Cassandra source using this command:

```
>git clone git://git.apache.org/cassandra.git
```

Git is a source code management system created by Linus Torvalds to manage development of the Linux kernel. It's increasingly popular and is used by projects such as Android, Fedora, Ruby on Rails, Perl, and many Cassandra clients (as we'll see in Chapter 8). If you're on a Linux distribution such as Ubuntu, it couldn't be easier to get Git. At a console, just type *>apt-get install git* and it will be installed and ready for commands. For more information, visit *http://git-scm.com/*.

Because Ivy takes care of all the dependencies, it's easy to build Cassandra once you have the source. Just make sure you're in the root directory of your source download and execute the ant program, which will look for a file called *build.xml* in the current directory and execute the default build target. Ant and Ivy take care of the rest. To execute the Ant program and start compiling the source, just type:

```
>ant
```

That's it. Ivy will retrieve all of the necessary dependencies, and Ant will build the nearly 350 source files and execute the tests. If all went well, you should see a BUILD SUCCESSFUL message. If all did not go well, make sure that your path settings are all correct, that you have the most recent versions of the required programs, and that you downloaded a stable Cassandra build. You can check the Hudson report to make sure that the source you downloaded actually can compile.

If you want to see detailed information on what is happening during the build, you can pass Ant the -v option to cause it to output verbose details regarding each operation it performs.

Additional Build Targets

To compile the server, you can simply execute *ant* as shown previously. But there are a couple of other targets in the build file that you might be interested in:

test
Users will probably find this the most helpful, as it executes the battery of unit tests. You can also check out the unit test sources themselves for some useful examples of how to interact with Cassandra.

gen-thrift-java
This target generates the Apache Thrift client interface for interacting with the database in Java.

gen-thrift-py
This target generates the Thrift client interface for Python users.

build-jar
To create a Java Archive (JAR) file for distribution, execute the command >*ant jar*. This will perform a complete build and output a file into the *build* directory called *apache-cassandra-x.x.x.jar*.

Building with Maven

The original authors of Cassandra apparently didn't care much for Maven, so the early releases did not include any Maven POM file. But because so many Java developers have begun to favor Maven over Ant, and the tooling support in IDEs for Maven has become so strong, there's a *pom.xml* contribution to the project so you can build from Maven if you prefer.

To build the source from Maven, navigate to *<cassandra-home>/contrib/maven* and execute this command:

```
$ mvn clean install
```

If you have any difficulties building with Maven, you may have to get some of the required JARs manually. As of version 0.6.3, the Maven POM doesn't work out of the box because some dependencies, such as the *libthrift.jar* file, are unavailable in a repository.

Few developers are using Maven with Cassandra, so Maven lacks strong support. Which is to say, use caution, because the Maven POM is often broken.

Running Cassandra

In earlier versions of Cassandra, before you could start the server there was a bit of fiddling to be done with Ivy and setting environment variables. But the developers have done a terrific job of making it very easy to start using Cassandra immediately.

 Cassandra requires Java Standard Edition JDK 6. Preferably, use 1.6.0_20 or greater. It has been tested on both the Open JDK and Sun's JDK. You can check your installed Java version by opening a command prompt and executing >`java -version`. If you need a JDK, you can get one at *http://java.sun.com/javase/downloads*.

On Windows

Once you have the binary or the source downloaded and compiled, you're ready to start the database server.

You also might need to set your `JAVA_HOME` environment variable. To do this on Windows 7, click the Start button and then right-click on Computer. Click Advanced System Settings, and then click the Environment Variables... button. Click New... to create a new system variable. In the Variable Name field, type `JAVA_HOME`. In the Variable Value field, type the path to your JDK installation. This is probably something like *C:\Program Files\Java\jdk1.6.0_20*. Remember that if you create a new environment variable, you'll need to reopen any currently open terminals in order for the system to become aware of the new variable. To make sure your environment variable is set correctly and that Cassandra can subsequently find Java on Windows, execute this command in a new terminal: >*echo %JAVA_HOME%*. This prints the value of your environment variable.

Once you've started the server for the first time, Cassandra will add two directories to your system. The first is *C:\var\lib\cassandra*, which is where it will store its data in files called *commitlog*. The other is *C:\var\log\cassandra*; logs will be written to a file called *system.log*. If you encounter any difficulties, consult the files in these directories to see what might have happened. If you've been trying different versions of the database and aren't worried about losing data, you can delete these directories and restart the server as a last resort.

On Linux

The process on Linux is similar to that on Windows. Make sure that your `JAVA_HOME` variable is properly set to version 1.6.0_20 or better. Then, you need to extract the Cassandra gzipped tarball using *gunzip*. Finally, create a couple of directories for Cassandra to store its data and logs, and give them the proper permissions, as shown here:

```
ehewitt@morpheus$ cd /home/eben/books/cassandra/dist/apache-cassandra-0.7.0-beta1
ehewitt@morpheus$ sudo mkdir -p /var/log/cassandra
ehewitt@morpheus$ sudo chown -R ehewitt /var/log/cassandra
ehewitt@morpheus$ sudo mkdir -p /var/lib/cassandra
ehewitt@morpheus$ sudo chown -R ehewitt /var/lib/cassandra
```

Instead of ehewitt, of course, substitute your own username.

Starting the Server

To start the Cassandra server on any OS, open a command prompt or terminal window, navigate to the *<cassandra-directory>/bin* where you unpacked Cassandra, and run the following command to start your server. In a clean installation, you should see some log statements like this:

```
eben@morpheus$ bin/cassandra -f
 INFO 13:23:22,367 DiskAccessMode 'auto' determined to be standard, indexAccessMode
is standard
 INFO 13:23:22,475 Couldn't detect any schema definitions in local storage.
 INFO 13:23:22,476 Found table data in data directories.
Consider using JMX to call org.apache.cassandra.service.StorageService
.loadSchemaFromYaml().
 INFO 13:23:22,497 Cassandra version: 0.7.0-beta1
 INFO 13:23:22,497 Thrift API version: 10.0.0
 INFO 13:23:22,498 Saved Token not found. Using qFABQw5XJMvs47lg
 INFO 13:23:22,498 Saved ClusterName not found. Using Test Cluster
 INFO 13:23:22,502 Creating new commitlog segment /var/lib/cassandra/commitlog/
CommitLog-1282508602502.log
 INFO 13:23:22,507 switching in a fresh Memtable for LocationInfo at CommitLogContext(
file='/var/lib/cassandra/commitlog/CommitLog-1282508602502.log', position=276)
 INFO 13:23:22,510 Enqueuing flush of Memtable-LocationInfo@29857804(178 bytes,
4 operations)
 INFO 13:23:22,511 Writing Memtable-LocationInfo@29857804(178 bytes, 4 operations)
 INFO 13:23:22,691 Completed flushing /var/lib/cassandra/data/system/
LocationInfo-e-1-Data.db
 INFO 13:23:22,701 Starting up server gossip
 INFO 13:23:22,750 Binding thrift service to localhost/127.0.0.1:9160
 INFO 13:23:22,752 Using TFramedTransport with a max frame size of 15728640 bytes.
 INFO 13:23:22,753 Listening for thrift clients...
 INFO 13:23:22,792 mx4j successfuly loaded
HttpAdaptor version 3.0.2 started on port 8081
```

> Using the -f switch tells Cassandra to stay in the foreground instead of running as a background process, so that all of the server logs will print to standard out and you can see them in your terminal window, which is useful for testing.

Congratulations! Now your Cassandra server should be up and running with a new single node cluster called Test Cluster listening on port 9160.

The committers work hard to ensure that data is readable from one minor dot release to the next and from one major version to the next. The commit log, however, needs to be completely cleared out from version to version (even minor versions).

If you have any previous versions of Cassandra installed, you may want to clear out the data directories for now, just to get up and running. If you've messed up your Cassandra installation and want to get started cleanly again, you can delete the folders in *var/lib/cassandra* and *var/log/cassandra*.

Running the Command-Line Client Interface

Now that you have a Cassandra installation up and running, let's give it a quick try to make sure everything is set up properly. On Linux, running the command-line interface just works. On Windows, you might have to do a little additional work.

On Windows, navigate to the Cassandra home directory and open a new terminal in which to run our client process:

```
>bin\cassandra-cli
```

It's possible that on Windows you will see an error like this when starting the client:

```
Starting Cassandra Client
Exception in thread "main" java.lang.NoClassDefFoundError:
org/apache/cassandra/cli/CliMain
```

This probably means that you started Cassandra directly from within the *bin* directory, and it therefore sets up its Java classpath incorrectly and can't find the *CliMain* file to start the client. You can define an environment variable called `CASSANDRA_HOME` that points to the top-level directory where you have placed or built Cassandra, so you don't have to pay as much attention to where you're starting Cassandra from.

For a little reminder on setting environment variables on Windows, see the section "On Windows" on page 33.

To run the command-line interface program on Linux, navigate to the Cassandra home directory and run the `cassandra-cli` program in the *bin* directory:

```
>bin/cassandra-cli
```

The Cassandra client will start:

```
eben@morpheus$ bin/cassandra-cli
Welcome to cassandra CLI.

Type 'help' or '?' for help. Type 'quit' or 'exit' to quit.
[default@unknown]
```

You now have an interactive shell at which you can issue commands.

Note, however, that if you're used to Oracle's SQL*Plus or similar command-line database clients, you may become frustrated. The Cassandra CLI is not intended to be used as a full-blown client, as it's really for development. That makes it a good way to get started using Cassandra, because you don't have to write lots of code to test interactions with your database and get used to the environment.

Basic CLI Commands

Before we get too deep into how Cassandra works, let's get an overview of the client API so that you can see what kinds of commands you can send to the server. We'll see how to use the basic environment commands and how to do a round trip of inserting and retrieving some data.

Help

To get help for the command-line interface, type *help* or *?* to see the list of available commands. The following list shows only the commands related to metadata and configuration; there are other commands for getting and setting values that we explore later.

```
[default@Keyspace1] help
List of all CLI commands:
?                                               Display this message.
help                                              Display this help.
help <command>                    Display detailed, command-specific help.
connect <hostname>/<port>                     Connect to thrift service.
use <keyspace> [<username> 'password']           Switch to a keyspace.
describe keyspace <keyspacename>                    Describe keyspace.
exit                                                     Exit CLI.
quit                                                     Exit CLI.
show cluster name                              Display cluster name.
show keyspaces                               Show list of keyspaces.
show api version                             Show server API version.
create keyspace <keyspace> [with <att1>=<value1> [and <att2>=<value2> ...]]
              Add a new keyspace with the specified attribute and value(s).
create column family <cf> [with <att1>=<value1> [and <att2>=<value2> ...]]
          Create a new column family with the specified attribute and value(s).
drop keyspace <keyspace>                          Delete a keyspace.
drop column family <cf>                      Delete a column family.
rename keyspace <keyspace> <keyspace_new_name>    Rename a keyspace.
rename column family <cf> <new_name>      Rename a column family.
```

Connecting to a Server

Starting the client this way does not automatically connect to a Cassandra server instance. So to connect to a particular server after you have started Cassandra this way, use the *connect* command:

```
eben@morpheus:~/books/cassandra/dist/apache-cassandra-0.7.0-beta1$ bin/cassandra-cli
Welcome to cassandra CLI.

Type 'help' or '?' for help. Type 'quit' or 'exit' to quit.
[default@unknown] connect localhost/9160
Connected to: "Test Cluster" on localhost/9160
[default@unknown]
```

As a shortcut, you can start the client and connect to a particular server instance by passing the host and port parameters at startup, like this:

```
eben@morpheus:~/books/cassandra/dist/apache-cassandra-0.7.0-beta1$ bin/
cassandra-cli localhost/9160
Welcome to cassandra CLI.

Type 'help' or '?' for help. Type 'quit' or 'exit' to quit.
[default@unknown]
```

 If you see this error while trying to connect to a server:

```
Exception connecting to localhost/9160 - java.net.ConnectException:
Connection refused: connect
```

make sure that a Cassandra instance is started at that host and port and that you can ping the host you're trying to reach. There may be firewall rules preventing you from connecting. Also make sure that you're using the new 0.7 syntax as described earlier, as it has changed from previous versions.

The CLI indicates that you're connected to a Cassandra server cluster called "Test Cluster". That's because this cluster of one node at localhost is set up for you by default.

 In a production environment, be sure to remove the Test Cluster from the configuration.

Describing the Environment

After connecting to your Cassandra instance Test Cluster, if you're using the binary distribution, an empty *keyspace*, or Cassandra database, is set up for you to test with.

To see the name of the current cluster you're working in, type:

```
[default@unknown] show cluster name
Test Cluster
```

To see which keyspaces are available in the cluster, issue this command:

```
[default@unknown] show keyspaces
system
```

If you have created any of your own keyspaces, they will be shown as well. The `system` keyspace is used internally by Cassandra, and isn't for us to put data into. In this way, it's similar to the master and temp databases in Microsoft SQL Server. This keyspace contains the schema definitions and is aware of any modifications to the schema made at runtime. It can propagate any changes made in one node to the rest of the cluster based on timestamps.

To see the version of the API you're using, type:

```
[default@Keyspace1] show api version
10.0.0
```

There are a variety of other commands with which you can experiment. For now, let's add some data to the database and get it back out again.

Creating a Keyspace and Column Family

A Cassandra keyspace is sort of like a relational database. It defines one or more column families, which are very roughly analogous to tables in the relational world. When you start the CLI client without specifying a keyspace, the output will look like this:

```
>bin/cassandra-cli --host localhost --port 9160
Starting Cassandra Client
Connected to: "Test Cluster" on localhost/9160
Welcome to cassandra CLI.

Type 'help' or '?' for help. Type 'quit' or 'exit' to quit.
[default@unknown]
```

Your shell prompt is for `default@unknown` because you haven't authenticated as a particular user (which we'll see how to do in Chapter 6) and you didn't specify a keyspace.

 This authentication scheme is familiar if you've used MySQL before. Authentication and authorization are very much works in progress at the time of this writing. The recommended deployment is to put a firewall around your cluster.

Let's create our own keyspace so we have something to write data to:

```
[default@unknown] create keyspace MyKeyspace with replication_factor=1
ab67bad0-ae2c-11df-b642-e700f669bcfc
```

Don't worry about the `replication_factor` for now. That's a setting we'll look at in detail later. After you have created your own keyspace, you can switch to it in the shell by typing:

```
[default@unknown] use MyKeyspace
Authenticated to keyspace: MyKeyspace
[default@MyKeyspace]
```

We're "authorized" to the keyspace because MyKeyspace doesn't require credentials.

Now we can create a column family in our keyspace. To do this on the CLI, use the following command:

```
[default@MyKeyspace] create column family User
991590d3-ae2e-11df-b642-e700f669bcfc
[default@MyKeyspace]
```

This creates a new column family called "User" in our current keyspace, and takes the defaults for column family settings. We can use the CLI to get a description of a keyspace using the *describe keyspace* command, and make sure it has our column family definition, as shown here:

```
[default@MyKeyspace] describe keyspace MyKeyspace
Keyspace: MyKeyspace

Column Family Name: User
Column Family Type: Standard
Column Sorted By: org.apache.cassandra.db.marshal.BytesType
flush period: null minutes
------
[default@MyKeyspace]
```

We'll worry about the Type, Sorted By, and flush period settings later. For now, we have enough to get started.

Writing and Reading Data

Now that we have a keyspace and a column family, we'll write some data to the database and read it back out again. It's OK at this point not to know quite what's going on. We'll come to understand Cassandra's data model in depth later. For now, you have a keyspace (database), which has a column family. For our purposes here, it's enough to think of a column family as a multidimensional ordered map that you don't have to define further ahead of time. Column families hold columns, and columns are the atomic unit of data storage.

To write a value, use the set command:

```
[default@MyKeyspace] set User['ehewitt']['fname']='Eben'
Value inserted.
[default@MyKeyspace] set User['ehewitt']['email']='me@example.com'
Value inserted.
[default@MyKeyspace]
```

Here we have created two columns for the key ehewitt, to store a set of related values. The column names are fname and email. We can use the count command to make sure that we have written two columns for our single key:

```
[default@MyKeyspace] count User['ehewitt']
2 columns
```

Now that we know the data is there, let's read it, using the get command:

```
[default@MyKeyspace] get User['ehewitt']
=> (column=666e616d65, value=Eben, timestamp=1282510290343000)
=> (column=656d61696c, value=me@example.com, timestamp=1282510313429000)
Returned 2 results.
```

You can delete a column using the `del` command. Here we will delete the `email` column for the `ehewitt` row key:

```
[default@MyKeyspace] del User['ehewitt']['email']
column removed.
```

Now we'll clean up after ourselves by deleting the entire row. It's the same command, but we don't specify a column name:

```
[default@MyKeyspace] del User['ehewitt']
row removed.
```

To make sure that it's removed, we can query again:

```
[default@Keyspace1] get User['ehewitt']
Returned 0 results.
```

Summary

Now you should have a Cassandra installation up and running. You've worked with the CLI client to insert and retrieve some data, and you're ready to take a step back and get the big picture on Cassandra before really diving into the details.

CHAPTER 3

The Cassandra Data Model

In this chapter, we'll gain an understanding of Cassandra's design goals, data model, and some general behavior characteristics.

For developers and administrators coming from the relational world, the Cassandra data model can be very difficult to understand initially. Some terms, such as "keyspace," are completely new, and some, such as "column," exist in both worlds but have different meanings. It can also be confusing if you're trying to sort through the Dynamo or Bigtable source papers, because although Cassandra may be based on them, it has its own model.

So in this chapter we start from common ground and then work through the unfamiliar terms. Then, we do some actual modeling to help understand how to bridge the gap between the relational world and the world of Cassandra.

The Relational Data Model

In a relational database, we have the database itself, which is the outermost container that might correspond to a single application. The database contains tables. Tables have names and contain one or more columns, which also have names. When we add data to a table, we specify a value for every column defined; if we don't have a value for a particular column, we use null. This new entry adds a row to the table, which we can later read if we know the row's unique identifier (primary key), or by using a SQL statement that expresses some criteria that row might meet. If we want to update values in the table, we can update all of the rows or just some of them, depending on the filter we use in a "where" clause of our SQL statement.

For the purposes of learning Cassandra, it may be useful to suspend for a moment what you know from the relational world.

A Simple Introduction

In this section, we'll take a bottom-up approach to understanding Cassandra's data model.

The simplest data store you would conceivably want to work with might be an array or list. It would look like Figure 3-1.

Figure 3-1. A list of values

If you persisted this list, you could query it later, but you would have to either examine each value in order to know what it represented, or always store each value in the same place in the list and then externally maintain documentation about which cell in the array holds which values. That would mean you might have to supply empty place-holder values (nulls) in order to keep the uniform size in case you didn't have a value for an optional attribute (such as a fax number or apartment number). An array is a clearly useful data structure, but not semantically rich.

So we'd like to add a second dimension to this list: names to match the values. We'll give names to each cell, and now we have a map structure, as shown in Figure 3-2.

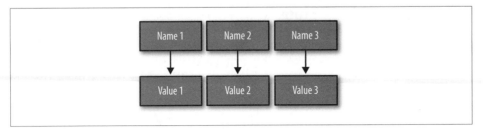

Figure 3-2. A map of name/value pairs

This is an improvement because we can know the names of our values. So if we decided that our map would hold User information, we could have column names like `first Name`, `lastName`, `phone`, `email`, and so on. This is a somewhat richer structure to work with.

But the structure we've built so far works only if we have one instance of a given entity, such as a single Person or User or Hotel or Tweet. It doesn't give us much if we want to store multiple entities with the same structure, which is certainly what we want to do. There's nothing to unify some collection of name/value pairs, and no way to repeat the same column names. So we need something that will group some of the column values together in a distinctly addressable group. We need a key to reference a group of columns that should be treated together as a set. We need rows. Then, if we get a single row, we can get all of the name/value pairs for a single entity at once, or just get the values for the names we're interested in. We could call these name/value pairs *columns*. We could call each separate entity that holds some set of columns *rows*. And the unique identifier for each row could be called a *row key*.

Cassandra defines a *column family* to be a logical division that associates similar data. For example, we might have a User column family, a Hotel column family, an AddressBook column family, and so on. In this way, a column family is somewhat analogous to a table in the relational world.

Putting this all together, we have the basic Cassandra data structures: the column, which is a name/value pair (and a client-supplied timestamp of when it was last updated), and a column family, which is a container for rows that have similar, but not identical, column sets.

In relational databases, we're used to storing column names as strings only—that's all we're allowed. But in Cassandra, we don't have that limitation. Both row keys and column names can be strings, like relational column names, but they can also be long integers, UUIDs, or any kind of byte array. So there's some variety to how your key names can be set.

This reveals another interesting quality to Cassandra's columns: they don't have to be as simple as predefined name/value pairs; you can store useful data in the key itself, not only in the value. This is somewhat common when creating indexes in Cassandra. But let's not get ahead of ourselves.

Now we don't need to store a value for every column every time we store a new entity. Maybe we don't know the values for every column for a given entity. For example, some people have a second phone number and some don't, and in an online form backed by Cassandra, there may be some fields that are optional and some that are required. That's OK. Instead of storing null for those values we don't know, which would waste space, we just won't store that column at all for that row. So now we have a sparse, multidimensional array structure that looks like Figure 3-3.

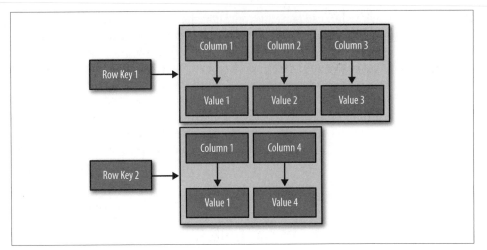

Figure 3-3. A column family

It may help to think of it in terms of JavaScript Object Notation (JSON) instead of a picture:

```
Musician:                               ColumnFamily 1
    bootsy:                             RowKey
        email: bootsy@pfunk.com,        ColumnName:Value
        instrument: bass                ColumnName:Value
    george:                             RowKey
        email: george@pfunk.com         ColumnName:Value

Band:                                   ColumnFamily 2
    george:                             RowKey
        pfunk: 1968-2010                ColumnName:Value
```

Here we have two column families, Musician and Band. The Musician column family has two rows, "bootsy" and "george". These two rows have a ragged set of columns associated with them: the bootsy record has two columns (email and instrument), and the george record has only one column. That's fine in Cassandra. The second column family is Band, and it also has a "george" row, with a column named "pfunk".

Columns in Cassandra actually have a third aspect: the timestamp, which records the last time the column was updated. This is not an automatic metadata property, however; clients have to provide the timestamp along with the value when they perform writes. You cannot query by the timestamp; it is used purely for conflict resolution on the server side.

Rows do not have timestamps. Only each individual column has a timestamp.

And what if we wanted to create a group of related columns, that is, add another dimension on top of this? Cassandra allows us to do this with something called a *super column family*. A super column family can be thought of as a map of maps. The super column family is shown in Figure 3-4.

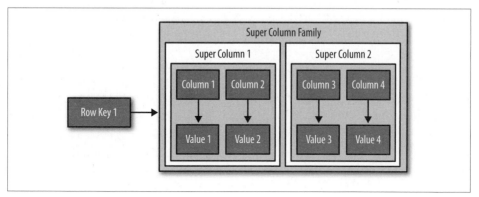

Figure 3-4. A super column family

Where a row in a column family holds a collection of name/value pairs, the super column family holds subcolumns, where subcolumns are named groups of columns. So the address of a value in a regular column family is a row key pointing to a column name pointing to a value, while the address of a value in a column family of type "super" is a row key pointing to a column name pointing to a subcolumn name pointing to a value. Put slightly differently, a row in a super column family still contains columns, each of which then contains subcolumns.

So that's the bottom-up approach to looking at Cassandra's data model. Now that we have this basic understanding, let's switch gears and zoom out to a higher level, in order to take a top-down approach. There is so much confusion on this topic that it's worth it to restate things in a different way in order to thoroughly understand the data model.

Clusters

Cassandra is probably not the best choice if you only need to run a single node. As previously mentioned, the Cassandra database is specifically designed to be distributed over several machines operating together that appear as a single instance to the end user. So the outermost structure in Cassandra is the *cluster*, sometimes called the *ring*, because Cassandra assigns data to nodes in the cluster by arranging them in a ring.

A node holds a replica for different ranges of data. If the first node goes down, a replica can respond to queries. The peer-to-peer protocol allows the data to replicate across nodes in a manner transparent to the user, and the *replication factor* is the number of machines in your cluster that will receive copies of the same data. We'll examine this in greater detail in Chapter 6.

Keyspaces

A cluster is a container for keyspaces—typically a single keyspace. A *keyspace* is the outermost container for data in Cassandra, corresponding closely to a relational database. Like a relational database, a keyspace has a name and a set of attributes that define keyspace-wide behavior. Although people frequently advise that it's a good idea to create a single keyspace per application, this doesn't appear to have much practical basis. It's certainly an acceptable practice, but it's perfectly fine to create as many keyspaces as your application needs. Note, however, that you will probably run into trouble creating thousands of keyspaces per application.

Depending on your security constraints and partitioner, it's fine to run multiple keyspaces on the same cluster. For example, if your application is called Twitter, you would probably have a cluster called `Twitter-Cluster` and a keyspace called `Twitter`. To my knowledge, there are currently no naming conventions in Cassandra for such items.

In Cassandra, the basic attributes that you can set per keyspace are:

Replication factor
> In simplest terms, the replication factor refers to the number of nodes that will act as copies (replicas) of each row of data. If your replication factor is 3, then three nodes in the ring will have copies of each row, and this replication is transparent to clients.
>
> The replication factor essentially allows you to decide how much you want to pay in performance to gain more consistency. That is, your consistency level for reading and writing data is based on the replication factor.

Replica placement strategy
> The replica placement refers to *how* the replicas will be placed in the ring. There are different strategies that ship with Cassandra for determining which nodes will get copies of which keys. These are SimpleStrategy (formerly known as RackUnawareStrategy), OldNetworkTopologyStrategy (formerly known as RackAwareStrategy), and NetworkTopologyStrategy (formerly known as DatacenterShardStrategy).

Column families
> In the same way that a database is a container for tables, a keyspace is a container for a list of one or more column families. A *column family* is roughly analogous to a table in the relational model, and is a container for a collection of rows. Each row contains ordered columns. Column families represent the structure of your data. Each keyspace has at least one and often many column families.

I mention the replication factor and replica placement strategy here because they are set per keyspace. However, they don't have an immediate impact on your data model per se.

It is possible, but generally not recommended, to create multiple keyspaces per application. The only time you would want to split your application into multiple keyspaces is if you wanted a different replication factor or replica placement strategy for some of the column families. For example, if you have some data that is of lower priority, you could put it in its own keyspace with a lower replication factor so that Cassandra doesn't have to work as hard to replicate it. But this may be more complicated than it's worth. It's probably a better idea to start with one keyspace and see whether you really need to tune at that level.

Column Families

A *column family* is a container for an ordered collection of rows, each of which is itself an ordered collection of columns. In the relational world, when you are physically creating your database from a model, you specify the name of the database (keyspace), the names of the tables (remotely similar to column families, but don't get stuck on the idea that column families equal tables—they don't), and then you define the names of the columns that will be in each table.

There are a few good reasons not to go too far with the idea that a column family is like a relational table. First, Cassandra is considered schema-free because although the column families are defined, the columns are not. You can freely add any column to any column family at any time, depending on your needs. Second, a column family has two attributes: a name and a comparator. The comparator value indicates how columns will be sorted when they are returned to you in a query—according to long, byte, UTF8, or other ordering.

In a relational database, it is frequently transparent to the user how tables are stored on disk, and it is rare to hear of recommendations about data modeling based on how the RDBMS might store tables on disk. That's another reason to keep in mind that a column family is *not* a table. Because column families are each stored in separate files on disk, it's important to keep related columns defined together in the same column family.

Another way that column families differ from relational tables is that relational tables define only columns, and the user supplies the values, which are the rows. But in Cassandra, a table can hold columns, or it can be defined as a super column family. The benefit of using a super column family is to allow for nesting.

For standard column families, which is the default, you set the type to Standard; for a super column family, you set the type to Super.

When you write data to a column family in Cassandra, you specify values for one or more columns. That collection of values together with a unique identifier is called a *row*. That row has a unique key, called the *row key*, which acts like the primary key unique identifier for that row. So while it's not incorrect to call it column-oriented, or columnar, it might be easier to understand the model if you think of rows as containers for columns. This is also why some people refer to Cassandra column families as similar to a four-dimensional hash:

```
[Keyspace][ColumnFamily][Key][Column]
```

We can use a JSON-like notation to represent a Hotel column family, as shown here:

```
Hotel {
    key: AZC_043 { name: Cambria Suites Hayden, phone: 480-444-4444,
        address: 400 N. Hayden Rd., city: Scottsdale, state: AZ, zip: 85255}
    key: AZS_011 { name: Clarion Scottsdale Peak, phone: 480-333-3333,
        address: 3000 N. Scottsdale Rd, city: Scottsdale, state: AZ, zip: 85255}
    key: CAS_021 { name: W Hotel, phone: 415-222-2222,
        address: 181 3rd Street, city: San Francisco, state: CA, zip: 94103}
    key: NYN_042 { name: Waldorf Hotel, phone: 212-555-5555,
        address: 301 Park Ave, city: New York, state: NY, zip: 10019}
}
```

 I'm leaving out the timestamp attribute of the columns here for simplicity, but just remember that every column has a timestamp.

In this example, the row key is a unique primary key for the hotel, and the columns are name, phone, address, city, state, and zip. Although these rows happen to define values for all of the same columns, you could easily have one row with 4 columns and another row in the same column family with 400 columns, and none of them would have to overlap.

 It's an inherent part of Cassandra's replica design that all data for a single row must fit on a single machine in the cluster. The reason for this limitation is that rows have an associated row key, which is used to determine the nodes that will act as replicas for that row. Further, the value of a single column cannot exceed 2GB. Keep these things in mind as you design your data model.

We can query a column family such as this one using the CLI, like this:

```
cassandra> get Hotelier.Hotel['NYN_042']
=> (column=zip, value=10019, timestamp=3894166157031651)
=> (column=state, value=NY, timestamp=3894166157031651)
=> (column=phone, value=212-555-5555, timestamp=3894166157031651)
=> (column=name, value=The Waldorf=Astoria, timestamp=3894166157031651)
=> (column=city, value=New York, timestamp=3894166157031651)
```

```
=> (column=address, value=301 Park Ave, timestamp=3894166157031651)
Returned 6 results.
```

This indicates that we have one hotel in New York, New York, but we see six results because the results are column-oriented, and there are six columns for that row in the column family. Note that while there are six columns for that row, other rows might have more or fewer columns.

Column Family Options

There are a few additional parameters that you can define for each column family. These are:

keys_cached
> The number of locations to keep cached per SSTable. This doesn't refer to column name/values at all, but to the number of keys, as locations of rows per column family, to keep in memory in least-recently-used order.

rows_cached
> The number of rows whose entire contents (the complete list of name/value pairs for that unique row key) will be cached in memory.

comment
> This is just a standard comment that helps you remember important things about your column family definitions.

read_repair_chance
> This is a value between 0 and 1 that represents the probability that read repair operations will be performed when a query is performed without a specified quorum, and it returns the same row from two or more replicas and at least one of the replicas appears to be out of date. You may want to lower this value if you are performing a much larger number of reads than writes.

preload_row_cache
> Specifies whether you want to prepopulate the row cache on server startup.

I have simplified these definitions somewhat, as they are really more about configuration and server behavior than they are about the data model. They are covered in detail in Chapter 6.

Columns

A *column* is the most basic unit of data structure in the Cassandra data model. A column is a triplet of a name, a value, and a clock, which you can think of as a timestamp for now. Again, although we're familiar with the term "columns" from the relational world, it's confusing to think of them in the same way in Cassandra. First of all, when designing a relational database, you specify the structure of the tables up front by assigning all of the columns in the table a name; later, when you write data, you're simply supplying values for the predefined structure.

But in Cassandra, you don't define the columns up front; you just define the column families you want in the keyspace, and then you can start writing data without defining the columns anywhere. That's because in Cassandra, all of a column's names are supplied by the client. This adds considerable flexibility to how your application works with data, and can allow it to evolve organically over time.

 Cassandra's clock was introduced in version 0.7, but its fate is uncertain. Prior to 0.7, it was called a timestamp, and was simply a Java long type. It was changed to support Vector Clocks, which are a popular mechanism for replica conflict resolution in distributed systems, and it's how Amazon Dynamo implements conflict resolution. That's why you'll hear the third aspect of the column referred to both as a timestamp and a clock. Vector Clocks may or may not ultimately become how timestamps are represented in Cassandra 0.7, which is in beta at the time of this writing.

The data types for the name and value are Java byte arrays, frequently supplied as strings. Because the name and value are binary types, they can be of any length. The data type for the clock is an `org.apache.cassandra.db.IClock`, but for the 0.7 release, a timestamp still works to keep backward compatibility. This column structure is illustrated in Figure 3-5.

 Cassandra 0.7 introduced an optional time to live (TTL) value, which allows columns to expire a certain amount of time after creation. This can potentially prove very useful.

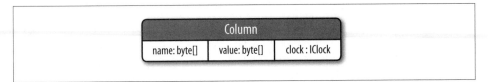

Figure 3-5. The structure of a column

Here's an example of a column you might define, represented with JSON notation just for clarity of structure:

```
{
    "name": "email",
    "value": "me@example.com",
    "timestamp": 1274654183103300
}
```

In this example, this column is named "email"; more precisely, the value of its name attribute is "email". But recall that a single column family will have multiple keys (or row keys) representing different rows that might also contain this column. This is why moving from the relational model is hard: we think of a relational table as holding the same set of columns for every row. But in Cassandra, a column family holds many rows, each of which may hold the same, or different, sets of columns.

On the server side, columns are immutable in order to prevent multithreading issues. The column is defined in Cassandra by the `org.apache.cassandra.db.IColumn` interface, which allows a variety of operations, including getting the value of the column as a byte array or, in the case of a super column, getting its subcolumns as a `Collection<IColumn>` and finding the time of the most recent change.

In a relational database, rows are stored together. This wasn't the case for early versions of Cassandra, but as of version 0.6, rows for the same column family are stored together on disk.

 You cannot perform joins in Cassandra. If you have designed a data model and find that you need something like a join, you'll have to either do the work on the client side, or create a denormalized second column family that represents the join results for you. This is common among Cassandra users. Performing joins on the client should be a very rare case; you really want to duplicate (denormalize) the data instead.

Wide Rows, Skinny Rows

When designing a table in a traditional relational database, you're typically dealing with "entities," or the set of attributes that describe a particular noun (Hotel, User, Product, etc.). Not much thought is given to the size of the rows themselves, because row size isn't negotiable once you've decided what noun your table represents. However, when you're working with Cassandra, you actually have a decision to make about the size of your rows: they can be wide or skinny, depending on the number of columns the row contains.

A wide row means a row that has lots and lots (perhaps tens of thousands or even millions) of columns. Typically there is a small number of rows that go along with so many columns. Conversely, you could have something closer to a relational model, where you define a smaller number of columns and use many different rows—that's the skinny model.

Wide rows typically contain automatically generated names (like UUIDs or time-stamps) and are used to store lists of things. Consider a monitoring application as an example: you might have a row that represents a time slice of an hour by using a modi-fied timestamp as a row key, and then store columns representing IP addresses that accessed your application within that interval. You can then create a new row key after an hour elapses.

Skinny rows are slightly more like traditional RDBMS rows, in that each row will contain similar sets of column names. They differ from RDBMS rows, however, because all columns are essentially optional.

Another difference between wide and skinny rows is that only wide rows will typically be concerned about sorting order of column names. Which brings us to the next section.

Column Sorting

Columns have another aspect to their definition. In Cassandra, you specify how column names will be compared for sort order when results are returned to the client. Columns are sorted by the "Compare With" type defined on their enclosing column family, and you can choose from the following: AsciiType, BytesType, LexicalUUIDType, Integer Type, LongType, TimeUUIDType, or UTF8Type.

AsciiType
> This sorts by directly comparing the bytes, validating that the input can be parsed as US-ASCII. US-ASCII is a character encoding mechanism based on the lexical order of the English alphabet. It defines 128 characters, 94 of which are printable.

BytesType
> This is the default, and sorts by directly comparing the bytes, skipping the validation step. BytesType is the default for a reason: it provides the correct sorting for most types of data (UTF-8 and ASCII included).

LexicalUUIDType
> A 16-byte (128-bit) Universally Unique Identifier (UUID), compared lexically (by byte value).

LongType
> This sorts by an 8-byte (64-bit) long numeric type.

IntegerType
> Introduced in 0.7, this is faster than LongType and allows integers of both fewer and more bits than the 64 bits provided by LongType.

TimeUUIDType
> This sorts by a 16-byte (128-bit) timestamp. There are five common versions of generating timestamp UUIDs. The scheme Cassandra uses is a version one UUID, which means that it is generated based on conflating the computer's MAC address and the number of 100-nanosecond intervals since the beginning of the Gregorian calendar.

UTF8Type
> A string using UTF-8 as the character encoder. Although this may seem like a good default type, that's probably because it's comfortable to programmers who are used to using XML or other data exchange mechanism that requires common encoding. In Cassandra, however, you should use UTF8Type only if you want your data validated.

Custom

> You can create your own column sorting mechanism if you like. This, like many things in Cassandra, is pluggable. All you have to do is extend the `org.apache` `.cassandra.db.marshal.AbstractType` and specify your class name.

Column names are stored in sorted order according to the value of `compare_with`. Rows, on the other hand, are stored in an order defined by the partitioner (for example, with RandomPartitioner, they are in random order, etc.). We examine partitioners in Chapter 6.

It is not possible in Cassandra to sort by value, as we're used to doing in relational databases. This may seem like an odd limitation, but Cassandra has to sort by column name in order to allow fetching individual columns from very large rows without pulling the entire row into memory. Performance is an important selling point of Cassandra, and sorting at read time would harm performance.

> Column sorting is controllable, but key sorting isn't; row keys always sort in byte order.

Super Columns

A *super column* is a special kind of column. Both kinds of columns are name/value pairs, but a regular column stores a byte array value, and the value of a super column is a map of subcolumns (which store byte array values). Note that they store only a map of columns; you cannot define a super column that stores a map of other super columns. So the super column idea goes only one level deep, but it can have an unbounded number of columns.

The basic structure of a super column is its name, which is a byte array (just as with a regular column), and the columns it stores (see Figure 3-6). Its columns are held as a map whose keys are the column names and whose values are the columns.

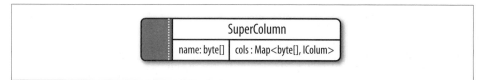

Figure 3-6. The basic structure of a super column

Each column family is stored on disk in its own separate file. So to optimize performance, it's important to keep columns that you are likely to query together in the same column family, and a super column can be helpful for this.

The `SuperColumn` class implements both the `IColumn` and the `IColumnContainer` classes, both from the `org.apache.cassandra.db` package. The Thrift API is the underlying RPC serialization mechanism for performing remote operations on Cassandra. Because the Thrift API has no notion of inheritance, you will sometimes see the API refer to a `ColumnOrSupercolumn` type; when data structures use this type, you are expected to know whether your underlying column family is of type `Super` or `Standard`.

 Fun fact: super columns were one of the updates that Facebook added to Google's Bigtable data model.

Here we see some more of the richness of the data model. When using regular columns, as we saw earlier, Cassandra looks like a four-dimensional hashtable. But for super columns, it becomes more like a *five*-dimensional hash:

```
[Keyspace][ColumnFamily][Key][SuperColumn][SubColumn]
```

To use a super column, you define your column family as type `Super`. Then, you still have row keys as you do in a regular column family, but you also reference the super column, which is simply a name that points to a list or map of regular columns (sometimes called the *subcolumns*).

Here is an example of a super column family definition called `PointOfInterest`. In the hotelier domain, a "point of interest" is a location near a hotel that travelers might like to visit, such as a park, museum, zoo, or tourist attraction:

```
PointOfInterest (SCF)
    SCkey: Cambria Suites Hayden
    {
        key: Phoenix Zoo
        {
            phone: 480-555-9999,
            desc: They have animals here.
        },
        key: Spring Training
        {
            phone: 623-333-3333,
            desc: Fun for baseball fans.

        },
    }, //end of Cambria row
    SCkey: (UTF8) Waldorf=Astoria
    {
        key: Central Park
            desc: Walk around. It's pretty.
        },
        key: Empire State Building
        {
            phone: 212-777-7777,
            desc: Great view from the 102nd floor.
```

```
            }
        }
    }
```

The `PointOfInterest` super column family has two super columns, each named for a different hotel (Cambria Suites Hayden and Waldorf=Astoria). The row keys are names of different points of interest, such as "Phoenix Zoo" and "Central Park". Each row has columns for a description (the "desc" column); some of the rows have a phone number, and some don't. Unlike relational tables, which group rows of identical structure, column families and super column families group merely *similar* records.

Using the CLI, we could query a super column family like this:

```
cassandra> get PointOfInterest['Central Park']['The Waldorf=Astoria']['desc']
=> (column=desc, value=Walk around in the park. It's pretty., timestamp=1281301988847)
```

This query is asking: in the `PointOfInterest` column family (which happens to be defined as type `Super`), use the row key "Central Park"; for the super column named "Waldorf=Astoria", get me the value of the "desc" column (which is the plain language text describing the point of interest).

Composite Keys

There is an important consideration when modeling with super columns: Cassandra does not index subcolumns, so when you load a super column into memory, all of its columns are loaded as well.

 This limitation was discovered by Ryan King, the Cassandra lead at Twitter. It might be fixed in a future release, but the change is pending an update to the underlying storage file (the SSTable).

You can use a composite key of your own design to help you with queries. A composite key might be something like `<userid:lastupdate>`.

This could just be something that you consider when modeling, and then check back on later when you come to a hardware sizing exercise. But if your data model anticipates more than several thousand subcolumns, you might want to take a different approach and not use super columns. The alternative involves creating a composite key. Instead of representing columns within a super column, the composite key approach means that you use a regular column family with regular columns, and then employ a custom delimiter in your key name and parse it on client retrieval.

Here's an example of a composite key pattern, used in combination with an example of a Cassandra design pattern I call Materialized View, as well as a common Cassandra design pattern I call Valueless Column:

```
HotelByCity (CF) Key: city:state {
  key: Phoenix:AZ {AZC_043: -, AZS_011: -}
  key: San Francisco:CA {CAS_021: -}
  key: New York:NY {NYN_042: -}
}
```

There are three things happening here. First, we already have defined hotel information in another column family called Hotel. But we can create a second column family called HotelByCity that denormalizes the hotel data. We repeat the same information we already have, but store it in a way that acts similarly to a view in RDBMS, because it allows us a quick and direct way to write queries. When we know that we're going to look up hotels by city (because that's how people tend to search for them), we can create a table that defines a row key for that search. However, there are many states that have cities with the same name (Springfield comes to mind), so we can't just name the row key after the city; we need to combine it with the state.

We then use another pattern called Valueless Column. All we need to know is what hotels are in the city, and we don't need to denormalize further. So *we use the column's name as the value*, and the column has no corresponding value. That is, when the column is inserted, we just store an empty byte array with it.

Design Differences Between RDBMS and Cassandra

There are several differences between Cassandra's model and query methods compared to what's available in RDBMS, and these are important to keep in mind.

No Query Language

SQL is the standard query language used in relational databases. Cassandra has no query language. It does have an API that you access through its RPC serialization mechanism, Thrift.

No Referential Integrity

Cassandra has no concept of referential integrity, and therefore has no concept of joins. In a relational database, you could specify foreign keys in a table to reference the primary key of a record in another table. But Cassandra does not enforce this. It is still a common design requirement to store IDs related to other entities in your tables, but operations such as cascading deletes are not available.

Secondary Indexes

Here's why secondary indexes are a feature: say that you want to find the unique ID for a hotel property. In a relational database, you might use a query like this:

```
SELECT hotelID FROM Hotel WHERE name = 'Clarion Midtown';
```

This is the query you'd have to use if you knew the name of the hotel you were looking for but not the unique ID. When handed a query like this, a relational database will perform a full table scan, inspecting each row's name column to find the value you're looking for. But this can become very slow once your table grows very large. So the relational answer to this is to create an index on the name column, which acts as a copy of the data that the relational database can look up very quickly. Because the hotelID is already a unique primary key constraint, it is automatically indexed, and that is the primary index; for us to create another index on the name column would constitute a secondary index, and Cassandra does not currently support this.

To achieve the same thing in Cassandra, you create a second column family that holds the lookup data. You create one column family to store the hotel names, and map them to their IDs. The second column family acts as an explicit secondary index.

 Support for secondary indexes is currently being added to Cassandra 0.7. This allows you to create indexes on column values. So, if you want to see all the users who live in a given city, for example, secondary index support will save you from doing it from scratch.

Sorting Is a Design Decision

In RDBMS, you can easily change the order in which records are returned to you by using ORDER BY in your query. The default sort order is not configurable; by default, records are returned in the order in which they are written. If you want to change the order, you just modify your query, and you can sort by any list of columns. In Cassandra, however, sorting is treated differently; it is a design decision. Column family definitions include a CompareWith element, which dictates the order in which your rows will be sorted on reads, but this is not configurable per query.

Where RDBMS constrains you to sorting based on the data type stored in the column, Cassandra only stores byte arrays, so that approach doesn't make sense. What you can do, however, is sort as if the column were one of several different types (ASCII, Long integer, TimestampUUID, lexicographically, etc.). You can also use your own pluggable comparator for sorting if you wish.

Otherwise, there is no support for ORDER BY and GROUP BY statements in Cassandra as there is in SQL. There is a query type called a SliceRange, which we examine in Chapter 4; it is similar to ORDER BY in that it allows a reversal.

Denormalization

In relational database design, we are often taught the importance of normalization. This is not an advantage when working with Cassandra because it performs best when the data model is denormalized. It is often the case that companies end up denormalizing data in a relational database. There are two common reasons for this. One is performance. Companies simply can't get the performance they need when they have to do so many joins on years' worth of data, so they denormalize along the lines of known queries. This ends up working, but goes against the grain of how relational databases are intended to be designed, and ultimately makes one question whether using a relational database is the best approach in these circumstances.

A second reason that relational databases get denormalized on purpose is a business document structure that requires retention. That is, you have an enclosing table that refers to a lot of external tables whose data could change over time, but you need to preserve the enclosing document as a snapshot in history. The common example here is with invoices. You already have Customer and Product tables, and you'd think that you could just make an invoice that refers to those tables. But this should never be done in practice. Customer or price information could change, and then you would lose the integrity of the Invoice document as it was on the invoice date, which could violate audits, reports, or laws, and cause other problems.

In the relational world, denormalization violates Codd's normal forms, and we try to avoid it. But in Cassandra, denormalization is, well, perfectly normal. It's not required if your data model is simple. But don't be afraid of it.

The important point is that instead of modeling the data first and then writing queries, with Cassandra you model the queries and let the data be organized around them. Think of the most common query paths your application will use, and then create the column families that you need to support them.

Detractors have suggested that this is a problem. But it is perfectly reasonable to expect that you should think hard about the queries in your application, just as you would, presumably, think hard about your relational domain. You may get it wrong, and then you'll have problems in either world. Or your query needs might change over time, and then you'll have to work to update your data set. But this is no different from defining the wrong tables, or needing additional tables, in RDBMS.

 For an interesting article on how Cloudkick is using Cassandra to store metrics and monitoring data, see *https://www.cloudkick.com/blog/2010/ mar/02/4_months_with_cassandra*.

Design Patterns

There are a few ways that people commonly use Cassandra that might be described as design patterns. I've given names to these common patterns: Materialized View, Valueless Column, and Aggregate Key.

Materialized View

It is common to create a secondary index that represents additional queries. Because you don't have a SQL WHERE clause, you can recreate this effect by writing your data to a second column family that is created specifically to represent that query.

For example, if you have a User column family and you want to find users in a particular city, you might create a second column family called UserCity that stores user data with the city as keys (instead of the username) and that has columns named for the users who live in that city. This is a denormalization technique that will speed queries and is an example of specifically designing your data around your queries (and not the other way around). This usage is common in the Cassandra world. When you want to query for users in a city, you just query the UserCity column family, instead of querying the User column family and doing a bunch of pruning work on the client across a potentially large data set.

Note that in this context, "materialized" means storing a full copy of the original data so that everything you need to answer a query is right there, without forcing you to look up the original data. If you are performing a second query because you're only storing column names that you use, like foreign keys in the second column family, that's a secondary index.

 As of 0.7, Cassandra has native support for secondary indexes.

Valueless Column

Let's build on our User/UserCity example. Because we're storing the reference data in the User column family, two things arise: one, you need to have unique and thoughtful keys that can enforce referential integrity; and two, the columns in the UserCity column family don't necessarily need values. If you have a row key of Boise, then the column names can be the names of the users in that city. Because your reference data is in the User column family, the columns don't really have any meaningful value; you're just using it as a prefabricated list, but you'll likely want to use values in that list to get additional data from the reference column family.

Aggregate Key

When you use the Valueless Column pattern, you may also need to employ the Aggregate Key pattern. This pattern fuses together two scalar values with a separator to create an aggregate. To extend our example further, city names typically aren't unique; many states in the US have a city called Springfield, and there's a Paris, Texas, and a Paris, Tennessee. So what will work better here is to fuse together the state name and the city name to create an Aggregate Key to use in our Materialized View. This key would look something like: TX:Paris or TN:Paris. By convention, many Cassandra users employ the colon as the separator, but it could be a pipe character or any other character that is not otherwise meaningful in your keys.

Some Things to Keep in Mind

Let's look briefly at a few things to keep in mind when you're trying to move from a relational mindset to Cassandra's data model. I'll just say it: if you have been working with relational databases for a long time, it's not always easy. Here are a few pointers:

- Start with your queries. Ask what queries your application will need, and model the data around that instead of modeling the data first, as you would in the relational world. This can be shocking to some people. Some very smart people have told me that this approach will cause trouble for the Cassandra practitioner down the line when new queries come up, as they tend to in business. Fair enough. My response is to ask why they assume their data types would be more static than their queries.

- You have to supply a timestamp (or clock) with each query, so you need a strategy to synchronize those with multiple clients. This is crucial in order for Cassandra to use the timestamps to determine the most recent write value. One good strategy here is the use of a Network Time Protocol (NTP) server. Again, some smart people have asked me, why not let the server take care of the clock? My response is that in a symmetrical distributed database, the server side actually has the same problem.

Summary

In this chapter we took a gentle approach to understanding Cassandra's data model of keyspaces, column families, columns, and super columns. We also explored a few of the contrasts between RDBMS and Cassandra.

## CHAPTER 4

Sample Application

In this chapter, we create a complete sample application so we can see how all the parts fit together. We will use various parts of the API to see how to insert data, perform batch updates, and search column families and super column families.

To create the example, we want to use something that is complex enough to show the various data structures and basic API operations, but not something that will bog you down with details. In order to get enough data in the database to make our searches work right (by finding stuff we're looking for and leaving out stuff we're not looking for), there's a little redundancy in the prepopulation of the database. Also, I wanted to use a domain that's familiar to everyone so we can concentrate on how to work with Cassandra, not on what the application domain is all about.

 The code in this chapter has been tested against the 0.7 beta 1 release, and works as shown. It is possible that API changes may necessitate minor tuning on your part, depending on your version.

Data Design

When you set out to build a new data-driven application that will use a relational database, you might start by modeling the domain as a set of properly normalized tables and use foreign keys to reference related data in other tables. Now that we have an understanding of how Cassandra stores data, let's create a little domain model that is easy to understand in the relational world, and then see how we might map it from a relational to a distributed hashtable model in Cassandra.

Relational modeling, in simple terms, means that you start from the conceptual domain and then represent the nouns in the domain in tables. You then assign primary keys and foreign keys to model relationships. When you have a many-to-many relationship, you create the join tables that represent just those keys. The join tables don't exist in the real world, and are a necessary side effect of the way relational models work. After you have all your tables laid out, you can start writing queries that pull together disparate data using the relationships defined by the keys. The queries in the relational world are very much secondary. It is assumed that you can always get the data you want as long as you have your tables modeled properly. Even if you have to use several complex subqueries or join statements, this is usually true.

By contrast, in Cassandra you don't start with the data model; you start with the query model.

For this example, let's use a domain that is easily understood and that everyone can relate to: a hotel that wants to allow guests to book a reservation.

Our conceptual domain includes hotels, guests that stay in the hotels, a collection of rooms for each hotel, and a record of the reservation, which is a certain guest in a certain room for a certain period of time (called the "stay"). Hotels typically also maintain a collection of "points of interest," which are parks, museums, shopping galleries, monuments, or other places near the hotel that guests might want to visit during their stay. Both hotels and points of interest need to maintain geolocation data so that they can be found on maps for mashups, and to calculate distances.

 Obviously, in the real world there would be many more considerations and much more complexity. For example, hotel rates are notoriously dynamic, and calculating them involves a wide array of factors. Here we're defining something complex enough to be interesting and touch on the important points, but simple enough to maintain the focus on learning Cassandra.

Here's how we would start this application design with Cassandra. First, determine your queries. We'll likely have something like the following:

- Find hotels in a given area.
- Find information about a given hotel, such as its name and location.
- Find points of interest near a given hotel.
- Find an available room in a given date range.
- Find the rate and amenities for a room.
- Book the selected room by entering guest information.

Hotel App RDBMS Design

Figure 4-1 shows how we might represent this simple hotel reservation system using a relational database model. The relational model includes a couple of "join" tables in order to resolve the many-to-many relationships of hotels-to-points of interest, and for rooms-to-amenities.

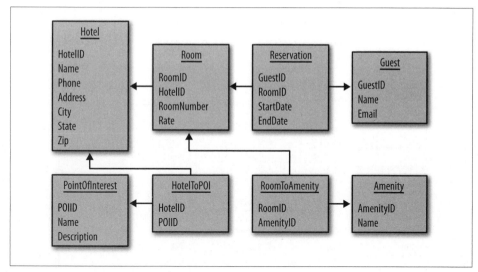

Figure 4-1. A simple hotel search system using RDBMS

Hotel App Cassandra Design

Although there are many possible ways to do it, we could represent the same logical data model using a Cassandra physical model such as that shown in Figure 4-2.

In this design, we're doing all the same things as in the relational design. We have transferred some of the tables, such as `Hotel` and `Guest`, to column families. Other tables, such as `PointOfInterest`, have been denormalized into a super column family. In the relational model, you can look up hotels by the city they're in using a SQL statement. But because we don't have SQL in Cassandra, we've created an index in the form of the `HotelByCity` column family.

I'm using a stereotype notation here, so `<<CF>>` refers to a column family, `<<SCF>>` refers to a super column family, and so on.

We have combined room and amenities into a single column family, `Room`. The columns such as type and rate will have corresponding values; other columns, such as hot tub, will just use the presence of the column name itself as the value, and be otherwise empty.

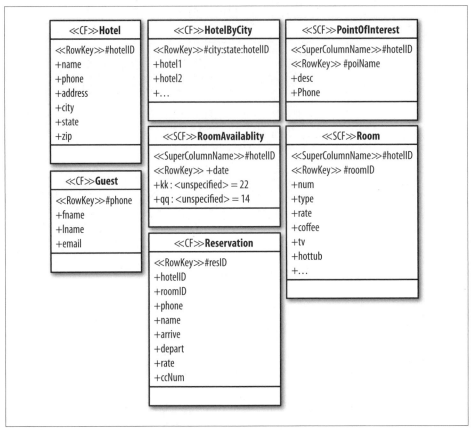

Figure 4-2. The hotel search represented with Cassandra's model

Hotel Application Code

In this section we walk through the code and show how to implement the given design. This is useful because it illustrates several different API functions in action.

The purpose of this sample application is to show how different ideas in Cassandra can be combined. It is by no means the only way to transfer the relational design into this model. There is a lot of low-level plumbing here that uses the Thrift API. Thrift is (probably) changing to Avro, so although the basic ideas here work, you don't want to follow this example in a real application. Instead, check out Chapter 8 and use one of the many available third-party clients for Cassandra, depending on the language that your application uses and other needs that you have.

The application we're building will do the following things:

1. Create the database structure.
2. Prepopulate the database with hotel and point of interest data. The hotels are stored in standard column families, and the points of interest are in super column families.
3. Search for a list of hotels in a given city. This uses a secondary index.
4. Select one of the hotels returned in the search, and then search for a list of points of interest near the chosen hotel.
5. Booking the hotel by doing an insert into the **Reservation** column family should be straightforward at this point, and is left to the reader.

Space doesn't permit implementing the entire application. But we'll walk through the major parts, and finishing the implementation is just a matter of creating a variation of what is shown.

Creating the Database

The first step is creating the schema definition. For this example, we'll define the schema in YAML and then load it, although you could also use client code to define it.

The YAML file shown in Example 4-1 defines the necessary keyspace and column families.

Example 4-1. Schema definition in cassandra.yaml

```
keyspaces:

    - name: Hotelier
      replica_placement_strategy: org.apache.cassandra.locator.RackUnawareStrategy
      replication_factor: 1
      column_families:
        - name: Hotel
          compare_with: UTF8Type

        - name: HotelByCity
          compare_with: UTF8Type

        - name: Guest
          compare_with: BytesType

        - name: Reservation
          compare_with: TimeUUIDType

        - name: PointOfInterest
          column_type: Super
          compare_with: UTF8Type
          compare_subcolumns_with: UTF8Type

        - name: Room
```

```
          column_type: Super
          compare_with: BytesType
          compare_subcolumns_with: BytesType

        - name: RoomAvailability
          column_type: Super
          compare_with: BytesType
          compare_subcolumns_with: BytesType
```

This definition provides all of the column families to run the example, and a couple more that we don't directly reference in the application code, because it rounds out the design as transferred from RDBMS.

Loading the schema

Once you have the schema defined in YAML, you need to load it. To do this, open a console, start the jconsole application, and connect to Cassandra via JMX. Then, execute the operation `loadSchemaFromYAML`, which is part of the `org.apache` `.cassandra.service.StorageService` MBean. Now Cassandra knows about your schema and you can start using it. You can also use the API itself to create keyspaces and column families.

Data Structures

The application requires some standard data structures that will just act as transfer objects for us. These aren't particularly interesting, but are required to keep things organized. We'll use a `Hotel` data structure to hold all of the information about a hotel, shown in Example 4-2.

Example 4-2. Hotel.java

```
package com.cassandraguide.hotel;

//data transfer object
public class Hotel {
    public String id;
    public String name;
    public String phone;
    public String address;
    public String city;
    public String state;
    public String zip;
}
```

This structure just holds the column information for convenience in the application.

We also have a `POI` data structure to hold information about points of interest. This is shown in Example 4-3.

Example 4-3. POI.java

```java
package com.cassandraguide.hotel;

//data transfer object for a Point of Interest
public class POI {
    public String name;
    public String desc;
    public String phone;
}
```

We also have a **Constants** class, which keeps commonly used strings in one easy-to-change place, shown in Example 4-4.

Example 4-4. Constants.java

```java
package com.cassandraguide.hotel;

import org.apache.cassandra.thrift.ConsistencyLevel;

public class Constants {

    public static final String CAMBRIA_NAME = "Cambria Suites Hayden";
    public static final String CLARION_NAME= "Clarion Scottsdale Peak";
    public static final String W_NAME = "The W SF";
    public static final String WALDORF_NAME = "The Waldorf=Astoria";

    public static final String UTF8 = "UTF8";
    public static final String KEYSPACE = "Hotelier";
    public static final ConsistencyLevel CL = ConsistencyLevel.ONE;
    public static final String HOST = "localhost";
    public static final int PORT = 9160;
}
```

Holding these commonly used strings make the code clearer and more concise, and you can easily change these values to reflect what makes sense in your environment.

Getting a Connection

For convenience, and to save repeating a bunch of boilerplate code, let's put the connection code into one class, called **Connector**, shown in Example 4-5.

Example 4-5. A connection client convenience class, Connector.java

```java
package com.cassandraguide.hotel;

import static com.cassandraguide.hotel.Constants.KEYSPACE;

import org.apache.cassandra.thrift.Cassandra;
import org.apache.cassandra.thrift.InvalidRequestException;
import org.apache.thrift.TException;
import org.apache.thrift.protocol.TBinaryProtocol;
import org.apache.thrift.protocol.TProtocol;
import org.apache.thrift.transport.TFramedTransport;
```

```
import org.apache.thrift.transport.TSocket;
import org.apache.thrift.transport.TTransport;
import org.apache.thrift.transport.TTransportException;

//simple convenience class to wrap connections, just to reduce repeat code
public class Connector {

    TTransport tr = new TSocket("localhost", 9160);

    // returns a new connection to our keyspace
    public Cassandra.Client connect() throws TTransportException,
            TException, InvalidRequestException {

        TFramedTransport tf = new TFramedTransport(tr);
        TProtocol proto = new TBinaryProtocol(tf);
        Cassandra.Client client = new Cassandra.Client(proto);
        tr.open();
        client.set_keyspace(KEYSPACE);
        return client;
    }

    public void close() {
        tr.close();
    }
}
```

When we need to execute a database operation, we can use this class to open a connection and then close the connection once we're done.

Prepopulating the Database

The Prepopulate class, shown in Example 4-6, does a bunch of inserts and batch_ mutates in order to prepopulate the database with the hotel information and points of interest information that users will search for.

Example 4-6. Prepopulate.java

```
package com.cassandraguide.hotel;

import static com.cassandraguide.hotel.Constants.CAMBRIA_NAME;
import static com.cassandraguide.hotel.Constants.CL;
import static com.cassandraguide.hotel.Constants.CLARION_NAME;
import static com.cassandraguide.hotel.Constants.UTF8;
import static com.cassandraguide.hotel.Constants.WALDORF_NAME;
import static com.cassandraguide.hotel.Constants.W_NAME;

import java.io.UnsupportedEncodingException;
import java.util.ArrayList;
import java.util.HashMap;
import java.util.List;
import java.util.Map;

import org.apache.cassandra.thrift.Cassandra;
import org.apache.cassandra.thrift.Clock;
```

```java
import org.apache.cassandra.thrift.Column;
import org.apache.cassandra.thrift.ColumnOrSuperColumn;
import org.apache.cassandra.thrift.ColumnParent;
import org.apache.cassandra.thrift.ColumnPath;
import org.apache.cassandra.thrift.Mutation;
import org.apache.cassandra.thrift.SuperColumn;
import org.apache.log4j.Logger;

/**
 * Performs the initial population of the database.
 * Fills the CFs and SCFs with Hotel, Point of Interest, and index data.
 * Shows batch_mutate and insert for Column Families and Super Column Families.
 *
 * I am totally ignoring exceptions to save space.
 */
public class Prepopulate {
    private static final Logger LOG = Logger.getLogger(Prepopulate.class);


    private Cassandra.Client client;
    private Connector connector;

    //constructor opens a connection so we don't have to
    //constantly recreate it
    public Prepopulate() throws Exception {
        connector = new Connector();
        client = connector.connect();
    }

    void prepopulate() throws Exception {
        //pre-populate the DB with Hotels
        insertAllHotels();

        //also add all hotels to index to help searches
        insertByCityIndexes();

        //pre-populate the DB with POIs
        insertAllPointsOfInterest();

        connector.close();
    }

    //also add hotels to lookup by city index
    public void insertByCityIndexes() throws Exception  {

        String scottsdaleKey = "Scottsdale:AZ";
        String sfKey = "San Francisco:CA";
        String newYorkKey = "New York:NY";

        insertByCityIndex(scottsdaleKey, CAMBRIA_NAME);
        insertByCityIndex(scottsdaleKey, CLARION_NAME);
        insertByCityIndex(sfKey, W_NAME);
        insertByCityIndex(newYorkKey, WALDORF_NAME);
}
    //use Valueless Column pattern
```

```java
private void insertByCityIndex(String rowKey, String hotelName)
    throws Exception {

    Clock clock = new Clock(System.nanoTime());

    Column nameCol = new Column(hotelName.getBytes(UTF8),
            new byte[0], clock);

    ColumnOrSuperColumn nameCosc = new ColumnOrSuperColumn();
    nameCosc.column = nameCol;

    Mutation nameMut = new Mutation();
    nameMut.column_or_supercolumn = nameCosc;

    //set up the batch
    Map<String, Map<String, List<Mutation>>> mutationMap =
        new HashMap<String, Map<String, List<Mutation>>>();

    Map<String, List<Mutation>> muts =
        new HashMap<String, List<Mutation>>();
    List<Mutation> cols = new ArrayList<Mutation>();
    cols.add(nameMut);

    String columnFamily = "HotelByCity";
    muts.put(columnFamily, cols);

    //outer map key is a row key
    //inner map key is the column family name
    mutationMap.put(rowKey, muts);


    //create representation of the column
    ColumnPath cp = new ColumnPath(columnFamily);
    cp.setColumn(hotelName.getBytes(UTF8));

    ColumnParent parent = new ColumnParent(columnFamily);
    //here, the column name IS the value (there's no value)
    Column col = new Column(hotelName.getBytes(UTF8), new byte[0], clock);

    client.insert(rowKey.getBytes(), parent, col, CL);

    LOG.debug("Inserted HotelByCity index for " + hotelName);

} //end inserting ByCity index

//POI
public void insertAllPointsOfInterest() throws Exception {

    LOG.debug("Inserting POIs.");

    insertPOIEmpireState();
    insertPOICentralPark();
    insertPOIPhoenixZoo();
    insertPOISpringTraining();
```

```
        LOG.debug("Done inserting POIs.");
    }

    private void insertPOISpringTraining() throws Exception {
        //Map<byte[],Map<String,List<Mutation>>>
        Map<byte[], Map<String, List<Mutation>>> outerMap =
            new HashMap<byte[], Map<String, List<Mutation>>>();
        List<Mutation> columnsToAdd = new ArrayList<Mutation>();

        Clock clock = new Clock(System.nanoTime());
        String keyName = "Spring Training";
        Column descCol = new Column("desc".getBytes(UTF8),
            "Fun for baseball fans.".getBytes("UTF-8"), clock);
        Column phoneCol = new Column("phone".getBytes(UTF8),
                "623-333-3333".getBytes(UTF8), clock);

        List<Column> cols = new ArrayList<Column>();
        cols.add(descCol);
        cols.add(phoneCol);

        Map<String, List<Mutation>> innerMap =
            new HashMap<String, List<Mutation>>();

        Mutation columns = new Mutation();
        ColumnOrSuperColumn descCosc = new ColumnOrSuperColumn();
        SuperColumn sc = new SuperColumn();
        sc.name = CAMBRIA_NAME.getBytes();
        sc.columns = cols;

        descCosc.super_column = sc;
        columns.setColumn_or_supercolumn(descCosc);

        columnsToAdd.add(columns);

        String superCFName = "PointOfInterest";
        ColumnPath cp = new ColumnPath();
        cp.column_family = superCFName;
        cp.setSuper_column(CAMBRIA_NAME.getBytes());
        cp.setSuper_columnIsSet(true);

        innerMap.put(superCFName, columnsToAdd);
        outerMap.put(keyName.getBytes(), innerMap);

        client.batch_mutate(outerMap, CL);

        LOG.debug("Done inserting Spring Training.");
    }


    private void insertPOIPhoenixZoo() throws Exception {

        Map<byte[], Map<String, List<Mutation>>> outerMap =
            new HashMap<byte[], Map<String, List<Mutation>>>();
        List<Mutation> columnsToAdd = new ArrayList<Mutation>();
```

```java
    long ts = System.currentTimeMillis();
    String keyName = "Phoenix Zoo";
    Column descCol = new Column("desc".getBytes(UTF8),
        "They have animals here.".getBytes("UTF-8"), new Clock(ts));

    Column phoneCol = new Column("phone".getBytes(UTF8),
            "480-555-9999".getBytes(UTF8), new Clock(ts));

    List<Column> cols = new ArrayList<Column>();
    cols.add(descCol);
    cols.add(phoneCol);

    Map<String, List<Mutation>> innerMap =
        new HashMap<String, List<Mutation>>();

    String cambriaName = "Cambria Suites Hayden";

    Mutation columns = new Mutation();
    ColumnOrSuperColumn descCosc = new ColumnOrSuperColumn();
    SuperColumn sc = new SuperColumn();
    sc.name = cambriaName.getBytes();
    sc.columns = cols;

    descCosc.super_column = sc;
    columns.setColumn_or_supercolumn(descCosc);

    columnsToAdd.add(columns);

    String superCFName = "PointOfInterest";
    ColumnPath cp = new ColumnPath();
    cp.column_family = superCFName;
    cp.setSuper_column(cambriaName.getBytes());
    cp.setSuper_columnIsSet(true);

    innerMap.put(superCFName, columnsToAdd);
    outerMap.put(keyName.getBytes(), innerMap);

    client.batch_mutate(outerMap, CL);

    LOG.debug("Done inserting Phoenix Zoo.");
}


private void insertPOICentralPark() throws Exception {

    Map<byte[], Map<String, List<Mutation>>> outerMap =
        new HashMap<byte[], Map<String, List<Mutation>>>();
    List<Mutation> columnsToAdd = new ArrayList<Mutation>();

    Clock clock = new Clock(System.nanoTime());
    String keyName = "Central Park";
    Column descCol = new Column("desc".getBytes(UTF8),
        "Walk around in the park. It's pretty.".getBytes("UTF-8"), clock);

    //no phone column for park
```

```
    List<Column> cols = new ArrayList<Column>();
    cols.add(descCol);

    Map<String, List<Mutation>> innerMap =
        new HashMap<String, List<Mutation>>();

    Mutation columns = new Mutation();
    ColumnOrSuperColumn descCosc = new ColumnOrSuperColumn();
    SuperColumn waldorfSC = new SuperColumn();
    waldorfSC.name = WALDORF_NAME.getBytes();
    waldorfSC.columns = cols;

    descCosc.super_column = waldorfSC;
    columns.setColumn_or_supercolumn(descCosc);

    columnsToAdd.add(columns);

    String superCFName = "PointOfInterest";
    ColumnPath cp = new ColumnPath();
    cp.column_family = superCFName;
    cp.setSuper_column(WALDORF_NAME.getBytes());
    cp.setSuper_columnIsSet(true);

    innerMap.put(superCFName, columnsToAdd);
    outerMap.put(keyName.getBytes(), innerMap);

    client.batch_mutate(outerMap, CL);

    LOG.debug("Done inserting Central Park.");
}

private void insertPOIEmpireState()  throws Exception {

    Map<byte[], Map<String, List<Mutation>>> outerMap =
        new HashMap<byte[], Map<String, List<Mutation>>>();

    List<Mutation> columnsToAdd = new ArrayList<Mutation>();

    Clock clock = new Clock(System.nanoTime());
    String esbName = "Empire State Building";
    Column descCol = new Column("desc".getBytes(UTF8),
            "Great view from 102nd floor.".getBytes("UTF-8"), clock);
    Column phoneCol = new Column("phone".getBytes(UTF8),
            "212-777-7777".getBytes(UTF8), clock);

    List<Column> esbCols = new ArrayList<Column>();
    esbCols.add(descCol);
    esbCols.add(phoneCol);

    Map<String, List<Mutation>> innerMap = new HashMap<String, List<Mutation>>();

    Mutation columns = new Mutation();
    ColumnOrSuperColumn descCosc = new ColumnOrSuperColumn();
    SuperColumn waldorfSC = new SuperColumn();
```

```java
    waldorfSC.name = WALDORF_NAME.getBytes();
    waldorfSC.columns = esbCols;

    descCosc.super_column = waldorfSC;
    columns.setColumn_or_supercolumn(descCosc);

    columnsToAdd.add(columns);

    String superCFName = "PointOfInterest";
    ColumnPath cp = new ColumnPath();
    cp.column_family = superCFName;
    cp.setSuper_column(WALDORF_NAME.getBytes());
    cp.setSuper_columnIsSet(true);

    innerMap.put(superCFName, columnsToAdd);
    outerMap.put(esbName.getBytes(), innerMap);

    client.batch_mutate(outerMap, CL);

    LOG.debug("Done inserting Empire State.");
}

//convenience method runs all of the individual inserts
public void insertAllHotels() throws Exception {

    String columnFamily = "Hotel";

    //row keys
    String cambriaKey = "AZC_043";
    String clarionKey = "AZS_011";
    String wKey = "CAS_021";
    String waldorfKey = "NYN_042";

    //conveniences
    Map<byte[], Map<String, List<Mutation>>> cambriaMutationMap =
        createCambriaMutation(columnFamily, cambriaKey);

    Map<byte[], Map<String, List<Mutation>>> clarionMutationMap =
        createClarionMutation(columnFamily, clarionKey);

    Map<byte[], Map<String, List<Mutation>>> waldorfMutationMap =
        createWaldorfMutation(columnFamily, waldorfKey);

    Map<byte[], Map<String, List<Mutation>>> wMutationMap =
        createWMutation(columnFamily, wKey);

    client.batch_mutate(cambriaMutationMap, CL);
    LOG.debug("Inserted " + cambriaKey);
    client.batch_mutate(clarionMutationMap, CL);
    LOG.debug("Inserted " + clarionKey);
    client.batch_mutate(wMutationMap, CL);
    LOG.debug("Inserted " + wKey);
    client.batch_mutate(waldorfMutationMap, CL);
    LOG.debug("Inserted " + waldorfKey);
```

```
        LOG.debug("Done inserting at " + System.nanoTime());
}

//set up columns to insert for W
private Map<byte[], Map<String, List<Mutation>>> createWMutation(
        String columnFamily, String rowKey)
        throws UnsupportedEncodingException {

    Clock clock = new Clock(System.nanoTime());

    Column nameCol = new Column("name".getBytes(UTF8),
            W_NAME.getBytes("UTF-8"), clock);
    Column phoneCol = new Column("phone".getBytes(UTF8),
            "415-222-2222".getBytes(UTF8), clock);
    Column addressCol = new Column("address".getBytes(UTF8),
            "181 3rd Street".getBytes(UTF8), clock);
    Column cityCol = new Column("city".getBytes(UTF8),
            "San Francisco".getBytes(UTF8), clock);
    Column stateCol = new Column("state".getBytes(UTF8),
            "CA".getBytes("UTF-8"), clock);
    Column zipCol = new Column("zip".getBytes(UTF8),
            "94103".getBytes(UTF8), clock);

    ColumnOrSuperColumn nameCosc = new ColumnOrSuperColumn();
    nameCosc.column = nameCol;

    ColumnOrSuperColumn phoneCosc = new ColumnOrSuperColumn();
    phoneCosc.column = phoneCol;

    ColumnOrSuperColumn addressCosc = new ColumnOrSuperColumn();
    addressCosc.column = addressCol;

    ColumnOrSuperColumn cityCosc = new ColumnOrSuperColumn();
    cityCosc.column = cityCol;

    ColumnOrSuperColumn stateCosc = new ColumnOrSuperColumn();
    stateCosc.column = stateCol;

    ColumnOrSuperColumn zipCosc = new ColumnOrSuperColumn();
    zipCosc.column = zipCol;

    Mutation nameMut = new Mutation();
    nameMut.column_or_supercolumn = nameCosc;
    Mutation phoneMut = new Mutation();
    phoneMut.column_or_supercolumn = phoneCosc;
    Mutation addressMut = new Mutation();
    addressMut.column_or_supercolumn = addressCosc;
    Mutation cityMut = new Mutation();
    cityMut.column_or_supercolumn = cityCosc;
    Mutation stateMut = new Mutation();
    stateMut.column_or_supercolumn = stateCosc;
    Mutation zipMut = new Mutation();
    zipMut.column_or_supercolumn = zipCosc;

    //set up the batch
```

```
        Map<byte[], Map<String, List<Mutation>>> mutationMap =
            new HashMap<byte[], Map<String, List<Mutation>>>();

        Map<String, List<Mutation>> muts =
            new HashMap<String, List<Mutation>>();
        List<Mutation> cols = new ArrayList<Mutation>();
        cols.add(nameMut);
        cols.add(phoneMut);
        cols.add(addressMut);
        cols.add(cityMut);
        cols.add(stateMut);
        cols.add(zipMut);

        muts.put(columnFamily, cols);

        //outer map key is a row key
        //inner map key is the column family name
        mutationMap.put(rowKey.getBytes(), muts);
        return mutationMap;
    }

    //add Waldorf hotel to Hotel CF
    private Map<byte[], Map<String, List<Mutation>>> createWaldorfMutation(
            String columnFamily, String rowKey)
            throws UnsupportedEncodingException {

        Clock clock = new Clock(System.nanoTime());

        Column nameCol = new Column("name".getBytes(UTF8),
                WALDORF_NAME.getBytes("UTF-8"), clock);
        Column phoneCol = new Column("phone".getBytes(UTF8),
                "212-555-5555".getBytes(UTF8), clock);
        Column addressCol = new Column("address".getBytes(UTF8),
                "301 Park Ave".getBytes(UTF8), clock);
        Column cityCol = new Column("city".getBytes(UTF8),
                "New York".getBytes(UTF8), clock);
        Column stateCol = new Column("state".getBytes(UTF8),
                "NY".getBytes("UTF-8"), clock);
        Column zipCol = new Column("zip".getBytes(UTF8),
                "10019".getBytes(UTF8), clock);

        ColumnOrSuperColumn nameCosc = new ColumnOrSuperColumn();
        nameCosc.column = nameCol;

        ColumnOrSuperColumn phoneCosc = new ColumnOrSuperColumn();
        phoneCosc.column = phoneCol;

        ColumnOrSuperColumn addressCosc = new ColumnOrSuperColumn();
        addressCosc.column = addressCol;

        ColumnOrSuperColumn cityCosc = new ColumnOrSuperColumn();
        cityCosc.column = cityCol;

        ColumnOrSuperColumn stateCosc = new ColumnOrSuperColumn();
        stateCosc.column = stateCol;
```

```
        ColumnOrSuperColumn zipCosc = new ColumnOrSuperColumn();
        zipCosc.column = zipCol;

        Mutation nameMut = new Mutation();
        nameMut.column_or_supercolumn = nameCosc;
        Mutation phoneMut = new Mutation();
        phoneMut.column_or_supercolumn = phoneCosc;
        Mutation addressMut = new Mutation();
        addressMut.column_or_supercolumn = addressCosc;
        Mutation cityMut = new Mutation();
        cityMut.column_or_supercolumn = cityCosc;
        Mutation stateMut = new Mutation();
        stateMut.column_or_supercolumn = stateCosc;
        Mutation zipMut = new Mutation();
        zipMut.column_or_supercolumn = zipCosc;

        //set up the batch
        Map<byte[], Map<String, List<Mutation>>> mutationMap =
            new HashMap<byte[], Map<String, List<Mutation>>>();

        Map<String, List<Mutation>> muts =
            new HashMap<String, List<Mutation>>();
        List<Mutation> cols = new ArrayList<Mutation>();
        cols.add(nameMut);
        cols.add(phoneMut);
        cols.add(addressMut);
        cols.add(cityMut);
        cols.add(stateMut);
        cols.add(zipMut);

        muts.put(columnFamily, cols);

        //outer map key is a row key
        //inner map key is the column family name
        mutationMap.put(rowKey.getBytes(), muts);
        return mutationMap;
    }

    //set up columns to insert for Clarion
    private Map<byte[], Map<String, List<Mutation>>> createClarionMutation(
            String columnFamily, String rowKey)
            throws UnsupportedEncodingException {

        Clock clock = new Clock(System.nanoTime());

        Column nameCol = new Column("name".getBytes(UTF8),
                CLARION_NAME.getBytes("UTF-8"), clock);
        Column phoneCol = new Column("phone".getBytes(UTF8),
                "480-333-3333".getBytes(UTF8), clock);
        Column addressCol = new Column("address".getBytes(UTF8),
                "3000 N. Scottsdale Rd".getBytes(UTF8), clock);
        Column cityCol = new Column("city".getBytes(UTF8),
                "Scottsdale".getBytes(UTF8), clock);
        Column stateCol = new Column("state".getBytes(UTF8),
```

```
        "AZ".getBytes("UTF-8"), clock);
Column zipCol = new Column("zip".getBytes(UTF8),
        "85255".getBytes(UTF8), clock);

ColumnOrSuperColumn nameCosc = new ColumnOrSuperColumn();
nameCosc.column = nameCol;

ColumnOrSuperColumn phoneCosc = new ColumnOrSuperColumn();
phoneCosc.column = phoneCol;

ColumnOrSuperColumn addressCosc = new ColumnOrSuperColumn();
addressCosc.column = addressCol;

ColumnOrSuperColumn cityCosc = new ColumnOrSuperColumn();
cityCosc.column = cityCol;

ColumnOrSuperColumn stateCosc = new ColumnOrSuperColumn();
stateCosc.column = stateCol;

ColumnOrSuperColumn zipCosc = new ColumnOrSuperColumn();
zipCosc.column = zipCol;

Mutation nameMut = new Mutation();
nameMut.column_or_supercolumn = nameCosc;
Mutation phoneMut = new Mutation();
phoneMut.column_or_supercolumn = phoneCosc;
Mutation addressMut = new Mutation();
addressMut.column_or_supercolumn = addressCosc;
Mutation cityMut = new Mutation();
cityMut.column_or_supercolumn = cityCosc;
Mutation stateMut = new Mutation();
stateMut.column_or_supercolumn = stateCosc;
Mutation zipMut = new Mutation();
zipMut.column_or_supercolumn = zipCosc;

//set up the batch
Map<byte[], Map<String, List<Mutation>>> mutationMap =
    new HashMap<byte[], Map<String, List<Mutation>>>();

Map<String, List<Mutation>> muts =
    new HashMap<String, List<Mutation>>();
List<Mutation> cols = new ArrayList<Mutation>();
cols.add(nameMut);
cols.add(phoneMut);
cols.add(addressMut);
cols.add(cityMut);
cols.add(stateMut);
cols.add(zipMut);

muts.put(columnFamily, cols);

//outer map key is a row key
//inner map key is the column family name
mutationMap.put(rowKey.getBytes(), muts);
return mutationMap;
```

```
}

//set up columns to insert for Cambria
private Map<byte[], Map<String, List<Mutation>>> createCambriaMutation(
        String columnFamily, String cambriaKey)
        throws UnsupportedEncodingException {

    //set up columns for Cambria
    Clock clock = new Clock(System.nanoTime());

    Column cambriaNameCol = new Column("name".getBytes(UTF8),
            "Cambria Suites Hayden".getBytes("UTF-8"), clock);
    Column cambriaPhoneCol = new Column("phone".getBytes(UTF8),
            "480-444-4444".getBytes(UTF8), clock);
    Column cambriaAddressCol = new Column("address".getBytes(UTF8),
            "400 N. Hayden".getBytes(UTF8), clock);
    Column cambriaCityCol = new Column("city".getBytes(UTF8),
            "Scottsdale".getBytes(UTF8), clock);
    Column cambriaStateCol = new Column("state".getBytes(UTF8),
            "AZ".getBytes("UTF-8"), clock);
    Column cambriaZipCol = new Column("zip".getBytes(UTF8),
            "85255".getBytes(UTF8), clock);

    ColumnOrSuperColumn nameCosc = new ColumnOrSuperColumn();
    nameCosc.column = cambriaNameCol;

    ColumnOrSuperColumn phoneCosc = new ColumnOrSuperColumn();
    phoneCosc.column = cambriaPhoneCol;

    ColumnOrSuperColumn addressCosc = new ColumnOrSuperColumn();
    addressCosc.column = cambriaAddressCol;

    ColumnOrSuperColumn cityCosc = new ColumnOrSuperColumn();
    cityCosc.column = cambriaCityCol;

    ColumnOrSuperColumn stateCosc = new ColumnOrSuperColumn();
    stateCosc.column = cambriaStateCol;

    ColumnOrSuperColumn zipCosc = new ColumnOrSuperColumn();
    zipCosc.column = cambriaZipCol;

    Mutation nameMut = new Mutation();
    nameMut.column_or_supercolumn = nameCosc;
    Mutation phoneMut = new Mutation();
    phoneMut.column_or_supercolumn = phoneCosc;
    Mutation addressMut = new Mutation();
    addressMut.column_or_supercolumn = addressCosc;
    Mutation cityMut = new Mutation();
    cityMut.column_or_supercolumn = cityCosc;
    Mutation stateMut = new Mutation();
    stateMut.column_or_supercolumn = stateCosc;
    Mutation zipMut = new Mutation();
    zipMut.column_or_supercolumn = zipCosc;

    //set up the batch
```

```
        Map<byte[], Map<String, List<Mutation>>> cambriaMutationMap =
            new HashMap<byte[], Map<String, List<Mutation>>>();

        Map<String, List<Mutation>> cambriaMuts =
            new HashMap<String, List<Mutation>>();
        List<Mutation> cambriaCols = new ArrayList<Mutation>();
        cambriaCols.add(nameMut);
        cambriaCols.add(phoneMut);
        cambriaCols.add(addressMut);
        cambriaCols.add(cityMut);
        cambriaCols.add(stateMut);
        cambriaCols.add(zipMut);

        cambriaMuts.put(columnFamily, cambriaCols);

        //outer map key is a row key
        //inner map key is the column family name
        cambriaMutationMap.put(cambriaKey.getBytes(), cambriaMuts);
        return cambriaMutationMap;
    }
}
```

This is a rather long example, but it attempts to show something more than "hello, world"—there are a number of **insert** and **batch_mutate** operations shown with standard column families and super column families. I have also included multiple rows for each type so that more sophisticated queries are required.

This class is the first to execute in our sample application, and once the **prepopulate** method is complete, your database will have all the data that the search functions need to work with.

The Search Application

Example 4-7 is the Java class with the **main** method that you should execute. It relies on Log4J, so you'll want to point to your *log4j.properties* file when you run it. All you have to do is run this class, and the database gets prepopulated with all of the hotel and point of interest information; then, it allows the user to search for hotels in a given city. The user picks one hotel, and the application fetches the nearby points of interest. You can then implement the remaining parts of the application to book a reservation if you like.

Example 4-7. HotelApp.java

```
package com.cassandraguide.hotel;

import static com.cassandraguide.hotel.Constants.CL;
import static com.cassandraguide.hotel.Constants.UTF8;

import java.util.ArrayList;
import java.util.List;

import org.apache.cassandra.thrift.Cassandra;
```

```
import org.apache.cassandra.thrift.Column;
import org.apache.cassandra.thrift.ColumnOrSuperColumn;
import org.apache.cassandra.thrift.ColumnParent;
import org.apache.cassandra.thrift.KeyRange;
import org.apache.cassandra.thrift.KeySlice;
import org.apache.cassandra.thrift.SlicePredicate;
import org.apache.cassandra.thrift.SliceRange;
import org.apache.cassandra.thrift.SuperColumn;
import org.apache.log4j.Logger;

/**
 * Runs the hotel application. After the database is pre-populated,
 * this class mocks a user interaction to perform a hotel search based on
 * city, selects one, then looks at some surrounding points of interest for
 * that hotel.
 *
 * Shows using Materialized View pattern, get, get_range_slices, key slices.
 *
 * These exceptions are thrown out of main to reduce code size:
 * UnsupportedEncodingException,
   InvalidRequestException, UnavailableException, TimedOutException,
   TException, NotFoundException, InterruptedException

   Uses the Constants class for some commonly used strings.
 */
public class HotelApp {
    private static final Logger LOG = Logger.getLogger(HotelApp.class);

    public static void main(String[] args) throws Exception {

        //first put all of the data in the database
        new Prepopulate().prepopulate();
        LOG.debug("** Database filled. **");

        //now run our client
        LOG.debug("** Starting hotel reservation app. **");
        HotelApp app = new HotelApp();

        //find a hotel by city--try Scottsdale or New York...
        List<Hotel> hotels = app.findHotelByCity("Scottsdale", "AZ");
        //List<Hotel> hotels = app.findHotelByCity("New York", "NY");
        LOG.debug("Found hotels in city. Results: " + hotels.size());

        //choose one
        Hotel h = hotels.get(0);

        LOG.debug("You picked " + h.name);

        //find Points of Interest for selected hotel
        LOG.debug("Finding Points of Interest near " + h.name);
        List<POI> points = app.findPOIByHotel(h.name);

        //choose one
        POI poi = points.get(0);
        LOG.debug("Hm... " + poi.name + ". " + poi.desc + "--Sounds fun!");
```

```java
        LOG.debug("Now to book a room...");

        //show availability for a date
        //left as an exercise...

        //create reservation
        //left as an exercise...

        LOG.debug("All done.");
    }

    //use column slice to get from Super Column
    public List<POI> findPOIByHotel(String hotel) throws Exception {

        ///query
        SlicePredicate predicate = new SlicePredicate();
        SliceRange sliceRange = new SliceRange();
        sliceRange.setStart(hotel.getBytes());
        sliceRange.setFinish(hotel.getBytes());
        predicate.setSlice_range(sliceRange);

        // read all columns in the row
        String scFamily = "PointOfInterest";
        ColumnParent parent = new ColumnParent(scFamily);

        KeyRange keyRange = new KeyRange();
        keyRange.start_key = "".getBytes();
        keyRange.end_key = "".getBytes();

        List<POI> pois = new ArrayList<POI>();

        //instead of a simple list, we get a map whose keys are row keys
        //and the values the list of columns returned for each
        //only row key + first column are indexed
        Connector cl = new Connector();
        Cassandra.Client client = cl.connect();
        List<KeySlice> slices = client.get_range_slices(
                parent, predicate, keyRange, CL);

        for (KeySlice slice : slices) {
            List<ColumnOrSuperColumn> cols = slice.columns;

            POI poi = new POI();
            poi.name = new String(slice.key);

            for (ColumnOrSuperColumn cosc : cols) {
                SuperColumn sc = cosc.super_column;

                List<Column> colsInSc = sc.columns;

                for (Column c : colsInSc) {
                    String colName = new String(c.name, UTF8);
                    if (colName.equals("desc")) {
                        poi.desc = new String(c.value, UTF8);
```

```
            }
            if (colName.equals("phone")) {
                poi.phone = new String(c.value, UTF8);
            }
        }

        LOG.debug("Found something neat nearby: " + poi.name +
                ". \nDesc: " + poi.desc +
                ". \nPhone: " + poi.phone);
        pois.add(poi);
    }
}

cl.close();
return pois;
}

//uses key range
public List<Hotel> findHotelByCity(String city, String state)
    throws Exception {

    LOG.debug("Seaching for hotels in " + city + ", " + state);

    String key = city + ":" + state.toUpperCase();

    ///query
    SlicePredicate predicate = new SlicePredicate();
    SliceRange sliceRange = new SliceRange();
    sliceRange.setStart(new byte[0]);
    sliceRange.setFinish(new byte[0]);
    predicate.setSlice_range(sliceRange);

    // read all columns in the row
    String columnFamily = "HotelByCity";
    ColumnParent parent = new ColumnParent(columnFamily);

    KeyRange keyRange = new KeyRange();
    keyRange.setStart_key(key.getBytes());
    keyRange.setEnd_key((key+1).getBytes()); //just outside lexical range
    keyRange.count = 5;

    Connector cl = new Connector();
    Cassandra.Client client = cl.connect();
    List<KeySlice> keySlices =
        client.get_range_slices(parent, predicate, keyRange, CL);

    List<Hotel> results = new ArrayList<Hotel>();

    for (KeySlice ks : keySlices) {
        List<ColumnOrSuperColumn> coscs = ks.columns;
        LOG.debug(new String("Using key " + ks.key));

        for (ColumnOrSuperColumn cs : coscs) {

            Hotel hotel = new Hotel();
```

```
            hotel.name = new String(cs.column.name, UTF8);
            hotel.city = city;
            hotel.state = state;

            results.add(hotel);
            LOG.debug("Found hotel result for " + hotel.name);
        }
    }
    ///end query
    cl.close();

    return results;
    }
}
```

I interspersed the code with comments to illustrate the purpose of the different statements.

The output of running the application is shown in Example 4-8.

Example 4-8. Output of running the hotel application

```
DEBUG 09:49:50,858 Inserted AZC_043
DEBUG 09:49:50,861 Inserted AZS_011
DEBUG 09:49:50,863 Inserted CAS_021
DEBUG 09:49:50,864 Inserted NYN_042
DEBUG 09:49:50,864 Done inserting at 6902368219815217
DEBUG 09:49:50,873 Inserted HotelByCity index for Cambria Suites Hayden
DEBUG 09:49:50,874 Inserted HotelByCity index for Clarion Scottsdale Peak
DEBUG 09:49:50,875 Inserted HotelByCity index for The W SF
DEBUG 09:49:50,877 Inserted HotelByCity index for The Waldorf=Astoria
DEBUG 09:49:50,877 Inserting POIs.
DEBUG 09:49:50,880 Done inserting Empire State.
DEBUG 09:49:50,881 Done inserting Central Park.
DEBUG 09:49:50,885 Done inserting Phoenix Zoo.
DEBUG 09:49:50,887 Done inserting Spring Training.
DEBUG 09:49:50,887 Done inserting POIs.
DEBUG 09:49:50,887 ** Database filled. **
DEBUG 09:49:50,889 ** Starting hotel reservation app. **
DEBUG 09:49:50,889 Seaching for hotels in Scottsdale, AZ
DEBUG 09:49:50,902 Using key [B@15e9756
DEBUG 09:49:50,903 Found hotel result for Cambria Suites Hayden
DEBUG 09:49:50,903 Found hotel result for Clarion Scottsdale Peak
DEBUG 09:49:50,904 Found hotels in city. Results: 2
DEBUG 09:49:50,904 You picked Cambria Suites Hayden
DEBUG 09:49:50,904 Finding Points of Interest near Cambria Suites Hayden
DEBUG 09:49:50,911 Found something neat nearby: Phoenix Zoo.
Desc: They have animals here..
Phone: 480-555-9999
DEBUG 09:49:50,911 Found something neat nearby: Spring Training.
Desc: Fun for baseball fans..
Phone: 623-333-3333
DEBUG 09:49:50,911 Hm... Phoenix Zoo. They have animals here.--Sounds fun!
DEBUG 09:49:50,911 Now to book a room...
DEBUG 09:49:50,912 All done.
```

Again, you typically don't want to write against Thrift or Avro yourself, but instead should use one of the clients listed in Chapter 8. The purpose here is to give you an idea of how the plumbing works, and to show a complete, working application that performs inserts and various searches and that resembles real-world usage.

Twissandra

When you start thinking about how to design for Cassandra, take a look at Twissandra, written by Eric Florenzano. Visit *http://www.twissandra.com* to see a fully working Twitter clone that you can download and try out. The source is all in Python, and it has a few dependencies on Django and a JSON library to sort out, but it's a great place to start. You can use what's likely a familiar data model (Twitter's) and see how users, time lines, and tweets all fit into a simple Cassandra data model.

There is also a helpful post by Eric Evans explaining how to use Twissandra, which is available at *http://www.rackspacecloud.com/blog/2010/05/12/cassandra-by-example*.

Summary

In this chapter we saw how to create a complete, working Cassandra application. We also illustrated a typical relational model compared with how you might represent that model in Cassandra, and introduced a variety of commands for interacting with the database.

## CHAPTER 5

The Cassandra Architecture

In this chapter, we examine several aspects of Cassandra's internal design in order to understand how it does its job. We consider the peer-to-peer design and its corresponding gossip protocol, as well as what Cassandra does on read and write requests, and examine how these choices affect architectural considerations such as scalability, durability, availability, manageability, and more. We also discuss Cassandra's adoption of a Staged Event-Driven Architecture, which acts as the platform for request delegation.

The Cassandra architecture is very sophisticated and relies on the use of several different theoretical constructs. It is hard to discuss any one new term without referencing other terms we probably also haven't met yet. This can be frustrating, which is why I've included the Glossary in the back of the book for you to refer to.

System Keyspace

Cassandra has an internal keyspace called `system` that it uses to store metadata about the cluster to aid in operations. In Microsoft SQL Server, two meta-databases are maintained: `master` and `tempdb`. The `master` is used to keep information about disk space, usage, system settings, and general server installation notes; the `tempdb` is used as a workspace to store intermediate results and perform general tasks. The Oracle database always has a tablespace called `SYSTEM`, used for similar purposes. The Cassandra system keyspace is used much like these.

Specifically, the system keyspace stores metadata for the local node, as well as hinted handoff information. The metadata includes:

- The node's token
- The cluster name
- Keyspace and schema definitions to support dynamic loading
- Migration data
- Whether or not the node is bootstrapped

The schema definitions are stored in two column families: the Schema column family holds user keyspace and schema definitions, and the Migrations column family records the changes made to a keyspace.

You cannot modify the system keyspace.

Peer-to-Peer

In traditional databases that can be deployed on multiple machines (such as MySQL), and even in newer models such as Google's Bigtable, some nodes are designated masters and some slaves. They have different roles in the overall cluster: the master acts as the authoritative source for data, and slaves synchronize their data to the master. Any changes written to the master are passed on to slaves. This model is optimized for reading data, as it allows data to be read from any slave. But the replication is one-way, from master to slave. This has an important ramification: all writes must be sent to the master, which means that it is a potential single point of failure. In a master/slave setup, the master node can have far-reaching effects if it goes offline.

By contrast, Cassandra has a peer-to-peer distribution model, such that any given node is structurally identical to any other node—that is, there is no "master" node that acts differently than a "slave" node. The aim of Cassandra's design is overall system availability and ease of scaling. The peer-to-peer design can improve general database availability, because while taking any given Cassandra node offline may have a potential impact on overall throughput, it is a graceful degradation that does not interrupt service. Assuming that you are using a reasonable replication strategy, the data on a failed node will still be available for reads and writes.

This design also makes it easier to scale Cassandra by adding new nodes. Because the behavior of each node is identical, in order to add a new server, you simply need to add it to the cluster. The new node will not immediately accept requests so that it has time to learn the topology of the ring and accept data that it may also be responsible for. After it does this, it can join the ring as a full member and begin accepting requests. This is largely automatic and requires minimal configuration. For this reason, the P2P design makes both scaling up and scaling down an easier task than in master/slave replication.

Gossip and Failure Detection

To support decentralization and partition tolerance, Cassandra uses a gossip protocol for intra-ring communication so that each node can have state information about other nodes. The gossiper runs every second on a timer. Hinted handoff is triggered by gossip, when a node notices that a node it has hints for has just come back online. Anti-entropy, on the other hand, is a manual process; it is not triggered by gossip.

Gossip protocols (sometimes called "epidemic protocols") generally assume a faulty network, are commonly employed in very large, decentralized network systems, and are often used as an automatic mechanism for replication in distributed databases. They take their name from the concept of human gossip, a form of communication in which peers can choose with whom they want to exchange information.

 The term "gossip protocol" was originally coined in 1987 by Alan Demers, a researcher at Xerox's Palo Alto Research Center, who was studying ways to route information through unreliable networks.

The gossip protocol in Cassandra is primarily implemented by the `org.apache` `.cassandra.gms.Gossiper` class, which is responsible for managing gossip for the local node. When a server node is started, it registers itself with the gossiper to receive endpoint state information.

Because Cassandra gossip is used for failure detection, the `Gossiper` class maintains a list of nodes that are alive and dead.

Here is how the gossiper works:

1. Periodically (according to the settings in its `TimerTask`), the G=gossiper will choose a random node in the ring and initialize a gossip session with it. Each round of gossip requires three messages.
2. The gossip initiator sends its chosen friend a `GossipDigestSynMessage`.
3. When the friend receives this message, it returns a `GossipDigestAckMessage`.
4. When the initiator receives the `ack` message from the friend, it sends the friend a `GossipDigestAck2Message` to complete the round of gossip.

When the gossiper determines that another endpoint is dead, it "convicts" that endpoint by marking it as dead in its local list and logging that fact.

Cassandra has robust support for failure detection, as specified by a popular algorithm for distributed computing called Phi Accrual Failure Detection. This manner of failure detection originated at the Advanced Institute of Science and Technology in Japan in 2004.

Accrual failure detection is based on two primary ideas. The first general idea is that failure detection should be flexible, which is achieved by decoupling it from the application being monitored. The second and more novel idea challenges the notion of traditional failure detectors, which are implemented by simple "heartbeats" and decide whether a node is dead or not dead based on whether a heartbeat is received or not. But accrual failure detection decides that this approach is naive, and finds a place in between the extremes of dead and alive—a *suspicion level*.

Therefore, the failure monitoring system outputs a continuous level of "suspicion" regarding how confident it is that a node has failed. This is desirable because it can take into account fluctuations in the network environment. For example, just because one connection gets caught up doesn't necessarily mean that the whole node is dead. So suspicion offers a more fluid and proactive indication of the weaker or stronger possibility of failure based on interpretation (the sampling of heartbeats), as opposed to a simple binary assessment.

 You can read the original Phi Accrual Failure Detection paper by Naohiro Hayashibara et al. at *http://ddg.jaist.ac.jp/pub/HDY+04.pdf*.

Failure detection is implemented in Cassandra by the `org.apache.cassandra.gms` `.FailureDetector` class, which implements the `org.apache.cassandra.gms.IFailure` `Detector` interface. Together, they allow the following operations:

`isAlive(InetAddress)`
> What the detector will report about a given node's alive-ness.

`interpret(InetAddress)`
> Used by the gossiper to help it decide whether a node is alive or not based on suspicion level reached by calculating Phi (as described in the Hayashibara paper).

`report(InetAddress)`
> When a node receives a heartbeat, it invokes this method.

Anti-Entropy and Read Repair

Where you find gossip protocols, you will often find their counterpart, anti-entropy, which is also based on an epidemic theory of computing. *Anti-entropy* is the replica synchronization mechanism in Cassandra for ensuring that data on different nodes is updated to the newest version.

Here's how it works. During a major compaction, the server initiates a TreeRequest/ TreeReponse conversation to exchange Merkle trees with neighboring nodes. The Merkle tree is a hash representing the data in that column family. If the trees from the different nodes don't match, they have to be reconciled (or "repaired") in order to determine the latest data values they should all be set to. This tree comparison validation is the responsibility of the `org.apache.cassandra.service.AntiEntropyService` class. `AntiEntropyService` implements the Singleton pattern and defines the static `Dif` `ferencer` class as well, which is used to compare two trees; if it finds any differences, it launches a repair for the ranges that don't agree.

Anti-entropy is used in Amazon's Dynamo, and Cassandra's implementation is modeled on that (see Section 4.7 of the Dynamo paper).

Dynamo uses a Merkle tree for anti-entropy (see the definition of Merkle tree in the Glossary). Cassandra uses them too, but the implementation is a little different. In

Cassandra, each column family has its own Merkle tree; the tree is created as a snapshot during a major compaction operation (see "Compaction" in the Glossary), and is kept only as long as is required to send it to the neighboring nodes on the ring. The advantage of this implementation is that it reduces disk I/O.

After each update, the anti-entropy algorithm kicks in. This performs a checksum against the database and compares checksums of peers; if the checksums differ, then the data is exchanged. This requires using a time window to ensure that peers have had a chance to receive the most recent update so that the system is not constantly and unnecessarily executing anti-entropy. To keep the operation fast, nodes internally maintain an inverted index keyed by timestamp and only exchange the most recent updates.

In Cassandra, you have multiple nodes that make up your cluster, and one or more of the nodes act as replicas for a given piece of data. To read data, a client connects to any node in the cluster and, based on the consistency level specified by the client, a number of nodes are read. The read operation blocks until the client-specified consistency level is met. If it is detected that some of the nodes responded with an out-of-date value, Cassandra will return the most recent value to the client. After returning, Cassandra will perform what's called a read repair in the background. This operation brings the replicas with stale values up to date.

This design is observed by Cassandra as well as by straight key/value stores such as Project Voldemort and Riak. It acts as a performance improvement because the client does not block until all nodes are read, but the read repair stage manages the task of keeping the data fresh in the background. If you have lots of clients, it's important to read from a quorum of nodes in order to ensure that at least one will have the most recent value.

If the client specifies a weak consistency level (such as ONE), then the read repair is performed in the background after returning to the client. If you are using one of the two stronger consistency levels (QUORUM or ALL), then the read repair happens *before* data is returned to the client.

If a read operation shows different values stored for the same timestamp, Cassandra will compare the values directly as a tie-breaking mechanism to ensure that read re-pairing doesn't enter an infinite loop. This case should be exceedingly rare.

Memtables, SSTables, and Commit Logs

When you perform a write operation, it's immediately written to the commit log. The commit log is a crash-recovery mechanism that supports Cassandra's durability goals. A write will not count as successful until it's written to the commit log, to ensure that if a write operation does not make it to the in-memory store (the memtable, discussed in a moment), it will still be possible to recover the data.

After it's written to the commit log, the value is written to a memory-resident data structure called the *memtable*. When the number of objects stored in the memtable reaches a threshold, the contents of the memtable are flushed to disk in a file called an SSTable. A new memtable is then created. This flushing is a nonblocking operation; multiple memtables may exist for a single column family, one current and the rest waiting to be flushed. They typically should not have to wait very long, as the node should flush them very quickly unless it is overloaded.

Each commit log maintains an internal bit flag to indicate whether it needs flushing. When a write operation is first received, it is written to the commit log and its bit flag is set to **1**. There is only one bit flag per column family, because only one commit log is ever being written to across the entire server. All writes to all column families will go into the same commit log, so the bit flag indicates whether a particular commit log contains anything that hasn't been flushed for a particular column family. Once the memtable has been properly flushed to disk, the corresponding commit log's bit flag is set to **0**, indicating that the commit log no longer has to maintain that data for durability purposes. Like regular logfiles, commit logs have a configurable rollover threshold, and once this file size threshold is reached, the log will roll over, carrying with it any extant dirty bit flags.

The SSTable is a concept borrowed from Google's Bigtable. Once a memtable is flushed to disk as an SSTable, it is immutable and cannot be changed by the application. Despite the fact that SSTables are compacted, this compaction changes only their on-disk representation; it essentially performs the "merge" step of a mergesort into new files and removes the old files on success.

 The idea that "SSTable" is a compaction of "Sorted String Table" is somewhat of a misnomer for Cassandra, because the data is not stored as strings on disk.

Each SSTable also has an associated Bloom filter, which is used as an additional performance enhancer (see "Bloom Filters" on page 95).

All writes are sequential, which is the primary reason that writes perform so well in Cassandra. No reads or seeks of any kind are required for writing a value to Cassandra because all writes are append operations. This makes one key limitation on performance the speed of your disk. Compaction is intended to amortize the reorganization of data, but it uses sequential IO to do so. So the performance benefit is gained by splitting; the write operation is just an immediate append, and then compaction helps to organize for better future read performance. If Cassandra naively inserted values where they ultimately belonged, writing clients would pay for seeks up front.

On reads, Cassandra will check the memtable first to find the value. Memtables are implemented by the `org.apache.cassandra.db.Memtable` class.

Hinted Handoff

Consider the following scenario. A write request is sent to Cassandra, but the node where the write properly belongs is not available due to network partition, hardware failure, or some other reason. In order to ensure general availability of the ring in such a situation, Cassandra implements a feature called *hinted handoff*. You might think of a *hint* as a little post-it note that contains the information from the write request. If the node where the write belongs has failed, the Cassandra node that receives the write will create a hint, which is a small reminder that says, "I have the write information that is intended for node B. I'm going to hang onto this write, and I'll notice when node B comes back online; when it does, I'll send it the write request." That is, node A will "hand off" to node B the "hint" regarding the write.

This allows Cassandra to be always available for writes, and reduces the time that a failed node will be inconsistent after it does come back online. We discussed consistency levels previously, and you may recall that consistency level ANY, which was added in 0.6, means that a hinted handoff alone will count as sufficient toward the success of a write operation. That is, even if only a hint was able to be recorded, the write still counts as successful.

Some concern about hinted handoffs has been voiced by members of the Cassandra community. At first, it seems like a thoughtful and elegant design to ensure overall durability of the database, and appears unproblematic because it is familiar from many distributed computing paradigms, such as Java Message Service (JMS). In a durable guaranteed-delivery JMS queue, if a message cannot be delivered to a receiver, JMS will wait for a given interval and then resend the request until the message is received. But there is a practical problem with both guaranteed delivery in JMS and Cassandra's hinted handoffs: if a node is offline for some time, the hints can build up considerably on other nodes. Then, when the other nodes notice that the failed node has come back online, they tend to flood that node with requests, just at the moment it is most vulnerable (when it is struggling to come back into play after a failure).

In response to these concerns, it is now possible to disable hinted handoff entirely, or, as a less extreme measure, reduce the priority of hinted handoff messages against new write requests.

 In Cassandra 0.6 and earlier, `HintedHandoffManager.sendMessage` would read an entire row into memory, and then send the row back to the client in a single message. As of version 0.7, Cassandra will now page within a single hinted row instead. This can improve performance against very wide rows.

Compaction

A compaction operation in Cassandra is performed in order to merge SSTables. During compaction, the data in SSTables is merged: the keys are merged, columns are combined, tombstones are discarded, and a new index is created.

Compaction is the process of freeing up space by merging large accumulated datafiles. This is roughly analogous to rebuilding a table in the relational world. But as Stu Hood points out, the primary difference in Cassandra is that it is intended as a transparent operation that is amortized across the life of the server.

On compaction, the merged data is sorted, a new index is created over the sorted data, and the freshly merged, sorted, and indexed data is written to a single new SSTable (each SSTable consists of three files: *Data*, *Index*, and *Filter*). This process is managed by the class `org.apache.cassandra.db.CompactionManager`. `CompactionManager` implements an MBean interface so it can be introspected.

Another important function of compaction is to improve performance by reducing the number of required seeks. There are a bounded number of SSTables to inspect to find the column data for a given key. If a key is frequently mutated, it's very likely that the mutations will all end up in flushed SSTables. Compacting them prevents the database from having to perform a seek to pull the data from each SSTable.

There are different types of compaction in Cassandra. A *major* compaction is triggered one of two ways: via a node probe or automatically. A node probe sends a TreeRequest message to the nodes that neighbor the target. When a node receives a TreeRequest, it immediately performs a *read-only compaction* in order to validate the column family.

A *read-only* compaction has the following steps:

1. Get the key distribution from the column family.
2. Once the rows have been added to the validator, if the column family needs to be validated, it will create the Merkle tree and broadcast it to the neighboring nodes.
3. The Merkle trees are brought together in a "rendezvous" as a list of `Differencers` (trees that need validating or comparison).
4. The comparison is executed by the `StageManager` class, which is responsible for handling concurrency issues in executing jobs. In this case, the `StageManager` uses an Anti-Entropy Stage. This uses the `org.apache.cassandra.concurrent.JMXEnabled ThreadPoolExecutor` class, which executes the compaction within a single thread and makes the operation available as an MBean for inspection.

You can increase overall performance by reducing the priority of compaction threads. To do so, use the following flag:

```
-Dcassandra.compaction.priority=1
```

This will affect CPU usage, not IO.

Bloom Filters

Bloom filters are used as a performance booster. They are named for their inventor, Burton Bloom. Bloom filters are very fast, nondeterministic algorithms for testing whether an element is a member of a set. They are nondeterministic because it is possible to get a false-positive read from a Bloom filter, but not a false-negative. Bloom filters work by mapping the values in a data set into a bit array and condensing a larger data set into a digest string. The digest, by definition, uses a much smaller amount of memory than the original data would. The filters are stored in memory and are used to improve performance by reducing disk access on key lookups. Disk access is typically much slower than memory access. So, in a way, a Bloom filter is a special kind of cache. When a query is performed, the Bloom filter is checked first before accessing disk. Because false-negatives are not possible, if the filter indicates that the element does not exist in the set, it certainly doesn't; but if the filter thinks that the element is in the set, the disk is accessed to make sure.

A new JMX MBean feature will be added to Nodetool that allows you to check the number of false-positives that your Bloom filters are returning; this operation is called `getBloomFilterFalsePositives`.

 Apache Hadoop, Google Bigtable, and Squid Proxy Cache also employ Bloom filters.

Tombstones

In the relational world, you might be used to the idea of a "soft delete." Instead of actually executing a delete SQL statement, the application will issue an update statement that changes a value in a column called something like "deleted". Programmers sometimes do this to support audit trails, for example.

There's a similar concept in Cassandra called a *tombstone*. This is how all deletes work and is therefore automatically handled for you. When you execute a delete operation, the data is not immediately deleted. Instead, it's treated as an update operation that places a tombstone on the value. A tombstone is a deletion marker that is required to suppress older data in SSTables until compaction can run.

There's a related setting called Garbage Collection Grace Seconds. This is the amount of time that the server will wait to garbage-collect a tombstone. By default, it's set to 864,000 seconds, the equivalent of 10 days. Cassandra keeps track of tombstone age, and once a tombstone is older than `GCGraceSeconds`, it will be garbage-collected. The purpose of this delay is to give a node that is unavailable time to recover; if a node is down longer than this value, then it is treated as failed and replaced.

As of 0.7, this setting is configurable per column family (it used to be for the whole keyspace).

Staged Event-Driven Architecture (SEDA)

Cassandra implements a Staged Event-Driven Architecture (SEDA). SEDA is a general architecture for highly concurrent Internet services, originally proposed in a 2001 paper called "SEDA: An Architecture for Well-Conditioned, Scalable Internet Services" by Matt Welsh, David Culler, and Eric Brewer (who you might recall from our discussion of the CAP theorem).

> You can read the original SEDA paper at *http://www.eecs.harvard.edu/ ~mdw/proj/seda*.

In a typical application, a single unit of work is often performed within the confines of a single thread. A write operation, for example, will start and end within the same thread. Cassandra, however, is different: its concurrency model is based on SEDA, so a single operation may start with one thread, which then hands off the work to another thread, which may hand it off to other threads. But it's not up to the current thread to hand off the work to another thread. Instead, work is subdivided into what are called *stages*, and the thread pool (really, a `java.util.concurrent.ExecutorService`) associated with the stage determines execution. A stage is a basic unit of work, and a single operation may internally state-transition from one stage to the next. Because each stage can be handled by a different thread pool, Cassandra experiences a massive performance improvement. This SEDA design also means that Cassandra is better able to manage its own resources internally because different operations might require disk IO, or they might be CPU-bound, or they might be network operations, and so on, so the pools can manage their work according to the availability of these resources.

A stage consists of an incoming event queue, an event handler, and an associated thread pool. Stages are managed by a controller that determines scheduling and thread allocation; Cassandra implements this kind of concurrency model using the thread pool `java.util.concurrent.ExecutorService`. To see specifically how this works, check out the `org.apache.cassandra.concurrent.StageManager` class.

The following operations are represented as stages in Cassandra:

- Read
- Mutation
- Gossip
- Response
- Anti-Entropy

- Load Balance
- Migration
- Streaming

A few additional operations are also implemented as stages. There are stages for units of work performed on memtables (in the ColumnFamilyStore class), and the Consistency Manager is a stage in the StorageService.

The stages implement the IVerbHandler interface to support the functionality for a given verb. Because the idea of mutation is represented as a stage, it can play a role in both insert and delete operations.

SEDA is a powerful architecture. Because it is event-driven, as its name states, work can be performed with exceptional concurrency and minimal coupling.

Managers and Services

There is a set of classes that form Cassandra's basic internal control mechanisms. I'll present a brief overview of these here so that you can become familiar with some of the more important ones. The first one to consider is probably the org.apache.cassandra .thrift.CassandraServer class. This class implements the calls to the Thrift interface, and delegates most of the efforts of performing queries to org.apache.cassandra .service.StorageProxy.

Cassandra Daemon

The org.apache.cassandra.service.CassandraDaemon interface represents the life cycle of the Cassandra service running on a single node. It includes the typical life cycle operations that you might expect: start, stop, activate, deactivate, and destroy.

Storage Service

The Cassandra database service is represented by org.apache.cassandra.service .StorageService. The storage service contains the node's token, which is a marker indicating the range of data that the node is responsible for.

The server starts up with a call to the initServer method of this class, upon which the server registers the SEDA verb handlers, makes some determinations about its state (such as whether it was bootstrapped or not, and what its partitioner is), and registers itself as an MBean with the JMX server.

Messaging Service

The purpose of org.apache.cassandra.net.MessagingService is to create socket listeners for message exchange; inbound and outbound messages from this node come through this service. The `MessagingService.listen` method creates a thread. Each incoming connection then dips into the `ExecutorService` thread pool using `org.apache.cassandra.net.IncomingTcpConnection` (a class that extends `Thread`) to deserialize the message. The message is validated, and then it's determined whether this is a streaming message or not. Message streaming is Cassandra's optimized way of sending sections of SSTable files from one node to another; all other communication between nodes occurs via serialized messages. If it's streaming, the message is passed to an `IncomingStreamReader`; if it's not streaming, the message is handled by `Messaging Service`'s deserialization executor, which is handed the message in the form of a task that implements `Runnable`. Because this service also makes heavy use of stages and the pool it maintains is wrapped with an MBean, you can find out a lot about how this service is working (whether reads are getting backed up and so forth) through JMX.

Hinted Handoff Manager

As its name suggests, `org.apache.cassandra.db.HintedHandoffManager` is the class that manages hinted handoffs internally. To do so it maintains a thread pool, which is available for JMX monitoring as `HINTED-HANDOFF-POOL`.

Summary

In this chapter, we examined the main pillars of Cassandra's construction, including gossip, anti-entropy, accrual failure detection, and how the use of a Staged Event-Driven Architecture maximizes performance. We also looked at how Cassandra internally executes various operations, such as tombstones and read repair. Finally, we surveyed some of the major classes and interfaces, pointing out key points of interest in case you want to dive deeper into the code base.

## CHAPTER 6

Configuring Cassandra

In this chapter, we look at how to configure Cassandra. We walk through creating keyspaces, setting up replication, and using a proper replica placement strategy.

Cassandra works out of the box with no configuration at all; you can simply download and decompress, and then execute the program to start the server with its default configuration.

We will focus on aspects of Cassandra that affect node behavior in a cluster, performance, and meta-operations such as replication, partitioning, and snitches. Performance tuning is considered a separate topic and gets its own treatment in Chapter 11.

 Cassandra development is moving quickly, and there have been many inveterate changes. I've tried my best to keep up with them here.

Keyspaces

Keyspaces used to be defined statically in an XML configuration file, but as of 0.7, you can use the API to create keyspaces and column families.

In Cassandra version 0.6 and prior, configuration for your cluster and column families was stored in a file called *storage-conf.xml*. Then there was a transitional conversion from XML to YAML, so you will see references to *storage-conf.xml* and *cassandra .yaml*. But version 0.7 introduced dynamic loading, so all creation and modification of keyspace and column family definition is done through the Thrift API or the command-line interface (CLI).

Starting with version 0.7 of Cassandra, you can use API operations to make changes to your schemas, much like you would in SQL by issuing Data Definition Language (DDL) statements, such as CREATE TABLE or ALTER TABLE.

Once your schema has been loaded into the system keyspace (Cassandra's internal keyspace for cluster metadata), any changes to your schema must be done using the Thrift interface. These methods are all prefixed with "system", presumably in order to remind you that they are highly impactful schema modification operations that modify the system keyspace:

system_add_keyspace
> Creates a keyspace.

system_rename_keyspace
> Changes the name of a keyspace after taking a snapshot of it. Note that this method blocks until its work is done.

system_drop_keyspace
> Deletes an entire keyspace after taking a snapshot of it.

system_add_column_family
> Creates a column family.

system_drop_column_family
> Deletes a column family after taking a snapshot of it.

system_rename_column_family
> Changes the name of a column family after taking a snapshot of it. Note that this method blocks until its work is done.

For example, to create a new keyspace using the CLI in 0.7, you can launch the command-line client as shown here:

```
[default@unknown] connect 127.0.0.1/9160
Connected to: "Test Cluster" on 127.0.0.1/9160
[default@unknown] create keyspace Test1 with replication_factor=0
610d06ed-a8d8-11df-93db-e700f669bcfc
[default@unknown] describe keyspace Test1
Keyspace: Test1
```

The convention default@unknown is similar to MySQL, where the authenticated username (if one is required) and the keyspace name you're currently using act as the prompt. So we can switch to a different keyspace using the use keyspace command:

```
use <keyspace> [<username> 'password']
```

Now that we've switched to our new keyspace on the CLI, we can add a column family to it:

```
[default@Test1] create column family MyCF
4105a82f-ad51-11df-93db-e700f669bcfc
```

You can specify additional settings as you like when creating the keyspace or column family using the with flag, and more settings using the and flag:

```
[default@MyKeyspace] create keyspace NewKs with replication_factor=1
```

There are other keyspace-related CLI commands you can invoke as necessary:

```
drop keyspace <keyspace>
drop column family <cf>
rename keyspace <keyspace> <keyspace_new_name>
rename column family <cf> <new_name>
```

It's also possible to use the API to do this, as shown in Example 6-1.

Example 6-1. Using the API to dynamically create a keyspace and column family

```java
package com.cassandraguide.config;

import java.util.ArrayList;
import java.util.List;

import org.apache.cassandra.thrift.Cassandra;
import org.apache.cassandra.thrift.CfDef;
import org.apache.cassandra.thrift.KsDef;
import org.apache.thrift.protocol.TBinaryProtocol;
import org.apache.thrift.protocol.TProtocol;
import org.apache.thrift.transport.TFramedTransport;
import org.apache.thrift.transport.TSocket;
import org.apache.thrift.transport.TTransport;

public class ConfigAPI {

    private static final String HOST = "localhost";
    private static final int PORT = 9160;

    /**
     * Creates a new keyspace and CF.
     */
    public static void main(String... args) throws Exception {

        String keyspaceName = "DynamicKeyspace";
        System.out.println("Creating new keyspace: "+ keyspaceName);

        //Create Keyspace
        KsDef k = new KsDef();
        k.setName(keyspaceName);
        k.setReplication_factor(1);
        k.setStrategy_class("org.apache.cassandra.locator.RackUnawareStrategy");

        List<CfDef> cfDefs = new ArrayList<CfDef>();
        k.setCf_defs(cfDefs);

        //Connect to Server
        TTransport tr = new TSocket(HOST, PORT);
        TFramedTransport tf = new TFramedTransport(tr);
        TProtocol proto = new TBinaryProtocol(tf);
        Cassandra.Client client = new Cassandra.Client(proto);
        tr.open();

        //Add the new keyspace
        client.system_add_keyspace(k);
```

```
        System.out.println("Added keyspace: "+ keyspaceName);

    }
}
```

So all you need to do to create a new keyspace is give it a name, a replica placement strategy (see "Replica Placement Strategies" on page 104), and a replication factor, then define any column families you want that keyspace to hold, and you're set. Now you are ready to start inserting values into your new MyCF column family.

 Cassandra will provide the default replication strategy if you don't name one; I'm just trying to be explicit in this example to show the syntax.

Creating a Column Family

To create a column family, you also use the CLI or the API. Here are the options available when creating a column family:

column_type
> Either Super or Standard.

clock_type
> The only valid value is Timestamp.

comparator
> Valid options include AsciiType, BytesType, LexicalUUIDType, LongType, TimeUUID Type, and UTF8Type.

subcomparator
> Name of comparator used for subcolumns when the column_type is Super. Valid options are the same as *comparator*.

reconciler
> Name of the class that will reconcile conflicting column versions. The only valid value at this time is Timestamp.

comment
> Any human-readable comment in the form of a string.

rows_cached
> The number of rows to cache.

preload_row_cache
> Set this to true to automatically load the row cache.

key_cache_size
> The number of keys to pull into the cache.

read_repair_chance
> Valid values are a number between 0.0 and 1.0.

Here's an example:

```
[default@Keyspace1] create column family MyRadCF with
column_type='Standard' and comparator='UTF8Type' and rows_cached=40000
3ae948aa-ae14-11df-a254-e700f669bcfc
```

Transitioning from 0.6 to 0.7

The *cassandra.yaml* file in the *conf* directory appears to be the replacement for *storage-conf.xml*, the configuration file from version 0.6 and earlier. But this YAML file is intended only for users upgrading their config files from XML to YAML. Instead, use the Thrift API calls prefixed with `system_` to configure your keyspaces and column families, as shown previously.

If you do have an existing *storage-conf.xml* file from using version 0.6, you will first need to convert it to YAML using the *bin/config-converter* tool, which can generate a *cassandra.yaml* file from a *storage-conf.xml*. There is an operation exposed through JMX in the `org.apache.cassandra.service.StorageServiceMBean` called `loadSchemaFromYAML`, which you can invoke to force Cassandra to load your schema changes from the *cassandra.yaml* file in your seed node. New nodes in your cluster will get schema updates as they are started. The seed node is not special here. You can run this method against any one node (though running it against more than one node is not recommended), and all nodes will receive the schema changes and gossip about changes to the schema. This is a one-time operation that stores the definition in Cassandra's system keyspace, and you don't want to modify the YAML file after running this. For any subsequent changes, you'll need to use the API or CLI. This operation will be deprecated once the transition is complete.

Although it's simple enough for testing to just use the defaults, let's examine how to configure the replica placement strategy, replication factor, and end point snitch. These settings are configurable within a keyspace, so that different keyspaces can have different settings for each.

Replicas

The replica placement strategy becomes more important the more nodes you add to your cluster. In Cassandra, the term *node* refers to the most general case; it means a server running the Cassandra software, participating in a ring of one or more Cassandra servers.

Every Cassandra node is a replica for something. For a given key range, there may be some Cassandra nodes that are not replicas for that range. If the replication factor is set to 1, writes are written only to a single node. If that node goes down, the values stored on that node are not accessible. If the replication factor is set to 2, two of the nodes in your cluster will get the value written to them on every write, and they will be replicas for each other. So if your replication factor is set to N, then each node will act as a replica for N ranges, even if N is set to 1.

A Cassandra cluster, or collection of hosts, is typically referred to as a *ring*, for reasons we'll see now. Each node in the ring is assigned a single, unique token. Each node claims ownership of the range of values from its token to the token of the previous node. This is captured in the `org.apache.cassandra.dht.Range` class. Exactly how a token is represented is dependent on the partitioner you're using. (For more information on partitioners, see "Partitioners" on page 110 later in this chapter.)

When creating a replica, the first replica is always placed in the node claiming the key range of its token. All remaining replicas are distributed according to a configurable replication strategy, which we'll look at now.

Replica Placement Strategies

In its simplest terms, to satisfy the replica placement strategy for the configuration file, you just need to provide the name of a Java class that extends the `org.apache` `.cassandra.locator.AbstractReplicationStrategy` class. The purpose of this setting is to configure the way that the node picker works.

For determining replica placement, Cassandra implements the Gang of Four Strategy pattern. The strategy is outlined in the common abstract class, allowing different implementations of an algorithm (different strategies for accomplishing the same work). Each algorithm implementation is encapsulated inside a single class that adheres to the interface. So you can provide the strategy framework a variety of different implementations of the algorithm, all of which are interchangeable to the runtime. Clients do not have to be concerned about which strategy is used. A common use of the Strategy pattern is for sorting. Imagine a `SortStrategy` interface with a single `sort` operation and different implementations for `Quicksort`, `Mergesort`, and so on. Each sorts in different ways, depending on your needs.

The interface provides 11 public methods that require implementation; if your strategy can make use of some of the method implementations provided in the abstract parent, then you can override only the methods you want. Of course, you don't have to implement this yourself. Out of the box, Cassandra provides three implementations of this interface (extensions of the abstract class): Rack-Aware Strategy, Rack-Unaware Strategy, and Data Center Shard Strategy.

Choosing the right replication strategy is important because the strategy determines which nodes are responsible for which key ranges. The implication is that you're also determining which nodes should receive which write operations, which can have a big impact on efficiency in different scenarios. If you set up your cluster such that all writes are going to two data centers—one in Australia and one in Reston, Virginia—you will see a matching performance degradation. The variety of pluggable strategies allows you greater flexibility, so that you can tune Cassandra according to your network topology and needs.

The first replica will always be the node that claims the range in which the token falls, but the remainder of the replicas are placed according to the replica placement strategy you use.

As I write this chapter, the names of the strategies are changing. The new names in 0.7 will be `SimpleStrategy` (formerly known as `RackUnaware Strategy`), `OldNetworkTopologyStrategy` (formerly known as `RackAwareS trategy`), and `NetworkTopologyStrategy` (formerly known as `Datacen terShardStrategy`).

Simple Strategy

Simple Strategy is the new name for Rack-Unaware Strategy.

The strategy used by default in the configuration file is `org.apache.cassandra .locator.RackUnawareStrategy`. This strategy only overrides the `calculateNatural Endpoints` method from the abstract parent implementation. This strategy places replicas in a single data center, in a manner that is not aware of their placement on a data center rack. This means that the implementation is theoretically fast, but not if the next node that has the given key is in a different rack than others. This is shown in Figure 6-1.

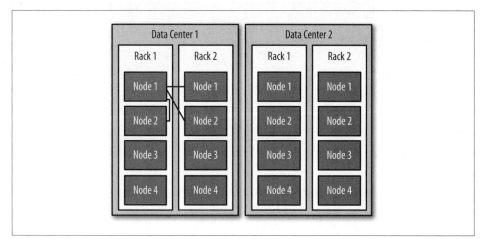

Figure 6-1. The Simple Strategy places replicas in a single data center, without respect to topology

What's happening here is that the next N nodes on the ring are chosen to hold replicas, and the strategy has no notion of data centers. A second data center is shown in the diagram to highlight the fact that the strategy is unaware of it.

Old Network Topology Strategy

The second strategy for replica placement that Cassandra provides out of the box is org.apache.cassandra.locator.RackAwareStrategy, now called Old Network Topology Strategy. It's mainly used to distribute data across different racks in the same data center. Like RackUnawareStrategy, this strategy only overrides the calculateNaturalEnd points method from the abstract parent implementation. This class, as the original name suggests, is indeed aware of the placement in data center racks.

Say you have two data centers, DC1 and DC2, and a set of Cassandra servers. This strategy will place some replicas in DC1, putting each in a different available rack. It will also ensure that another replica is placed in DC2. The Rack-Aware Strategy is specifically for when you have nodes in the same Cassandra cluster spread over two data centers and you are using a replication factor of 3. This strategy is depicted in Figure 6-2.

Use this strategy when you want to ensure higher availability at the potential cost of some additional latency while the third node in the alternate data center is contacted. There is no point in using Rack-Aware Strategy if you are only running Cassandra in a single data center. Cassandra is optimized for running in different data centers, however, and taking advantage of its high availability may be an important consideration for you. If your Cassandra cluster does span multiple data centers, consider using this strategy.

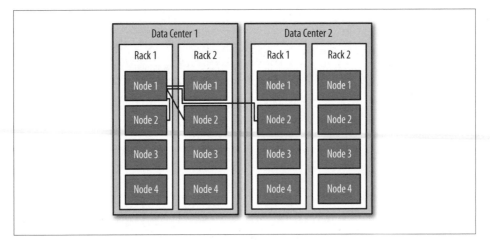

Figure 6-2. The Old Network Topology Strategy places the second replica in a different data center and others on different racks in the same data center

If you use the Rack-Aware Strategy, you must also use the Rack-Aware Snitch. Snitches are described in "Snitches" on page 111.

Network Topology Strategy

This strategy, included with the 0.7 release of Cassandra, allows you to specify more evenly than the `RackAwareStrategy` how replicas should be placed across data centers. To use it, you supply parameters in which you indicate the desired replication strategy for each data center. This file is read and executed by the `org.apache.cassandra` `.locator.DataCenterShardStrategy` class, so the implementation is somewhat flexible. The data center shard strategy is depicted in Figure 6-3.

This strategy used to employ a file called *datacenter.properties*. But as of 0.7, this metadata is attached directly to the keyspace and strategy as a map of configuration options.

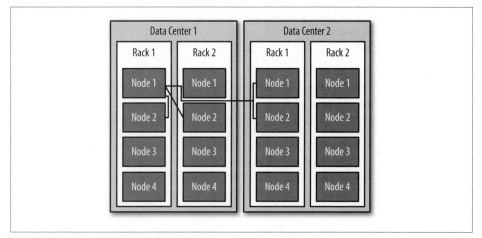

Figure 6-3. The Network Topology Strategy places some replicas in another data center and the remainder in other racks in the first data center, as specified

Replication Factor

The replication factor specifies how many copies of each piece of data will be stored and distributed throughout the Cassandra cluster. It is specified by the `replication_factor` setting.

It may seem intuitive that the more nodes you have in your cluster, the more you want to increase the replication factor. However, you don't want to follow this rule of thumb alone; instead, increase the replication factor in order to satisfy your required service level.

With a replication factor of one, your data will exist only in a single node in the cluster. Losing that node means that data becomes unavailable. It also means that Cassandra will have to do more work as coordinator among nodes; if all the data for a given key is on node B, every client request for that key that enters through node A will need to be forwarded.

You must not set this value higher than the number of nodes in your cluster, as this wouldn't make any sense. But you also don't want to use this setting to tune Cassandra. Cassandra will achieve high consistency when the read replica count plus the write replica count is greater than the replication factor.

So if you have 10 nodes in your cluster, you *could* set the replication factor to 10 as the maximum. But you might not want to do that, as it robs Cassandra of what it's good at and stymies its availability, because if a single node goes down, you won't be able to have high consistency. Instead, set the replication factor to a reasonable number and then tune the consistency level up or down. The consistency level never allows you to write to more than the number of nodes specified by the replication factor. A "reasonable number" here is probably fairly low. ONE seems like the lowest number; however, ANY is similar to ONE but even less consistent, since you might not see the written value until a long time after you wrote it. If any node in the cluster is alive, ANY should succeed.

 If you're new to Cassandra, the replication factor can sometimes be confused with the consistency level. The replication factor is set per keyspace, and is specified in the server's config file. The consistency level is specified per query, by the client. The replication factor indicates how many nodes you want to use to store a value during each write operation. The consistency level specifies how many nodes the client has decided must respond in order to feel confident of a successful read or write operation. The confusion arises because the consistency level is based on the replication factor, not on the number of nodes in the system.

Increasing the Replication Factor

The replication factor is not a setting that is intended to be changed on a live cluster and should be determined ahead of time. But as your application grows and you need to add nodes, you can increase the replication factor. There are some simple guidelines to follow when you do this. First, keep in mind that you'll have to restart the nodes after a simple increase in the replication factor value. A repair will then be performed after you restart the nodes, as Cassandra will have to redistribute some data in order to account for the increased replication factor. For as long as the repair takes, it is possible that some clients will receive a notice that data does not exist if they connect to a replica that doesn't have the data yet.

A faster way of increasing the replication factor from 1 to 2 is to use the node tool. First, execute a drain on the original node to ensure that all the data is flushed to the SSTables. Then, stop that node so it doesn't accept any more writes. Next, copy the datafiles from your keyspaces (the files under the directory that is your value for the DataFile Directory element in the config). Make sure not to copy the values in the internal Cassandra keyspace. Paste those datafiles to the new node. Change the settings in the configuration of both nodes so that the replication factor is set to 2. Make sure that autobootstrap is set to false in both nodes. Then, restart both nodes and run node tool repair. These steps will ensure that clients will not have to endure the potential of false empty reads for as long.

To illustrate this, I have three nodes with IP addresses ending in 1.5, 1.7, and 1.8, and their replication factor is set to 1. I will connect to node 1.5 and perform a write to a column that hasn't previously existed anywhere:

```
cassandra> connect 192.168.1.5/9160
Connected to: "TDG Cluster" on 192.168.1.5/9160
cassandra> set Keyspace1.Standard2['mykey']['rf']='1'
Value inserted.
```

Now I shut down node 1.5 and connect to the other node, 1.7, and try to get the value I just set:

```
cassandra> connect 192.168.1.7/9160
Connected to: "TDG Cluster" on 192.168.1.7/9160
cassandra> get Keyspace1.Standard2['mykey']['rf']
Exception null
```

Because my replication factor was 1, the value was written only to the 1.5 node, so when I lost that node, the other node in the cluster didn't have the value. No client will be able to read the value of the rf column until 1.5 comes back online.

But let's see the effect of updating the replication factor. We change it from 1 to 2 in the 1.5 and 1.7 nodes and restart. Let's insert a new value to our rf column on node 1.7:

```
cassandra> connect 192.168.1.7/9160
Connected to: "TDG Cluster" on 192.168.1.7/9160
cassandra> get Keyspace1.Standard2['mykey']['rf']
Exception null
cassandra> set Keyspace1.Standard2['mykey']['rf']='2'
Value inserted.
```

The Exception null response in the preceding example proves that the value didn't exist on node 1.7 beforehand. Now we shut down node 1.7 and connect to 1.5, and we see the value because it was replicated to 1.5 on our write to 1.7, due to our replication factor:

```
cassandra> connect 192.168.1.5/9160
Connected to: "TDG Cluster" on 192.168.1.5/9160
cassandra> get Keyspace1.Standard2['mykey']['rf']
=> (column=rf, value=2, timestamp=1279491483449000)
```

As a general guideline, you can anticipate that your write throughput capacity will be the number of nodes divided by your replication factor. So in a 10-node cluster that typically does 10,000 writes per second with a replication factor of 1, if you increase the replication factor to 2, you can expect to do around 5,000 writes per second.

Partitioners

The purpose of the partitioner is to allow you to specify how row keys should be sorted, which has a significant impact on how data will be distributed across your nodes. It also has an effect on the options available for querying ranges of rows. There are a few different partitioners you can use, which we look at now.

> The choice of partitioner does not apply to column sorting, only row key sorting.

You set the partitioner by updating the value of the `Partitioner` element in the config file or in the API. It takes as a value the name of a class that implements the `org.apache.cassandra.dht.IPartitioner` interface. Out of the box, Cassandra provides three of these: the random partitioner, which is the default; the order-preserving partitioner; and collating order-preserving partitioner. Because of Cassandra's generally pluggable design, you can also create your own partitioner by implementing the `org.apache.cassandra.dht.IPartitioner` class and placing it on Cassandra's classpath.

> Keep in mind that the partitioner can modify the on-disk SSTable representations. So if you change the partitioner type, you will have to delete your data directories.

Random Partitioner

The random partitioner is implemented by `org.apache.cassandra.dht.Random Partitioner` and is Cassandra's default. It uses a `BigIntegerToken` with an MD5 hash applied to it to determine where to place the keys on the node ring. This has the advantage of spreading your keys evenly across your cluster, because the distribution is random. It has the disadvantage of causing inefficient range queries, because keys within a specified range might be placed in a variety of disparate locations in the ring, and key range queries will return data in an essentially random order.

Order-Preserving Partitioner

The order-preserving partitioner is implemented by `org.apache.cassandra.dht.Order PreservingPartitioner`, which implements `IPartitioner<StringToken>`. Using this type of partitioner, the token is a UTF-8 string, based on a key. Rows are therefore stored by key order, aligning the physical structure of the data with your sort order.

Configuring your column family to use order-preserving partitioning (OPP) allows you to perform range slices.

It's worth noting that OPP isn't more efficient for range queries than random partitioning—it just provides ordering. It has the disadvantage of creating a ring that is potentially very lopsided, because real-world data typically is not written to evenly. As an example, consider the value assigned to letters in a Scrabble game. Q and Z are rarely used, so they get a high value. With OPP, you'll likely eventually end up with lots of data on some nodes and much less data on other nodes. The nodes on which lots of data is stored, making the ring lopsided, are often referred to as "hot spots." Because of the ordering aspect, users are commonly attracted to OPP early on. However, using OPP means that your operations team will need to manually rebalance nodes periodically using Nodetool's `loadbalance` or `move` operations.

If you want to perform range queries from your clients, you must use an order-preserving partitioner or a collating order-preserving partitioner.

Collating Order-Preserving Partitioner

This partitioner orders keys according to a United States English locale (`EN_US`). Like OPP, it requires that the keys are UTF-8 strings. Although its name might imply that it extends the OPP, it doesn't. Instead, this class extends `AbstractByteOrdered Partitioner`. This partitioner is rarely employed, as its usefulness is limited.

Byte-Ordered Partitioner

New for 0.7, the team added `ByteOrderedPartitioner`, which is an order-preserving partitioner that treats the data as raw bytes, instead of converting them to strings the way the order-preserving partitioner and collating order-preserving partitioner do. If you need an order-preserving partitioner that doesn't validate your keys as being strings, BOP is recommended for the performance improvement.

Snitches

The job of a snitch is simply to determine relative host proximity. Snitches gather some information about your network topology so that Cassandra can efficiently route requests. The snitch will figure out where nodes are in relation to other nodes. Inferring data centers is the job of the replication strategy.

Simple Snitch

By default, Cassandra uses `org.apache.cassandra.locator.EndPointSnitch`. It operates by simply comparing different octets in the IP addresses of each node. If two hosts have the same value in the second octet of their IP addresses, then they are determined to be in the same data center. If two hosts have the same value in the third octet of their IP addresses, then they are determined to be in the same rack. "Determined to be" really means that Cassandra has to guess based on an assumption of how your servers are located in different VLANs or subnets.

 Simple Snitch was renamed in 0.7; prior to that it was called endpoint snitch.

You configure which endpoint snitch implementation to use by updating the value for the `<EndPointSnitch>` element in the configuration file. The other choice is the `PropertyFileSnitch`.

PropertyFileSnitch

The `org.apache.cassandra.locator.PropertyFileSnitch` used to be in `contrib`, but was moved into the main code base in 0.7. This snitch allows you more control when using a Rack-Aware Strategy by specifying node locations in a standard key/value properties file called *cassandra-rack.properties*.

This snitch was contributed by Digg, which uses Cassandra and regularly contributes to its development. This snitch helps Cassandra know for certain if two IPs are in the same data center or on the same rack—because you tell it that they are. This is perhaps most useful if you move servers a lot, as operations often need to, or if you have inherited an unwieldy IP scheme.

The default configuration of *cassandra-rack.properties* looks like this:

```
# Cassandra Node IP=Data Center:Rack
10.0.0.10=DC1:RAC1
10.0.0.11=DC1:RAC1
10.0.0.12=DC1:RAC2

10.20.114.10=DC2:RAC1
10.20.114.11=DC2:RAC1
10.20.114.15=DC2:RAC2

# default for unknown nodes
default=DC1:r1
```

Here we see that there are two data centers, each with two racks. Cassandra can determine an even distribution with good performance.

Update the values in this file to record each node in your cluster to specify which rack contains the node with that IP and which data center it's in. Although this may seem difficult to maintain if you expect to add or remove nodes with some frequency, remember that it's one alternative, and it trades away a little flexibility and ease of maintenance in order to give you more control and better runtime performance, as

Cassandra doesn't have to figure out where nodes are. Instead, you just tell it where they are.

The `PropertyFileSnitch` used to be called `PropertyFileEndPoint Snitch` and was in the `contrib` directory before being promoted to part of the standard distribution, in case you see references to that online.

Creating a Cluster

You can run Cassandra on a single machine, which is fine for getting started as you learn how to read and write data. But Cassandra is specifically engineered to be used in a cluster of many machines that can share the load in very high-volume situations. In this section, we see what you have to do to get multiple Cassandra instances to talk to each other in a ring.

During the writing of this book, the entire configuration mechanism was changing dramatically. This section covers how to create a cluster using version 0.6.

What we want to do here is just use the sample keyspace that ships with Cassandra to make sure that we can get multiple machines in a ring together. So we'll start with the default configuration file and keyspace definition, and change only those settings required to create a simple cluster.

For this exercise, let's say that we have two boxes we want to set up as a Cassandra cluster, with the IP addresses 192.168.1.5 and 192.168.1.7. When you start Cassandra, it reads the configuration file to determine how you want the current node to broadcast —that is, what host or IP address and what port to use. You need to tell the current node about the other nodes with which it should participate in a ring. Doing this is a simple matter of opening the config file in a text editor and updating a few values, as we'll examine here.

A new node in a cluster needs what's called a *seed node*. If node A acts as a seed for node B, when node B comes online, it will use node A as a reference point from which to get data. Seed nodes will ignore the `AutoBootstrap` setting because it is assumed that they will be the first nodes in the cluster.

Changing the Cluster Name

Cassandra clusters are given names in order to prevent machines in one cluster from joining another that you don't want them to be a part of. The name of the default cluster in the config file is "Test Cluster". You can change the name of the cluster by updating the `<ClusterName>` element—just make sure that you have done this on all nodes that you want to participate in this cluster.

 If you have written data to an existing Cassandra cluster and then change the cluster name, Cassandra will warn you with a cluster name mismatch error as it tries to read the datafiles on startup, and then it will shut down.

Adding Nodes to a Cluster

The configuration file has an element that is set to false by default. Say that you have been running a cluster or a single node and added data to it, and now you want to introduce more nodes to the cluster. You can do this using the **autobootstrap** element. I have a single Cassandra server running on an IP ending in 1.5, as shown by NodeTool:

```
$ bin/nodetool -h 192.168.1.5 ring
Address         Status    Load       Range                                         Ring
192.168.1.5     Up        433.43 MB  12680467166164945006580981054963333334036    |<--|
```

This server has its own address as a seed. We leave autobootstrap set to false, because this node is acting as a seed. If you want to add a new seed node, then you should autobootstrap it first, and then change it to a seed afterward. For node B to use node A as a seed, node B needs to reference node A as its seed in its configuration file. But node A does not have to declare itself as a seed.

Now I'd like to add another node to share the load. This node's address ends in 1.7. First, make sure that the nodes in the cluster all have the same name and the same keyspace definitions so that the new node can accept data. Edit the config file on the second node to indicate that the first one will act as the seed. Then, set autobootstrap to true.

When the second node is started up, it immediately recognizes the first node, but then sleeps for 90 seconds to allow time for nodes to gossip information about how much data they are storing locally. It then gets the bootstrap token from the first node, so it knows what section of the data it should accept. The bootstrap token is a token that splits the load of the most-loaded node in half. Again, the second node sleeps for 30 seconds and then starts bootstrapping.

```
INFO 11:45:43,652 Starting up server gossip
INFO 11:45:43,886 Joining: getting load information
INFO 11:45:43,901 Sleeping 90000 ms to wait for load information...
INFO 11:45:45,742 Node /192.168.1.5 is now part of the cluster
INFO 11:45:46,818 InetAddress /192.168.1.5 is now UP
INFO 11:45:46,818 Started hinted handoff for endPoint /192.168.1.5
INFO 11:45:46,865 Finished hinted handoff of 0 rows to endpoint /192.168.1.5
INFO 11:47:13,913 Joining: getting bootstrap token
INFO 11:47:16,004 New token will be 41707658470746813056713124104091156313 to a
ssume load from /192.168.1.5
```

```
INFO 11:47:16,019 Joining: sleeping 30000 ms for pending range setup
INFO 11:47:46,034 Bootstrapping
```

Depending on how much data you have, you could see your new node in this state for some time. You can use Nodetool's **streams** command to watch the data being transferred for bootstrap. Watching the logfile is a good way to determine that the node is *finished* bootstrapping, but to watch for progress while it's happening, use **nodetool streams**. Eventually, the new node will accept the load from the first node, and you'll see a successful indication that the new node has started up:

```
INFO 11:52:29,361 Sampling index for /var/lib/cassandra/data\Keyspace1\Standard
1-1-Data.db
INFO 11:52:34,073 Streaming added /var/lib/cassandra/data\Keyspace1\Standard1-1
-Data.db
INFO 11:52:34,088 Bootstrap/move completed! Now serving reads.
INFO 11:52:34,354 Binding thrift service to /192.168.1.7:9160
INFO 11:52:34,432 Cassandra starting up...
```

As you can see, it took around four minutes to transfer data.

During bootstrapping, the first (seed) node at 1.5 looks like this:

```
INFO 11:48:12,955 Sending a stream initiate message to /192.168.1.7 ...
INFO 11:48:12,955 Waiting for transfer to /192.168.1.7 to complete
INFO 11:52:28,903 Done with transfer to /192.168.1.7
```

Now we can run node tool again to make sure that everything is set up properly:

```
$ bin/nodetool -h 192.168.1.5 ring
Address         Status    Load      Range                                              Ring
                                    126804671661649450065809810549633334036
192.168.1.7     Up        229.56 MB 41707658470746813056713124104091156313             |<--|
192.168.1.5     Up        459.26 MB 126804671661649450065809810549633334036            |-->|
```

Cassandra has automatically bootstrapped the 1.7 node by sending it half of the data from the previous node (1.5). So now we have a two-node cluster. To ensure that it works, let's add a value to the 1.5 node:

```
cassandra> connect 192.168.1.5/9160
Connected to: "TDG Cluster" on 192.168.1.5/9160
cassandra> set Keyspace1.Standard2['mykey']['col0']='value0'
Value inserted.
```

Now let's open a second CLI client and read that value from the 1.7 node:

```
cassandra> connect 192.168.1.7/9160
Connected to: "TDG Cluster" on 192.168.1.7/9160
cassandra> get Keyspace1.Standard2['mykey']['col0']
=> (column=col0, value=value0, timestamp=1278878907805000)
```

You can repeat these steps to add additional nodes to your cluster.

If there's something wrong with one of the nodes in your cluster (perhaps it's offline, but Cassandra is not sure), you may see a question mark when you run node tool:

```
$ bin/nodetool -h 192.168.1.5 ring
Address         Status    Load       Range                                               Ring
                                     112711146095673746066359353163476425700
192.168.1.5     Up        459.26 MB  276472753532973138865478084465147049912             |<--|
192.168.1.7     ?         229.53 MB  112711146095673746066359353163476425700             |-->|
```

Multiple Seed Nodes

Cassandra allows you to specify multiple seed nodes. A seed node is used as a contact point for other nodes, so Cassandra can learn the topology of the cluster, that is, what hosts have what ranges.

By default, the configuration file will have only a single **seed** entry:

```
seeds:
    - 127.0.0.1
```

To add more seed nodes to your ring, just add another seed element. We can set two servers to be seeds just by indicating the IP address or hostname of this node and then adding our second instance:

```
seeds:
    - 192.168.1.5
    - 192.168.1.7
```

 Make sure that the autobootstrap element is set to false if you're using a node's own IP address as a seed. One approach is to make the first three or five nodes in a cluster seeds, without autobootstrap—that is, by manually choosing tokens or by allowing Cassandra to pick random tokens. The rest of your nodes will not be seeds, so they can be added using autobootstrap.

Next, we need to update the listen address for this machine so it's not just on loopback. Listen address is how nodes identify each other, and it's used for all internal communication.

```
listen_address: 192.168.1.5
```

Finally, we need to change the address on which our RPC client will broadcast because this is how other nodes will see this one. By default, the configuration file will have an **rpc_address** entry that uses localhost. We'll change this value to the actual IP address of each machine:

```
rpc_address: 192.168.1.5
```

The **rpc_address** setting is used only for connections made directly from clients to Cassandra nodes.

rpc_address used to be called ThriftAddress, but because of the up-coming possible change to Avro instead of Thrift as the RPC mechanism, it has been changed to a more general name.

Now you can restart Cassandra and start the installations on the other machines. If you have successfully added multiple nodes to your cluster, you will see output similar to this (yours might be a little less verbose, as I'm showing debug-level output here):

```
INFO 15:45:15,629 Starting up server gossip
INFO 15:45:15,677 Binding thrift service to /192.168.1.5:9160
INFO 15:45:15,681 Cassandra starting up...
DEBUG 15:45:16,636 GC for ParNew: 13 ms, 12879912 reclaimed leaving 11233080 used;
max is 1177812992
DEBUG 15:45:16,647 attempting to connect to /192.168.1.7
DEBUG 15:45:17,638 Disseminating load info ...
INFO 15:45:19,744 Node /192.168.1.7 is now part of the cluster
DEBUG 15:45:19,746 Node /192.168.1.7 state normal, token
41654880048427970483049687892424207188
DEBUG 15:45:19,746 No bootstrapping or leaving nodes -> empty pending ranges
for Keyspace1
INFO 15:45:20,789 InetAddress /192.168.1.7 is now UP
DEBUG 15:45:20,789 Started hinted handoff for endPoint /192.168.1.7
DEBUG 15:45:20,800 Finished hinted handoff for endpoint /192.168.1.7
DEBUG 15:46:17,638 Disseminating load info ...
```

This output shows that I have two nodes in my cluster: the node I just started, which is listening on 192.168.1.5, and the node that was already up and running, which is listening on 192.168.1.7.

Dynamic Ring Participation

Nodes in a Cassandra cluster can be brought down and brought back up without disruption to the rest of the cluster (assuming a reasonable replication factor and consistency level). Say that we have started a two-node cluster as described earlier in "Creating a Cluster" on page 113. We can cause an error to occur that will take down one of the nodes, and then make sure that the rest of the cluster is still OK:

```
INFO 15:34:18,953 Starting up server gossip
INFO 15:34:19,281 Binding thrift service to /192.168.1.7:9160
INFO 15:34:19,343 Cassandra starting up...
INFO 15:45:19,396 Node /192.168.1.5 is now part of the cluster
INFO 15:45:20,176 InetAddress /192.168.1.5 is now UP
INFO 16:13:36,476 error writing to /192.168.1.5
INFO 16:13:40,517 InetAddress /192.168.1.5 is now dead.
INFO 16:21:02,466 error writing to /192.168.1.5
INFO 16:21:02,497 error writing to /192.168.1.5
```

The error message will repeat until the 1.5 node comes back up. Running Nodetool will indicate that it's down now, while the other node is still up.

So we bring it back up and check the logs at 1.7. Sure enough, Cassandra has automatically detected that the other participant has returned to the cluster and is again open for business:

```
INFO 16:33:48,193 error writing to /192.168.1.5
INFO 16:33:51,235 error writing to /192.168.1.5
INFO 16:34:20,126 Standard2 has reached its threshold; switching in a fresh Mem
table at CommitLogContext(file='/var/lib/cassandra/commitlog\CommitLog-127759165
782.log', position=752)
INFO 16:34:20,173 Enqueuing flush of Memtable(Standard2)@7481705
INFO 16:34:20,251 Writing Memtable(Standard2)@7481705
INFO 16:34:20,282 LocationInfo has reached its threshold; switching in a fresh
Memtable at CommitLogContext(file='/var/lib/cassandra/commitlog\CommitLog-127759
658782.log', position=752)
INFO 16:34:20,298 Enqueuing flush of Memtable(LocationInfo)@24804063
INFO 16:34:20,579 Completed flushing c:\var\lib\cassandra\data\Keyspace1\Standa
d2-1-Data.db
INFO 16:34:20,594 Writing Memtable(LocationInfo)@24804063
INFO 16:34:20,797 Completed flushing c:\var\lib\cassandra\data\system\LocationI
fo-2-Data.db
INFO 16:34:58,159 Node /192.168.1.5 has restarted, now UP again
INFO 16:34:58,159 Node /192.168.1.5 state jump to normal
```

The state jump to normal for the 1.5 node indicates that it's part of the cluster again:

```
eben@morpheus$ bin/nodetool -host 192.168.1.5 ring
Address        Status    Load      Range                                              Ring
                                   416548800484279704830496878924242207188
192.168.1.5    Up        1.71 KB   208466712622890044293293447172905883342            |<--|
192.168.1.7    Up        2 KB      416548800484279704830496878924242207188            |-->|
```

Security

By default, Cassandra allows any client on your network to connect to your cluster. This does not mean that no security is set up out of the box, but rather that Cassandra is configured to use an authentication mechanism that allows all clients, without requiring that they provide credentials. The security mechanism is pluggable, which means that you can easily swap out one authentication method for another, or write your own.

The authenticator that's plugged in by default is the org.apache.cassandra.auth.Allow AllAuthenticator. If you want to force clients to provide credentials, another alternative ships with Cassandra, the org.apache.cassandra.auth.SimpleAuthenticator. In this section, we see how to use this second authenticator.

Using SimpleAuthenticator

There are two files included in the *config* directory: *access.properties* and *passwd* *.properties*. The access file uses a key/value pair to specify which users are allowed access to which keyspaces, specified by a comma-separated list. The example provided looks like this:

```
Keyspace1=jsmith,Elvis Presley,dilbert
```

This indicates that there are three users allowed to access **Keyspace1**, and spaces are allowed in the usernames.

The file *passwd.properties* must contain a list of these users and specify the password for each of them. Here is the example *passwd.properties* file:

```
jsmith=havebadpass
Elvis\ Presley=graceland4evar
dilbert=nomoovertime
```

Note that because the user Elvis Presley has a space in his username, a backslash must be used to escape the space.

To use the Simple Authenticator, replace the value for the authenticator element in *cassandra.yaml*. Change it from **org.apache.cassandra.auth.AllowAllAuthenticator** to the name of the implementing class that requires a login: **org.apache.cassandra.auth.SimpleAuthenticator**.

If you haven't configured the authentication files properly, you'll see an error like this:

```
ERROR 10:44:27,928 Fatal error: When using org.apache.cassandra.auth.SimpleAuth
enticator
access.properties and passwd.properties properties must be defined.
```

That's because there is one more step: we have to tell Cassandra the location of the access and passwords files, using the *bin/cassandra.in.sh* include script. We pass the file locations to the JVM by pasting the following code at the bottom of this file. My include file now looks like the snippet here, indicating the full path to the files:

```
JVM_OPTS="
        -Dpasswd.properties=/home/eben/books/cassandra/dist/
apache-cassandra-0.7.0-beta1/
conf/passwd.properties
        -Daccess.properties=/home/eben/books/cassandra/dist/
apache-cassandra-0.7.0-beta1/
conf/access.properties"
```

If you have specified an incorrect location or name for either of these files, the server log will let you know:

```
ERROR 11:13:55,755 Internal error processing login
java.lang.RuntimeException: Authentication table file given by property
passwd.properties
could not be found: /somebadpath/my.properties (No such file or directory)
```

Now we can log into the command-line interface with a username and password combination:

```
[default@unknown] connect localhost/9160
Connected to: "Test Cluster" on localhost/9160
[default@unknown] use Keyspace1 jsmith 'havebadpass'
```

```
Authenticated to keyspace: Keyspace1
[jsmith@Keyspace1]
```

If you enter an incorrect password, the CLI tells you:

```
[default@unknown] use Keyspace1 jsmith 'havebadpassfdfdfd'
Exception during authentication to the cassandra node: verify keyspace exists,
and you are using correct credentials.
```

If you enter a username that doesn't exist or try to authenticate to a keyspace that the user doesn't have access to, you'll see something like this:

```
[default@unknown] use Keyspace1 dude 'dude'
Login failure. Did you specify 'keyspace', 'username' and 'password'?
[default@unknown]
```

Somewhat confusingly, if you just try to use a keyspace that you don't have access to, you'll see an authentication message, but then you won't be able to perform operations. In the following example, we switch to a keyspace that requires authentication. The CLI appears to let us do that, but then we can't read a column:

```
[default@Keyspace1] get Standard1['user123']['name']
Your credentials are not sufficient to perform READONLY operations
[default@Keyspace1]
```

Assuming we have set the 'name' value for this user, if we supply the proper credentials, we can perform the operation:

```
[default@Keyspace1] use Keyspace1 eben 'pass'
Authenticated to keyspace: Keyspace1
[eben@Keyspace1] get Standard1['user123']['name']
=> (column=6e616d65, value=bootsy, timestamp=1284316537496000)
[eben@Keyspace1]
```

We can also specify the username and password combination when we connect on the CLI:

```
eben@morpheus:~/books/cassandra/dist/apache-cassandra-0.7.0-beta1$
   bin/cassandra-cli --host localhost --port 9160
   --username jsmith --password havebadpass --keyspace Keyspace1

Connected to: "Test Cluster" on localhost/9160
Welcome to cassandra CLI.

Type 'help' or '?' for help. Type 'quit' or 'exit' to quit.
[jsmith@Keyspace1] get Standard1['user123']['name']
=> (column=6e616d65, value=bootsy, timestamp=1284316537496000)
[jsmith@Keyspace1]
```

Executing a query now returns us a result.

 In 0.6, there was no login operation provided by the Thrift API, so if you've gotten used to starting the CLI and then connecting in a separate operation, that won't work if you are requiring authentication. A login operation was added in 0.7.

In 0.7, authenticators have been split into an IAuthenticator (which handles authentication) and IAuthority (which handles authorization). The SimpleAuthenticator class has had authorization split out into SimpleAuthority. SimpleAuthenticator reads only *passwd.properties*, and SimpleAuthority reads only *access.properties*.

Programmatic Authentication

If you have set up authentication on your keyspace, your client application code will need to log in. You can use Example 6-2 as a guide.

Example 6-2. Programmatic authentication to a keyspace

```
package com.cassandraguide.config;

import java.util.HashMap;
import java.util.Map;

import org.apache.cassandra.thrift.AccessLevel;
import org.apache.cassandra.thrift.AuthenticationRequest;
import org.apache.cassandra.thrift.Cassandra;
import org.apache.thrift.protocol.TBinaryProtocol;
import org.apache.thrift.protocol.TProtocol;
import org.apache.thrift.transport.TFramedTransport;
import org.apache.thrift.transport.TSocket;
import org.apache.thrift.transport.TTransport;

/**
 * How to connect if you've set up SimpleAuthenticator
 */
public class AuthExample {

    public static void main(String[] args) throws Exception {

        TTransport tr = new TSocket("localhost", 9160);
        TFramedTransport tf = new TFramedTransport(tr);
        TProtocol proto = new TBinaryProtocol(tf);
        Cassandra.Client client = new Cassandra.Client(proto);
        tr.open();

        AuthenticationRequest authRequest = new AuthenticationRequest();
        Map<String, String> credentials = new HashMap<String, String>();
        credentials.put("username", "jsmith");
        credentials.put("password", "havebadpass");
        authRequest.setCredentials(credentials);

        client.set_keyspace("Keyspace1");

        AccessLevel access = client.login(authRequest);
        System.out.println("ACCESS LEVEL: " + access);
        tr.close();
    }
}
```

In this case, the program just prints out FULL because that's this user's access level.

There are a couple of things to note here. First, the credentials map uses username and password as keys; it's not username as the key and password as the value. Second, you need to call set_keyspace separately, to indicate what keyspace you're trying to authenticate to.

Using MD5 Encryption

The SimpleAuthenticator class has two modes for specifying passwords: plain text and MD5 encrypted. So far, we've used the default, plain text. Let's look at how to improve security a bit by using MD5. MD5 is a cryptographical algorithm that stands for "Message-Digest algorithm version 5" (the "5" indicates an improvement in strength over version 4). It's a widely used one-way hash function that generates a 128-bit hash value from an input. It's also worth noting that MD5 is not going to be radically secure for you; it's just a little harder to break in.

You enable MD5 in the *cassandra.in.sh* file by passing the passwd.mode switch to the JVM:

```
JVM_OPTS=" \
        -da \
//other stuff...
        -Dpasswd.mode=MD5"
```

Now if you try to authenticate using an unencrypted password, you'll see an error like this:

```
Exception during authentication to the cassandra node, verify you are using correct
credentials.
```

You can use a variety of tools to generate an MD5-encrypted version of the plain-text username and password as a one-way hash. Here's a short Python program to create an MD5 hash from a plain string:

```
$ python
Python 2.6.5 ...
>>> from hashlib import md5
>>> p = "havebadpass"
>>> h = md5(p).hexdigest()
>>> print h
e1a31eee2136eb73e8e47f9e9d13ab0d
```

Now you can replace the password for jsmith in the *passwd.properties* file with the encrypted value.

Providing Your Own Authentication

You can provide your own method of authenticating to Cassandra if you want to make special requirements, such as a Kerberos ticket or encryption, or if you want to store passwords in a different location, such as an LDAP directory. To create your own authentication scheme, simply implement the IAuthenticator interface. This interface requires two methods, as shown here:

```
public AccessLevel login(String keyspace, AuthenticationRequest authRequest)
    throws AuthenticationException, AuthorizationException;

public void validateConfiguration() throws ConfigurationException;
```

The login method must return a Thrift AccessLevel instance, indicating what degree of access the authenticating user is allowed. The validateConfiguration method simply allows a check to ensure that the authentication mechanism is properly set up. For example, with the SimpleAuthenticator, it just checks that the required *access* and *passwd* files have been specified.

Miscellaneous Settings

There are a few settings related to general configuration that don't quite seem to belong in any other category, so I've grouped them together here.

column_index_size_in_kb
>   This indicates the size in kilobytes that a row is allowed to grow to before its columns will be indexed. If you have very large column values, you'll want to increase this value. Super columns are not indexed, so this setting refers only to column indexes. You do not want this setting to be very large because all the index data is read for each read access, so you could slow Cassandra down if you make it read more than is necessary. This becomes especially important if you frequently read partial rows.

in_memory_compaction_limit_in_mb
>   This value represents the size limit for rows being compacted in memory. If a row is larger than this, it will be staged onto disk and compacted in a slower, two-step process. The setting's value is set to 64MB by default. Prior to Cassandra version 0.7, this was called the row_warning_threshold_in_mb.

gc_grace_seconds
>   This indicates the amount of time in seconds to wait before garbage-collecting tombstones. Tombstones are markers indicating that a value was deleted, but they persist until this threshold is met. By default it is set to 864,000, which is 10 days. This might seem like an inordinately long time, but you have to allow enough time for tombstones to propagate through the entire cluster to any replicas. That may still seem like a long time, but the idea is that you could have hardware failures, and you'll need time to get those nodes back up and operational so that tombstones can replicate to them too. If a downed node that did not receive tombstone notifications comes back up after the tombstones have been truly deleted, read repair will allow the untombstoned, undeleted data to slowly be introduced back into the cluster.

Of course, if you do a lot of deleting, you could tune this setting back for the sake of tidiness, but it's probably not going to make a huge difference.

phi_convict_threshold

This marks the Phi value that must be reached in order for Cassandra to conclude that the server is down. By default, this is set to 8, and in general you will not want to change this setting. However, if your network is not performing optimally or you have other reasons to suspect that Cassandra could get a false read on this, you can increase this setting to allow more leniency in determining whether a node is actually down.

Phi Threshold and Accrual Failure Detectors

Since its inception at Facebook, Cassandra has employed what is called an Accrual Failure Detector. This is a failure detector that outputs a value associated with each process (or node). This value is called Phi. The value is output in a manner that is designed from the ground up to be adaptive in the face of volatile network conditions, so it's not a binary condition that simply checks whether a server is up or down.

The Phi convict threshold in the configuration adjusts the sensitivity of the failure detector. Lower values increase the sensitivity and higher values decrease it, but not in a linear fashion.

The Phi value refers to a level of *suspicion* that a server might be down. Applications such as Cassandra that employ an AFD can specify variable conditions for the Phi value they emit. Cassandra can generally detect a failed node in about 10 seconds using this mechanism.

You can read the original Phi Accrual Failure Detection paper on which Cassandra's design is based at *http://ddg.jaist.ac.jp/pub/HDY+04.pdf*.

Additional Tools

This section discusses miscellaneous tools that ship with Cassandra to help you configure it.

Viewing Keys

You can see which keys are in your SSTables using a script called **sstablekeys**. To run it, just use the location of the SSTable for which you want to see keys, as shown here:

```
eben@morpheus$ bin/sstablekeys /var/lib/cassandra/data/Hotelier/Hotel-1-Data.db
 WARN 10:56:05,928 Schema definitions were defined both locally and in cassandra.yaml.
Definitions in cassandra.yaml were ignored.
415a435f303433
415a535f303131
4341535f303231
4e594e5f303432
```

Importing Previous Configurations

If you had a keyspace defined in 0.6 using the configuration file that you'd like to import into Cassandra 0.7 or higher, you can use a special JMX operation, `Storage Service.loadSchemaFromYaml()`. Note that this method has two important caveats: first, it is intended to be used only once; second, it will probably be removed by version 0.8.

Starting with version 0.7, the user keyspaces defined in *cassandra.yaml* are not loaded by default when the server starts. So you might see a message like this as your Cassandra server starts up for the first time:

```
INFO config.DatabaseDescriptor: Found table data in data directories.
Consider using JMX to call org.apache.cassandra.service.StorageService.
loadSchemaFromYaml().
```

In order to load them, you need to invoke the `loadSchemaFromYaml` JMX operation. But in order to invoke this command, you need to do a couple of things. First, get *mx4j-tools.jar* from Sourceforge.net. Download and extract the ZIP file into any directory. Then, copy the JAR named *mx4j-tools.jar* in its *lib* directory into Cassandra's *lib* directory. This will allow you to make JMX connections to interact with Cassandra in really rich ways. We'll see more about using JMX with Cassandra later, but for now we just want to get a keyspace up for testing. Restart Cassandra after adding the JAR.

Next, open a new terminal and issue the command *jconsole*. A GUI will start and load the JConsole tool that ships with Java. This tool can introspect the Java Virtual Machine and allow you to view runtime data and invoke operations that are exposed via JMX.

To load the keyspaces defined in *cassandra.yaml*, click the MBeans tab in the JConsole GUI. Expand the `org.apache.cassandra.service` bean, then `StorageService`, then Operations. Click the `loadSchemaFromYAML` operation and click the button. This will execute the command on the Cassandra service and load your schemas in the *cassandra.yaml* file.

To perform the once-only operation to import a 0.6 configuration into 0.7, use the `loadSchemaFromYaml` operation on the `StorageService` MBean. This is shown in Figure 6-4.

Now you should see output similar to the following in your logs:

```
17:35:47 INFO thrift.CassandraDaemon: Cassandra starting up...
17:35:48 INFO utils.Mx4jTool: mx4j successfuly loaded
HttpAdaptor version 3.0.2 started on port 8081
17:40:43 INFO config.DatabaseDescriptor: UTF8Type
17:40:43 INFO config.DatabaseDescriptor: BytesType
17:40:43 INFO config.DatabaseDescriptor: UTF8Type
17:40:43 INFO config.DatabaseDescriptor: TimeUUIDType
17:40:43 INFO config.DatabaseDescriptor: BytesType
17:40:43 INFO config.DatabaseDescriptor: BytesType
17:40:43 INFO config.DatabaseDescriptor:
```

The database descriptor logs are a good thing, as this indicates that the operation loaded your schemas.

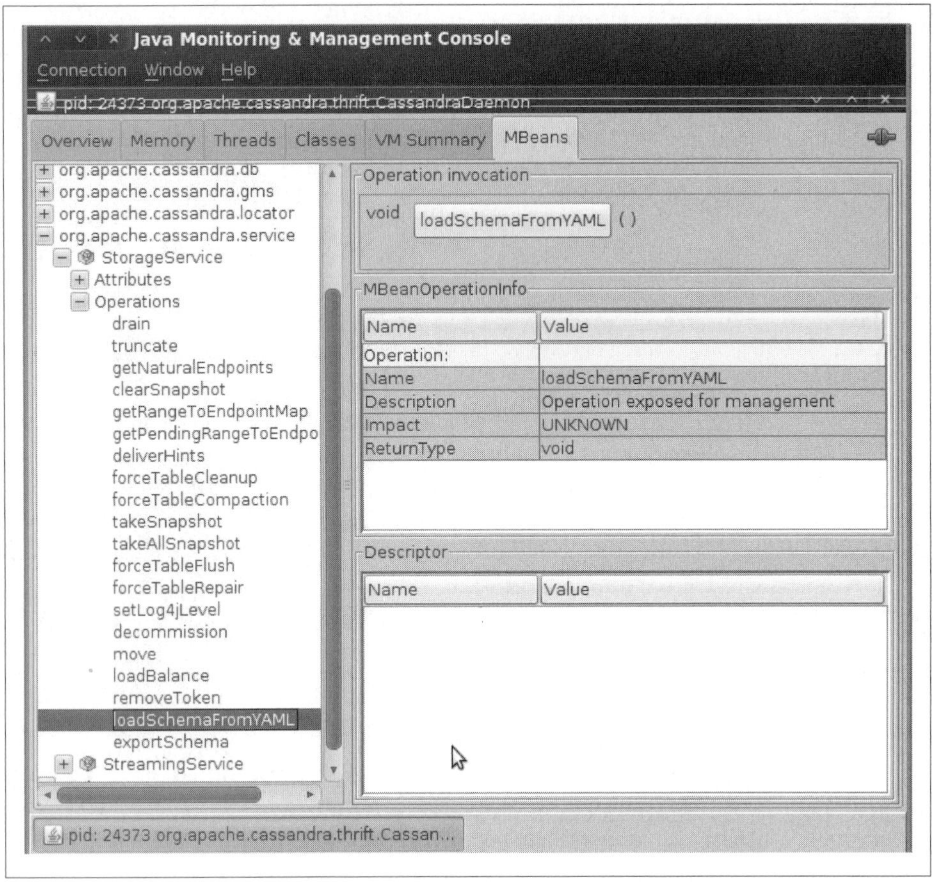

Figure 6-4. Using the jconsole tool to load old keyspaces defined in cassandra.yaml

You can also use the `org.apache.cassandra.config.Converter` class to assist you in converting from *storage-conf.xml* to a *cassandra.yaml* file. If you are upgrading from 0.6 to 0.7, this should be your first step. To run the converter, use the *config-converter* script in the *bin* directory. It will read in the old file, convert it, and dump the contents.

> If you need to import and export data, Cassandra comes with two scripts for working with JSON: one that imports JSON into Cassandra SSTables, and another that exports existing SSTables into JSON.

Summary

In this chapter we looked at how to configure Cassandra, including using the new dynamic configuration ability in the API and some of the utilities that ship with the server to dig into your raw datafiles. We saw how to set the replication factor and the snitch, and how to use a good replica placement strategy.

If you prefer to use a graphical interface instead of the CLI, you can get information regarding your Cassandra setup using Chiton, which is a Python GTK-based Cassandra browser written by Brandon Williams. You can find it at *http://github.com/driftx/chiton*.

## CHAPTER 7

Reading and Writing Data

Now that we understand the data model, we'll look at the different kinds of queries you can perform in Cassandra to read and write data. In this chapter, we use Cassandra 0.6.7-beta1, which is the most recent release version at the time of this writing.

Query Differences Between RDBMS and Cassandra

There are several differences between Cassandra's model and query methods and what's available in RDBMS, and these are important to keep in mind.

No Update Query

There is no first-order concept of an update in Cassandra, meaning that there is no client query called an "update." You can readily achieve the same effect, however, by simply performing an insert using an existing row key. If you issue an insert statement for a key that already exists, Cassandra will overwrite the values for any matching columns; if your query contains additional columns that don't already exist for that row key, then the additional columns will be inserted. This is all seamless.

Record-Level Atomicity on Writes

Cassandra automatically gives you record-level atomicity on every write operation. In RDBMS, you would have to specify row-level locking. Although Cassandra offers atomicity at the column family level, it does not guarantee isolation.

No Server-Side Transaction Support

Because you need to denormalize tables to create secondary indexes, you might need to insert data into two or more tables (one for your primary table and one for your inverted or secondary index). This means issuing two insert statements. So if it is applicable for your use case, you'll need to manually "roll back" writes by issuing a delete if one of the insert operations fails.

More to the point, perhaps, is that Cassandra doesn't have transactions, because it just wasn't built with that goal in mind.

No Duplicate Keys

It is possible in SQL databases to insert more than one row with identical values if you have not defined a unique primary key constraint on one of the columns. This is not possible in Cassandra. If you write a new record with a key that already exists in a column family, the values for any existing columns will be overwritten, and any columns that previously were not present for that row will be added to the row.

Basic Write Properties

There are a few basic properties of Cassandra's write ability that are worth noting. First, writing data is very fast in Cassandra, because its design does not require performing disk reads or seeks. The memtables and SSTables save Cassandra from having to perform these operations on writes, which slow down many databases. All writes in Cassandra are append-only.

Because of the database commit log and hinted handoff design, the database is always writeable, and within a column family, writes are always atomic.

Consistency Levels

Cassandra's tuneable consistency levels mean that you can specify in your queries how much consistency you require. A higher consistency level means that more nodes need to respond to the query, giving you more assurance that the values present on each replica are the same. If two nodes respond with different timestamps, the newest value wins, and that's what will be returned to the client. In the background, Cassandra will then perform what's called a *read repair*: it takes notice of the fact that one or more replicas responded to a query with an outdated value, and updates those replicas with the most current value so that they are all consistent.

There are several consistency levels that you can specify, and they mean something different for read operations than for write operations. The possible consistency levels, and the implications of specifying each one for read queries, are shown in Table 7-1.

 The consistency levels are based on the replication factor specified in the configuration file, *not* on the total number of nodes in the system.

Table 7-1. Read consistency levels

Consistency level	Implication
ZERO	Unsupported. You cannot specify CL.ZERO for read operations because it doesn't make sense. This would amount to saying "give me the data from no nodes."
ANY	Unsupported. Use CL.ONE instead.
ONE	Immediately return the record held by the first node that responds to the query. A background thread is created to check that record against the same record on other replicas. If any are out of date, a *read repair* is then performed to sync them all to the most recent value.
QUORUM	Query all nodes. Once a majority of replicas ((replication factor / 2) + 1) respond, return to the client the value with the most recent timestamp. Then, if necessary, perform a read repair in the background on all remaining replicas.
ALL	Query all nodes. Wait for all nodes to respond, and return to the client the record with the most recent timestamp. Then, if necessary, perform a read repair in the background. If any nodes fail to respond, fail the read operation.

As you can see from the table, there are certain consistency levels that are not supported for read operations: ZERO and ANY. Notice that the implication of consistency level ONE is that the first node to respond to the read operation is the value that the client will get—*even if it is out of date.* The read repair operation is performed *after* the record is returned, so any subsequent reads will all have a consistent value, regardless of the responding node.

Another item worth noting is in the case of consistency level ALL. If you specify CL.ALL, then you're saying that you require all replicas to respond, so if any node with that record is down or otherwise fails to respond before the timeout, the read operation fails.

 A node is considered unresponsive if it does not respond to a query before the value specified by rpc_timeout_in_ms in the configuration file. The default is 10 seconds.

You can specify these consistency levels for write operations as well, though their meanings are very different. The implications of using the different consistency levels on writes are shown in Table 7-2.

Table 7-2. Write consistency levels

Consistency level	Implication
ZERO	The write operation will return immediately to the client before the write is recorded; the write will happen asynchronously in a background thread, and there are no guarantees of success.
ANY	Ensure that the value is written to a minimum of one node, allowing hints to count as a write.
ONE	Ensure that the value is written to the commit log and memtable of at least one node before returning to the client.

Consistency level	Implication
QUORUM	Ensure that the write was received by at least a majority of replicas ((replication factor / 2) + 1).
ALL	Ensure that the number of nodes specified by replication factor received the write before returning to the client. If even one replica is unresponsive to the write operation, fail the operation.

The most notable consistency level for writes is the ANY level. This level means that the write is guaranteed to reach at least one node, but *it allows a hint to count as a successful write*. That is, if you perform a write operation and the node that the operation targets for that value is down, the server will make a note to itself, called a *hint*, which it will store until that node comes back up. Once the node is up, the server will detect this, look to see whether it has any writes that it saved for later in the form of a hint, and then write the value to the revived node. In many cases, the node that makes the hint actually *isn't* the node that stores it; instead, it sends it off to one of the nonreplica neighbors of the node that is down.

Using the consistency level of ONE on writes means that the write operation will be written to both the commit log and the memtable. That means that writes at CL.ONE are durable, so this level is the minimum level to use to achieve fast performance and durability. If this node goes down immediately after the write operation, the value will have been written to the commit log, which can be replayed when the server is brought back up to ensure that it still has the value.

For both reads and writes, the consistency levels of ZERO, ANY, and ONE are considered weak, whereas QUORUM and ALL are considered strong. Consistency is tuneable in Cassandra because clients can specify the desired consistency level on both reads and writes. There is an equation that is popularly used to represent the way to achieve strong consistency in Cassandra: $R + W > N$ = *strong consistency*. In this equation, R, W, and N are the read replica count, the write replica count, and the replication factor, respectively; all client reads will see the most recent write in this scenario, and you will have strong consistency.

Basic Read Properties

There are a few basic properties of reading data from Cassandra that are worth noting. First, it's easy to read data because clients can connect to any node in the cluster to perform reads, without having to know whether a particular node acts as a replica for that data. If a client connects to a node that doesn't have the data it's trying to read, the node it's connected to will act as coordinator node to read the data from a node that does have it, identified by token ranges.

To fulfill read operations, Cassandra does have to perform seeks, but you can speed these up by adding RAM. Adding RAM will help you if you find the OS doing a lot of paging on reads (in general, it is better to enable the various caches Cassandra has).

Cassandra has to wait for a number of responses synchronously (based on consistency level and replication factor), and then perform read repairs as necessary.

So reads are clearly slower than writes, for these various reasons. The partitioner doesn't influence the speed of reads. In the case of range queries, using OPP is significantly faster because it allows you to easily determine which nodes *don't* have your data. The partitioner's responsibility is to perform the consistent hash operation that maps keys to nodes. In addition, you can choose row caching and key caching strategies to give you a performance boost (see Chapter 11).

The API

This section presents an overview of the basic Cassandra API so that once we start reading and writing data, some of these exotic terms won't seem quite so difficult. We already know what a column, super column, and column family are: a column family contains columns or super columns; a super column contains only columns (you can't nest one super column inside another); and columns contain a name/value pair and a timestamp.

In a relational database, the terms SELECT, INSERT, UPDATE, and DELETE mean just what they mean colloquially, in regular life. But working with Cassandra's API structures is not exactly straightforward, and can be somewhat daunting to newcomers; after all, there's no such thing as a "slice range" in regular life, so these terms may take some getting used to.

There are two basic concepts that you'll want to learn quickly: ranges and slices. Many queries are defined using these terms, and they can be a bit confusing at first.

 Columns are sorted by their type (as specified by `CompareWith`), and rows are sorted by their partitioner.

Ranges and Slices

A *range* basically refers to a mathematical range, where you have a set of ordered elements and you want to specify some subset of those elements by defining a start element and a finish element. The range is the representation of all the elements between start and finish, inclusive.

Ranges typically refer to ranges of *keys* (rows). The term *slice* is used to refer to a range of columns within a row.

The range works according to the column family's comparator. That is, given columns a, b, c, d, and e, the range of (a,c) includes columns a, b, and c. So, if you have 1,000 columns with names that are long integers, you can see how you could easily specify a range of columns between 35 and 45. By using ranges, you can retrieve all of the columns in a range that you define (called a *range slice*), or you can perform the same update to the items in the range using a batch.

You may have many hundreds of columns defined on a row, but you might not want to retrieve all of them in a given query. Columns are stored in sorted order, so the range query is provided so that you can fetch columns within a range of column names.

> Range queries require using an `OrderPreservingPartitioner`, so that keys are returned in the order defined by the collation used by the partitioner.

When specifying a range query and using Random Partitioner, there's really no way to specify a range more narrow than "all". This is obviously an expensive proposition, because you might incur additional network operations. It can also potentially result in missed keys. That's because it's possible that an update happening at the same time as your row scan will miss the updates made earlier in the index than what you are currently processing.

There is another thing that can be confusing at first. When you are using Random Partitioner, you must recall that *range queries first hash the keys*. So if you are using a range of "Alice" to "Alison", the query will first run a hash on each of those keys and return not simply the natural values between Alice and Alison, but rather the values between the hashes of those values.

Here is the basic flow of a read operation that looks for a specific key when using Random Partitioner. First, the key is hashed, and then the client connects to any node in the cluster. That node will route the request to the node with that key. The memtable is consulted to see whether your key is present; if it's not found, then a scan is performed on the Bloom filter for each file, starting with the newest one. Once the key is found in the Bloom filter, it is used to consult the corresponding datafile and find the column values.

Setup and Inserting Data

We'll look at inserts first, because you need to have something in the database to query. In this section we set up a Java project and walk through a complete example that does an insert and then reads the data back.

First, download Cassandra from *http://cassandra.apache.org*. It's easiest to get started with the binary version. See Chapter 2 if you're having any trouble.

Now let's create a new project to test some of our work. For now, we'll use a Java project in Eclipse. First, create a new project, and then add a few JARs to your classpath: a Log4J JAR to output log statements (don't forget to set the properties file for your

own classes); the Thrift library called *libthrift-r917130.jar*, which contains the
`org.apache.thrift` classes; and the Cassandra JAR *apache-cassandra-x.x.x.jar*, which
contains the `org.apache.cassandra` classes. We also need to add the SLF4J logger (both
the API and the implementation JAR), which Cassandra requires. Finally, add an argument to your JVM to add the *log4j.properties* file to your classpath:

```
-Dlog4j.configuration=file:///home/eben/books/cassandra/log4j.properties
```

> In Eclipse, you can add the *log4j.properties* file by creating a new Run
> Configuration. Click the Arguments tab, and then in the VM Arguments
> text field, enter the parameter specified in the previous code sample—
> of course using the actual path to your properties file.

My *log4j.properties* file looks like this:

```
# output messages into a rolling log file as well as stdout
log4j.rootLogger=DEBUG,stdout,R

# stdout
log4j.appender.stdout=org.apache.log4j.ConsoleAppender
log4j.appender.stdout.layout=org.apache.log4j.PatternLayout
log4j.appender.stdout.layout.ConversionPattern=%5p %d{HH:mm:ss,SSS} %m%n

# rolling log file
log4j.appender.R=org.apache.log4j.RollingFileAppender
log4j.appender.file.maxFileSize=5MB
log4j.appender.file.maxBackupIndex=5
log4j.appender.R.layout=org.apache.log4j.PatternLayout
log4j.appender.R.layout.ConversionPattern=%5p [%t] %d{ISO8601} %C %F (line %L) %m%n

# This points to your logs directory
log4j.appender.R.File=cass-client.log
```

To keep this simple, we'll use the default keyspace and configuration. Now start the
server, and create a class that looks like the one shown in Example 7-1. This example
will open a connection to Cassandra and write a new row with two columns: `name` and
`age`. We then read back a single column value for that row, and then read the entire row.

Example 7-1. SimpleWriteRead.java

```
package com.cassandraguide.rw;

import java.io.UnsupportedEncodingException;
import java.util.List;

import org.apache.cassandra.thrift.Cassandra;
import org.apache.cassandra.thrift.Clock;
import org.apache.cassandra.thrift.Column;
import org.apache.cassandra.thrift.ColumnOrSuperColumn;
import org.apache.cassandra.thrift.ColumnParent;
import org.apache.cassandra.thrift.ColumnPath;
import org.apache.cassandra.thrift.ConsistencyLevel;
```

```
import org.apache.cassandra.thrift.InvalidRequestException;
import org.apache.cassandra.thrift.NotFoundException;
import org.apache.cassandra.thrift.SlicePredicate;
import org.apache.cassandra.thrift.SliceRange;
import org.apache.cassandra.thrift.TimedOutException;
import org.apache.cassandra.thrift.UnavailableException;
import org.apache.log4j.Logger;
import org.apache.thrift.TException;
import org.apache.thrift.protocol.TBinaryProtocol;
import org.apache.thrift.protocol.TProtocol;
import org.apache.thrift.transport.TFramedTransport;
import org.apache.thrift.transport.TSocket;
import org.apache.thrift.transport.TTransport;

public class SimpleWriteRead {

    private static final Logger LOG = Logger.getLogger(SimpleWriteRead.class);

    //set up some constants
    private static final String UTF8 = "UTF8";
    private static final String HOST = "localhost";
    private static final int PORT = 9160;
    private static final ConsistencyLevel CL = ConsistencyLevel.ONE;

    //not paying attention to exceptions here
    public static void main(String[] args) throws UnsupportedEncodingException,
            InvalidRequestException, UnavailableException, TimedOutException,
            TException, NotFoundException {

        TTransport tr = new TSocket(HOST, PORT);
        //new default in 0.7 is framed transport
        TFramedTransport tf = new TFramedTransport(tr);
        TProtocol proto = new TBinaryProtocol(tf);
        Cassandra.Client client = new Cassandra.Client(proto);
        tf.open();
        client.set_keyspace("Keyspace1");

        String cfName = "Standard1";
        byte[] userIDKey = "1".getBytes(); //this is a row key

        Clock clock = new Clock(System.currentTimeMillis());

        //create a representation of the Name column
        ColumnPath colPathName = new ColumnPath(cfName);
        colPathName.setColumn("name".getBytes(UTF8));

        ColumnParent cp = new ColumnParent(cfName);

        //insert the name column
        LOG.debug("Inserting row for key " + new String(userIDKey));
        client.insert(userIDKey, cp,
                new Column("name".getBytes(UTF8),
                        "George Clinton".getBytes(), clock), CL);

        //insert the Age column
```

```
client.insert(userIDKey, cp,
        new Column("age".getBytes(UTF8),
                "69".getBytes(), clock), CL);

LOG.debug("Row insert done.");

// read just the Name column
LOG.debug("Reading Name Column:");
Column col = client.get(userIDKey, colPathName,
        CL).getColumn();

LOG.debug("Column name: " + new String(col.name, UTF8));
LOG.debug("Column value: " + new String(col.value, UTF8));
LOG.debug("Column timestamp: " + col.clock.timestamp);

//create a slice predicate representing the columns to read
//start and finish are the range of columns--here, all
SlicePredicate predicate = new SlicePredicate();
SliceRange sliceRange = new SliceRange();
sliceRange.setStart(new byte[0]);
sliceRange.setFinish(new byte[0]);
predicate.setSlice_range(sliceRange);

LOG.debug("Complete Row:");
// read all columns in the row
ColumnParent parent = new ColumnParent(cfName);
List<ColumnOrSuperColumn> results =
    client.get_slice(userIDKey,
            parent, predicate, CL);

//loop over columns, outputting values
for (ColumnOrSuperColumn result : results) {
    Column column = result.column;
    LOG.debug(new String(column.name, UTF8) + " : "
            + new String(column.value, UTF8));
}
tf.close();

LOG.debug("All done.");
    }
}
```

Running this example will output the following:

```
DEBUG 14:02:09,572 Inserting row for key 1
DEBUG 14:02:09,580 Row insert done.
DEBUG 14:02:09,580 Reading Name Column:
DEBUG 14:02:09,585 Column name: name
DEBUG 14:02:09,586 Column value: George Clinton
DEBUG 14:02:09,586 Column timestamp: 1284325329569
DEBUG 14:02:09,589 Complete Row:
DEBUG 14:02:09,594 age : 69
DEBUG 14:02:09,594 name : George Clinton
DEBUG 14:02:09,594 All done.
```

This isn't Cassandra-specific, but in Java you can easily get a more user-friendly representation of a date by wrapping the `long` timestamp output with a new `Date` object, like this: `new Date(col.timestamp);`.

Let's unpack what we've done here. First, we create a connection to the Cassandra server:

```
TTransport tr = new TSocket(HOST, PORT);
//new default in 0.7 is framed transport
TFramedTransport tf = new TFramedTransport(tr);
TProtocol proto = new TBinaryProtocol(tf);
Cassandra.Client client = new Cassandra.Client(proto);
tf.open();
client.set_keyspace("Keyspace1");
```

Here we're using the framed transport, which is the new default in Cassandra 0.7. This code connects to Cassandra at the specified keyspace.

Then, we create representations for the column family we'll use, and convenience values for the row key and clock that indicate when this insert was performed:

```
String cfName = "Standard1";
byte[] userIDKey = "1".getBytes(); //this is a row key

Clock clock = new Clock(System.currentTimeMillis());
```

Next, we use the client object with the column path to insert a new value:

```
ColumnParent cp = new ColumnParent(cfName);

//insert the name column
LOG.debug("Inserting row for key " + new String(userIDKey));
client.insert(userIDKey, cp,
        new Column("name".getBytes(UTF8),
                "George Clinton".getBytes(), clock), CL);
```

The insert operation requires a row key, as well as the column object that includes the column name and the value we want to assign to it for this row key. We also specify the clock representing when this insert was performed, and the consistency level to apply.

We then basically repeat this operation to write to the same row, but now to the age column, giving it a value of 69:

```
client.insert(userIDKey, cp,
        new Column("age".getBytes(UTF8),
                "69".getBytes(), clock), CL);
```

So at this point we have inserted two columns into a single row and are ready to read it back to verify.

To ensure our insert went well by reading it back, we use the client **get** method, passing the row key and the path to the column we want to read (the **name** column below), and then specify the consistency level we require for this operation:

```
ColumnPath colPathName = new ColumnPath(cfName);
colPathName.setColumn("name".getBytes(UTF8));
Column col = client.get(userIDKey, colPathName,
        CL).getColumn();

LOG.debug("Column name: " + new String(col.name, UTF8));
LOG.debug("Column value: " + new String(col.value, UTF8));
LOG.debug("Column timestamp: " + col.clock.timestamp);
```

So each column value has its own timestamp (wrapped in a clock) because it's the column, not the row, that is the atomic unit. This can be confusing when you first come to Cassandra if you're used to adding a timestamp column to a relational table to indicate when it was last updated. But there's no such thing in Cassandra as the last time a row was updated; it's granular at the column level.

Because Cassandra returns a byte array for column names and values, we create a **String** object around the byte array so we can do application stuff with it (like write it to a log here). The clock is stored as a long (representing the milliseconds since the Unix epoch), so we could wrap this in a new **java.util.Date** object if we wanted to.

So using the **get** method and specifying the column path and other parameters, we read a single column's value. But now we want to get a "range" of columns for a single row (called a *slice*). So we use a slice predicate:

```
SlicePredicate predicate = new SlicePredicate();
SliceRange sliceRange = new SliceRange();
sliceRange.setStart(new byte[0]);
sliceRange.setFinish(new byte[0]);
predicate.setSlice_range(sliceRange);
```

The *slice predicate* is a container object that allows us to specify the range of columns that we want to read between a start and a finish. By specifying **new byte[0]** as the start and finish positions of the range, we're saying that we want all of the columns.

Now that our predicate is set up, we can execute the range slice query that will get all of the columns for our row, so we can loop over them one by one:

```
ColumnParent parent = new ColumnParent(cfName);
List<ColumnOrSuperColumn> results =
  client.get_slice(userIDKey, parent, predicate, CL);
```

This **get_slice** query uses the predicate we created as well as two new things: the **ColumnOrSuperColumn** class and a column parent. The **ColumnOrSuperColumn** class is just what it says: it represents either a column or a super column returned by Thrift. Thrift does not have support for inheritance, so this class is used to pack up both columns and super columns in this one object (depending on what you're querying). The client just reads the values if a column is returned; if a super column is returned, the client gets a column out of the super column and reads that.

The column parent is the path to the parent of a set of columns. Because we're retrieving a set of columns in a `get_slice` by definition, we need to specify the column family that is the parent of the columns we're looking up. Now we can loop over columns for this row, printing out each column's three attributes, and then close the connection:

```
for (ColumnOrSuperColumn result : results) {
    Column column = result.column;

    LOG.debug(new String(column.name, UTF8) + " : "
        + new String(column.value, UTF8));
}
tf.close();
```

You use the `insert` operation to add values or to overwrite existing values. So to update a value, use the `insert` operation with the new column values you want for the same key.

You can also insert many values at once, which we see how to do later in this chapter in "Batch Mutates" on page 150.

Using a Simple Get

Use the `get` operation to retrieve columns or super columns, using a column path to access them:

```
ColumnOrSuperColumn get(byte[] key, ColumnPath column_path,
    ConsistencyLevel consistency_level)
```

Example 7-2 shows how to do this.

Example 7-2. Using the get operation

```
package com.cassandraguide.rw;

//imports left out

public class GetExample {

    private static final Logger LOG = Logger.getLogger(GetExample.class);

    private static final String UTF8 = "UTF8";
    private static final String HOST = "localhost";
    private static final int PORT = 9160;
    private static final ConsistencyLevel CL = ConsistencyLevel.ONE;

    public static void main(String[] args) throws UnsupportedEncodingException,
            InvalidRequestException, UnavailableException, TimedOutException,
            TException, NotFoundException {

        TTransport tr = new TSocket(HOST, PORT);
        //new default in 0.7 is framed transport
        TFramedTransport tf = new TFramedTransport(tr);
        TProtocol proto = new TBinaryProtocol(tf);
```

```
Cassandra.Client client = new Cassandra.Client(proto);
tf.open();
client.set_keyspace("Keyspace1");

String cfName = "Standard1";
byte[] userIDKey = "1".getBytes(); //this is the row key

Clock clock = new Clock(System.currentTimeMillis());

//create a representation of the Name column
ColumnParent cp = new ColumnParent(cfName);

//insert the name column
LOG.debug("Inserting row for key " + new String(userIDKey));
client.insert(userIDKey, cp,
        new Column("name".getBytes(UTF8),
                "George Clinton".getBytes(), clock), CL);

LOG.debug("Row insert done.");

/** Do the GET */

LOG.debug("Get result:");
// read all columns in the row
ColumnPath path = new ColumnPath();
path.column_family = cfName;
path.column = "name".getBytes();

ColumnOrSuperColumn cosc = client.get(userIDKey, path, CL);
Column column = cosc.column;
LOG.debug(new String(column.name, UTF8) + " : "
        + new String(column.value, UTF8));
//END GET

tr.close();

LOG.debug("All done.");
    }
}
```

Here, we perform an insert so that we have something to get. We create a client object and then call its **get** method, which takes the row key, a column path, and a consistency level as arguments. The column path sets the name of the column that we're looking for. Remember that the column names and values are binary (in a Java client they're byte arrays), so we have to convert the string column name to a byte array for the query. Then when we get the column's value, it's a byte array too, so we convert it to a string to work with the result.

In this example, we add values for both the name and the age columns, but because our column path represents only the single column we're interested in querying, we just get the age. The output is shown here:

```
DEBUG 14:36:42,265 Inserting row for key 1
DEBUG 14:36:42,273 Row insert done.
```

```
DEBUG 14:36:42,273 Get result:
DEBUG 14:36:42,282 name : George Clinton
DEBUG 14:36:42,282 All done.
```

Seeding Some Values

Here we'll just use the command-line interface to quickly create a couple of keys with
some different columns to serve as data for the following queries:

```
[default@Keyspace1] set Standard1['k1']['a']='1'
Value inserted.
[default@Keyspace1] set Standard1['k1']['b']='2'
Value inserted.
[default@Keyspace1] set Standard1['k1']['c']='3'
Value inserted.
[default@Keyspace1] set Standard1['k2']['a']='2.1'
Value inserted.
[default@Keyspace1] set Standard1['k2']['b']='2.2'
```

So we have two rows; the first has three columns and the second has two columns.

Slice Predicate

A *slice predicate* is used in both read and write operations, acting as a limiting factor
for specifying a set of columns. You can specify the predicate one of two ways: with a
list of column names or with a slice range. If you know the names of a few columns
that you want to retrieve, then you can specify them explicitly by name. If you don't
know their names, or for another reason want to retrieve a range of columns, you use
a slice range object to specify the range.

 I'm using contained examples to be concise. But it is not uncommon to
see many, many columns defined per row in Cassandra, so don't let
these examples mislead you. It's a big data store and can hold two billion
columns per row in version 0.7.

To use the slice predicate, you create a predicate object populated with the column
names you want, and pass it to your read operation.

Getting Particular Column Names with Get Slice

If you want to get just the columns called "a" and "b" in a single row, you can use the
predicate with the column names specified.

You can get a set of columns contained in a column parent using a `get_slice` operation.
It will retrieve values by column name or a range of names, and will return either columns or super columns. The `get_slice` operation has this signature:

```
List<ColumnOrSuperColumn> get_slice(byte[] key,
    ColumnParent column_parent, SlicePredicate predicate, ConsistencyLevel cl)
```

This is shown in Example 7-3.

Example 7-3. SlicePredicate.java

```
package com.cassandraguide.rw;

// imports omitted

public class SlicePredicateExample {

    public static void main(String[] args) throws Exception {
        Connector conn = new Connector();
        Cassandra.Client client = conn.connect();

        SlicePredicate predicate = new SlicePredicate();
        List<byte[]> colNames = new ArrayList<byte[]>();
        colNames.add("a".getBytes());
        colNames.add("b".getBytes());
        predicate.column_names = colNames;

        ColumnParent parent = new ColumnParent("Standard1");

        byte[] key = "k1".getBytes();
        List<ColumnOrSuperColumn> results =
            client.get_slice(key, parent, predicate, ConsistencyLevel.ONE);

        for (ColumnOrSuperColumn cosc : results) {
            Column c = cosc.column;
            System.out.println(new String(c.name, "UTF-8") + " : "
                    + new String(c.value, "UTF-8"));
        }

        conn.close();

        System.out.println("All done.");
    }
}
```

In this example, only the specified columns will be retrieved, and the other columns will be ignored. The query returns a list of `ColumnOrSuperColumn` objects. Because we know that we're querying a regular column family, we get the column out of the `ColumnOrSuperColumn` data structure returned by the underlying RPC mechanism (Thrift), and finally retrieve the names and values from it in a loop.

The output is as follows:

```
a : 1
b : 2
All done.
```

Getting a Set of Columns with Slice Range

Sometimes you don't want to specify each and every column you want to retrieve, perhaps because you have a lot of columns to retrieve or because you don't know all of their names.

To read a *range* of the columns in a row, you can specify the start and finish columns, and Cassandra will give you the start and finish columns as well as any columns in between, according to the sorting order based on the comparator for that column family. Create your slice predicate, then create your range, and then set the range into the predicate before passing the predicate to your read operation. Here's an example:

```
SlicePredicate predicate = new SlicePredicate();
SliceRange sliceRange = new SliceRange();
sliceRange.setStart("age".getBytes());
sliceRange.setFinish("name".getBytes());
predicate.setSlice_range(sliceRange);
```

When executed with a `get_slice` operation, this query will return the two columns specified, as well as any columns that a comparison operation would sort within that range (between them lexicographically, numerically, or whatever). For example, if this row also had an "email" column, it would be returned in the results as well.

You must consider the column names according to their comparator, and specify start and finish in the proper order. For example, trying to set a start of `name` and a finish of `age` will throw an exception like this:

```
InvalidRequestException(why:range finish must come after start in the order of
traversal)
```

 Recall that "returning a column" doesn't mean that you get the value, as in SQL; it means that you get the complete column data structure, which is the name, the value, and the timestamp.

Counts

You can limit the number of columns returned by your slice range by using the count attribute of the `Slice Range` structure. Let's say we have a row with hundreds of columns. We could specify a range that might include many of these columns, but limit our result set to only the first 10 columns like this:

```
SliceRange sliceRange = new SliceRange();
sliceRange.setStart("a".getBytes());
sliceRange.setFinish("d".getBytes());
sliceRange.count = 10;
```

Again, the "first" columns are those according to the order dictated by the column family's comparator.

Reversed

You can also reverse the order in which the columns are fetched by setting the reversed = true attribute on the slice range. If you have columns age, email, and name, then setting reversed to true returns them in the order name, email, age.

Getting All Columns in a Row

To read *all* of the columns in a row, you still need the predicate using a slice range, but you pass it empty byte arrays for the start and finish parameters, like this:

```
SlicePredicate predicate = new SlicePredicate();
SliceRange sliceRange = new SliceRange();
sliceRange.setStart(new byte[0]);
sliceRange.setFinish(new byte[0]);
predicate.setSlice_range(sliceRange);
```

Then, you can pass this populated predicate object to your get_slice operation along with the other necessary parameters (such as consistency level and so on).

Get Range Slices

In the same way that you access a set of columns by using a range, you can also access a range of keys or tokens. Using the get_range_slices operation, you can pass it a KeyRange object that defines the range of keys you want.

One major distinction here is that you can get either keys or tokens in a range using the same KeyRange data structure as the parameter to get_range_slices. Key ranges are start-inclusive, whereas token ranges are start-exclusive; because of ring distribution, tokens can wrap around so that the end token is less than the start token.

The API defines the operation get_range_slices for you to use. The operation is structured like this:

```
List<KeySlice> results = client.get_range_slices(parent, predicate, keyRange,
    ConsistencyLevel);
```

For a complete listing that shows using a range slice, see Example 7-4.

Example 7-4. GetRangeSliceExample.java

```
package com.cassandraguide.rw;

//imports omitted

public class GetRangeSliceExample {

    public static void main(String[] args) throws Exception {
        Connector conn = new Connector();
        Cassandra.Client client = conn.connect();

        System.out.println("Getting Range Slices.");
```

```
SlicePredicate predicate = new SlicePredicate();
List<byte[]> colNames = new ArrayList<byte[]>();
colNames.add("a".getBytes());
colNames.add("b".getBytes());
predicate.column_names = colNames;

ColumnParent parent = new ColumnParent("Standard1");

KeyRange keyRange = new KeyRange();
keyRange.start_key = "k1".getBytes();
keyRange.end_key = "k2".getBytes();

//a key slice is returned
List<KeySlice> results =
    client.get_range_slices(parent, predicate, keyRange,
            ConsistencyLevel.ONE);

for (KeySlice keySlice : results) {
    List<ColumnOrSuperColumn> cosc = keySlice.getColumns();

    System.out.println("Current row: " +
            new String(keySlice.getKey()));

    for (int i = 0; i < cosc.size(); i++) {
        Column c = cosc.get(i).getColumn();
        System.out.println(new String(c.name, "UTF-8") + " : "
                + new String(c.value, "UTF-8"));
    }
}

conn.close();

System.out.println("All done.");
    }
}
```

 This program assumes that you've added a few values for a few different row keys to work with, as shown in "Seeding Some Values" on page 142.

The program outputs the following:

```
Getting Range Slices.
Current row: k1
a : 1
b : 2
Current row: k2
a : 2.1
b : 2.2
All done.
```

Though the names involving "slice" and "range" may seem unusual at first, they turn out to be innocuous. Just remember that slices mean sets of columns and ranges mean sets of keys. So in this example, we're getting multiple columns for multiple row keys.

Multiget Slice

With `get_slice`, we saw how to get a set of column names for a single specified row key. `multiget_slice` lets you retrieve a subset of columns for a set of row keys based on a column parent and a predicate. That is, given *more than one* row key, retrieve the value of the named columns for each key. So a multiget slice is more than one named column for more than one row.

 There used to be a method called `multiget`, but it is now deprecated in favor of `multiget_slice`.

The operation looks like this:

```
Map<byte[],List<ColumnOrSuperColumn>> results =
            client.multiget_slice(rowKeys, parent, predicate, CL);
```

You specify the parent and the predicate as usual, and also provide the operation with the set of row keys you want to query. The row keys are just specified as a list of byte arrays, which are the key names.

The results come back to us as a `Map<byte[],List<ColumnOrSuperColumn>>`. This may seem like a complicated data structure, but it's actually simple. A map is a key/value pair, and in this case the byte array key is the row key, so in this example there will be two keys: one for each row key we get. Each `byte[]` key in the results map points to a list containing one or more `ColumnOrSuperColumn` objects. This structure is used because Thrift does not support inheritance. You have to know whether your column family is of type `Standard` or `Super`, and then you just get the right one from the data structure. From the `ColumnOrSuperColumn`, you extract the column (in this case, the `super_column` will be empty), and then use the column object to get the name and value. You could also get the timestamp from it if you wanted to.

An example of using multiget slice is shown in Example 7-5.

Example 7-5. MultigetSliceExample.java

```
package com.cassandraguide.rw;

//imports omitted

public class MultigetSliceExample {

    private static final ConsistencyLevel CL = ConsistencyLevel.ONE;
```

```
    private static final String columnFamily = "Standard1";

    public static void main(String[] args) throws UnsupportedEncodingException,
            InvalidRequestException, UnavailableException, TimedOutException,
            TException, NotFoundException {

        Connector conn = new Connector();
        Cassandra.Client client = conn.connect();

        System.out.println("Running Multiget Slice.");

        SlicePredicate predicate = new SlicePredicate();
        List<byte[]> colNames = new ArrayList<byte[]>();
        colNames.add("a".getBytes());
        colNames.add("c".getBytes());
        predicate.column_names = colNames;

        ColumnParent parent = new ColumnParent(columnFamily);

        //instead of one row key, we specify many
        List<byte[]> rowKeys = new ArrayList<byte[]>();
        rowKeys.add("k1".getBytes());
        rowKeys.add("k2".getBytes());

        //instead of a simple list, we get a map, where the keys are row keys
        //and the values the list of columns returned for each
        Map<byte[],List<ColumnOrSuperColumn>> results =
            client.multiget_slice(rowKeys, parent, predicate, CL);

        for (byte[] key : results.keySet()) {
            List<ColumnOrSuperColumn> row = results.get(key);

            System.out.println("Row " + new String(key) + " --> ");
            for (ColumnOrSuperColumn cosc : row) {
                Column c = cosc.column;
                System.out.println(new String(c.name, "UTF-8") + " : "
                        + new String(c.value, "UTF-8"));
            }
        }

        conn.close();

        System.out.println("All done.");
    }
}
```

So we have a couple of row keys in the database, with identifiers I've kept purposefully
short and clear in order to help you visualize the structure. We have a variety of column
sets between the two rows but we're only interested in retrieving the a and c columns,
so we use a slice predicate and specify the column_names to limit the results. We also
want to specify more than one row, so we use a list of byte arrays to indicate which row
keys we're after.

Running this code elicits the following result:

```
Running Multiget Slice.
Row k2 -->
a : 2.1
Row k1 -->
a : 1
c : 3
All done.
```

As you can see, there was no column named "b" defined for the row with key "k2", and Cassandra didn't return anything for it. There was a value for column "b" in row "k1", but we didn't ask for it in our slice, so we didn't get it.

> Because we're using Thrift as the underlying RPC mechanism to communicate with Cassandra, the results will come back to you unordered and you'll have to sort them on the client. That's because Thrift can't preserve order. A multiget is actually just a wrapper over a series of get requests.

Deleting

Deleting data is not the same in Cassandra as it is in a relational database. In RDBMS, you simply issue a delete statement that identifies the row or rows you want to delete. In Cassandra, a delete does not actually remove the data immediately. There's a simple reason for this: Cassandra's durable, eventually consistent, distributed design. If Cassandra had a straightforward design for deletes and a node goes down, that node would therefore not receive the delete. Once that node comes back online, it would mistakenly think that all of the nodes that had received the delete had actually missed a write (the data that it still has because it missed the delete), and it would start repairing all of the other nodes. So Cassandra needs a more sophisticated mechanism to support deletes. That mechanism is called a *tombstone*.

A tombstone is a special marker issued in a delete that overwrites the deleted values, acting as a placeholder. If any replica did not receive the delete operation, the tombstone can later be propagated to those replicas when they are available again. The net effect of this design is that your data store will not immediately shrink in size following a delete. Each node keeps track of the age of all its tombstones. Once they reach the age as configured in `gc_grace_seconds` (which is 10 days by default), then a compaction is run, the tombstones are garbage-collected, and the corresponding disk space is recovered.

> Remember that SSTables are immutable, so the data is not deleted from the SSTable. On compaction, tombstones are accounted for, merged data is sorted, a new index is created over the sorted data, and the freshly merged, sorted, and indexed data is written to a single new file.

The assumption is that 10 days is plenty of time for you to bring a failed node back online before compaction runs. If you feel comfortable doing so, you can reduce that grace period to reclaim disk space more quickly.

Let's run an example that will delete some data that we previously inserted. Note that there is no "delete" operation in Cassandra, it's remove, and there's really no "remove," it's just a write (of a tombstone flag). Because a remove operation is really a tombstone write, you still have to supply a timestamp with the operation, because if there are multiple clients writing, the highest timestamp wins—and those writes might include a tombstone or a new value. Cassandra doesn't discriminate here; whichever operation has the highest timestamp will win.

A simple delete looks like this:

```
Connector conn = new Connector();
Cassandra.Client client = conn.connect();

String columnFamily = "Standard1";
byte[] key = "k2".getBytes(); //this is the row key

Clock clock = new Clock(System.currentTimeMillis());

ColumnPath colPath = new ColumnPath();
colPath.column_family = columnFamily;
colPath.column = "b".getBytes();

client.remove(key, colPath, clock, ConsistencyLevel.ALL);

System.out.println("Remove done.");

conn.close();
```

Batch Mutates

There were many examples of using batch mutate to perform multiple inserts in Chapter 4, so I won't rehash that here. I'll just present an overview.

To perform many insert or update operations at once, use the batch_mutate method instead of the insert method. Like a batch update in the relational world, the batch_mutate operation allows grouping calls on many keys into a single call in order to save on the cost of network round trips. If batch_mutate fails in the middle of its list of mutations, there will be no rollback, so any updates that have already occured up to this point will remain intact. In the case of such a failure, the client can retry the batch_mutate operation.

 There used to be an operation called batch_insert, but it is deprecated.

Batch Deletes

The sample application doesn't include any delete operations, so let's look at that in a little more depth.

You use remove to delete a single column, but you can use a Deletion structure with a batch_mutate operation to perform a set of complex delete operations at once.

You can create a list of column names that you want to delete, and then indirectly pass it to batch_mutate. I say "indirectly" because there are several data structures that you need to create in order to run a deletion.

First, create the list of column names to delete. Pass that list to a SlicePredicate, pass the SlicePredicate to a Deletion object, pass that to a Mutation object, and finally, pass that to a batch_mutate.

The following code snippet shows how to do this. First, you create a SlicePredicate object to hold the names of the columns you want to delete. Here we just want to delete the "b" column. Then, you create a Deletion object that sets this predicate, and create a Mutation that sets this Deletion.

Once you have the Deletion object set up, you can create your mutation map. This map uses a byte array key to point to the deletions you want to make, so you can use different keys with the same or different mutation objects to perform the batch delete. These keys point to another map, which itself uses a string as the key to name the column family to modify. That map key points to a list of mutations that should be performed.

```
String columnFamily = "Standard1";
byte[] key = "k2".getBytes(); //this is the row key

Clock clock = new Clock(System.currentTimeMillis());

SlicePredicate delPred = new SlicePredicate();
List<byte[]> delCols = new ArrayList<byte[]>();

//let's delete the column named 'b', though we could add more
delCols.add("b".getBytes());
delPred.column_names = delCols;

Deletion deletion = new Deletion();
deletion.predicate = delPred;
deletion.clock = clock;
Mutation mutation = new Mutation();
mutation.deletion = deletion;

Map<byte[], Map<String, List<Mutation>>> mutationMap =
new HashMap<byte[], Map<String, List<Mutation>>>();

List<Mutation> mutationList = new ArrayList<Mutation>();
mutationList.add(mutation);

Map<String, List<Mutation>> m = new HashMap<String, List<Mutation>>();
m.put(columnFamily, mutationList);
```

```
                //just for this row key, though we could add more
                mutationMap.put(key, m);
                client.batch_mutate(mutationMap, ConsistencyLevel.ALL);
```

There is a second way to specify items to delete using the `Deletion` structure: you can use a `SliceRange` instead of a `List` of columns, so you can delete by range instead of explicitly listing column names.

Range Ghosts

You may sometimes hear people refer to "range ghosts" in Cassandra. This means that even if you have deleted all of the columns for a given row, you will still see a result returned for that row in a range slice, but the column data will be empty. This is valid, and is just something to keep in mind as you iterate result sets on the client.

Programmatically Defining Keyspaces and Column Families

You can create keyspaces and column families through the API as well. Example 7-6 shows you how.

Example 7-6. DefineKeyspaceExample.java

```java
package com.cassandraguide.rw;

//imports omitted

/**
 * Shows how to define a keyspace and CF programmatically.
 */
public class DefineKeyspaceExample {

    public static void main(String[] args) throws UnsupportedEncodingException,
            InvalidRequestException, UnavailableException, TimedOutException,
            TException, NotFoundException, InterruptedException {

        Connector conn = new Connector();
        Cassandra.Client client = conn.connect();

        System.out.println("Defining new keyspace.");

        KsDef ksdef = new KsDef();
        ksdef.name = "ProgKS";
        ksdef.replication_factor = 1;
        ksdef.strategy_class =
            "org.apache.cassandra.locator.RackUnawareStrategy";

        List<CfDef> cfdefs = new ArrayList<CfDef>();
        CfDef cfdef1 = new CfDef();
        cfdef1.name = "ProgCF1";
        cfdef1.keyspace = ksdef.name;
        cfdefs.add(cfdef1);
```

```
        ksdef.cf_defs = cfdefs;

        client.system_add_keyspace(ksdef);

        System.out.println("Defining new cf.");
        CfDef cfdef2 = new CfDef();
        cfdef2.keyspace = ksdef.name;
        cfdef2.column_type = "Standard";
        cfdef2.name = "ProgCF";

        client.system_add_column_family(cfdef2);

        conn.close();

        System.out.println("All done.");
    }
}
```

Summary

In this chapter we saw how to read and write data using a variety of operations offered by Cassandra's rich API.

## CHAPTER 8

Clients

We're used to connecting to relational databases using drivers. For example, in Java, JDBC is an API that abstracts the vendor implementation of the relational database to present a consistent way of storing and retrieving data using Statements, Prepared-Statements, ResultSets, and so forth. To interact with the database you get a driver that works with the particular database you're using, such as Oracle, SQL Server, or MySQL; the implementation details of this interaction are hidden from the developer. Given the right driver, you can use a wide variety of programming languages to connect to a wide variety of databases.

Cassandra is somewhat different in that there are no drivers for it. If you've decided to use Python to interact with Cassandra, you don't go out and find a Cassandra driver for Python; there is no such thing. Instead of just abstracting the database interactions from the developer's point of view, the way JDBC does, an entirely different mechanism is used. This is a client generation layer, provided by the Thrift API and the Avro project. But there are also high-level Cassandra clients for Java, Scala, Ruby, C#, Python, Perl, PHP, C++, and other languages, written as conveniences by third-party developers.

There are benefits to these clients, in that you can easily embed them in your own applications (which we'll see how to do) and that they frequently offer more features than the basic Thrift interface does, including connection pooling and JMX integration and monitoring.

In the following sections, we see how Thrift and Avro work and how they're used with Cassandra. Then, we move on to examine more robust client projects that independent developers have written in various languages to offer different options for working with the database.

 If you're going to write a Cassandra application, use one of these clients instead of writing all of that plumbing code yourself. The only difficulty is in choosing a client that will continue to stay in lockstep with updates to Cassandra itself.

Basic Client API

In Cassandra version 0.6 and earlier, Thrift served as the foundation for the entire client API. With version 0.7, Avro started being supported due to certain limitations of the Thrift interface and the fact that Thrift development is no longer particularly active. For example, there are a number of bugs in Thrift that have remained open for over a year, and the Cassandra committers wanted to provide a client layer that is more active and receives more attention. Thrift is currently in version 0.2, with no release since 2009, and there is precious little documentation.

It is not clear at the time of this writing how long Thrift will be supported in addition to Avro; they're both in the now-current tree. Because it is currently unclear which will ultimately be supported, I've included a little about them both here.

Thrift

Thrift is the driver-level interface; it provides the API for client implementations in a wide variety of languages. Thrift was developed at Facebook and donated as an Apache project with Incubator status in 2008. It's available at *http://incubator.apache.org/thrift*, though you don't need to download it separately to use Cassandra.

Thrift is a code generation library for clients in C++, C#, Erlang, Haskell, Java, Objective C/Cocoa, OCaml, Perl, PHP, Python, Ruby, Smalltalk, and Squeak. Its goal is to provide an easy way to support efficient RPC calls in a wide variety of popular languages, without requiring the overhead of something like SOAP.

To use it, you create a language-neutral service definition file that describes your data types and service interface. This file is then used as input into the engine that generates RPC client code libraries for each of the supported languages. The effect of the static generation design choice is that it is very easy for the developer to use, and the code can perform efficiently because validation happens at compile time instead of runtime.

 You can read the full paper that describes the Thrift implementation, written by its creators, at *http://incubator.apache.org/thrift/static/thrift -20070401.pdf*.

The design of Thrift offers the following features:

Language-independent types
> Because types are defined in a language-neutral manner using the definition file, they can be shared between different languages. For example, a C++ struct can be exchanged with a Python dictionary.

Common transport interface
    The same application code can be used whether you are using disk files, in-memory data, or a streaming socket.

Protocol independence
    Thrift encodes and decodes the data types for use across protocols.

Versioning support
    The data types are capable of being versioned to support updates to the client API.

The data definitions are created using a file ending with a *.thrift* extension. Under your Cassandra source folder, there's a folder called interface. In it is a file called *cassandra.thrift*. This file holds the data definitions for Cassandra. I won't include the whole file contents here, but it looks like this:

```
//data structures
struct Column {
    1: required binary name,
    2: required binary value,
    3: required i64 timestamp,
}
struct SuperColumn {
    1: required binary name,
    2: required list<Column> columns,
}

//exceptions
exception NotFoundException {
}
//etc...

//service API structures
enum ConsistencyLevel {
    ZERO = 0,
    ONE = 1,
    QUORUM = 2,
    DCQUORUM = 3,
    DCQUORUMSYNC = 4,
    ALL = 5,
    ANY = 6,
}
struct SliceRange {
    1: required binary start,
    2: required binary finish,
    3: required bool reversed=0,
    4: required i32 count=100,
}
struct SlicePredicate {
    1: optional list<binary> column_names,
    2: optional SliceRange    slice_range,
}
struct KeyRange {
    1: optional string start_key,
    2: optional string end_key,
    3: optional string start_token,
```

```
    4: optional string end_token,
    5: required i32 count=100
}

//service operations
service Cassandra {
  # auth methods
  void login(1: required string keyspace, 2:required AuthenticationRequest
auth_request)
            throws (1:AuthenticationException authnx, 2:AuthorizationException
authzx),

  i32 get_count(1:required string keyspace,
                2:required string key,
                3:required ColumnParent column_parent,
                4:required ConsistencyLevel consistency_level=ONE)
      throws (1:InvalidRequestException ire, 2:UnavailableException ue,
3:TimedOutException te),
//etc...

//meta-APIs
  /** list the defined keyspaces in this cluster */
  set<string> describe_keyspaces(),

//etc...
```

Here I have shown a representative sample of what's in the Thrift definition source file that makes up the Cassandra API. By looking at this file you can understand how Thrift definitions are made, what types of operations are available from the Cassandra client interface, and what kind of data structures they use.

In the Cassandra distribution, the same *interface* folder that has this *.thrift* file also has a folder called *thrift*. This folder contains subfolders, one for each language that has bindings generated from Thrift based on the definitions.

When Cassandra is built, here's what happens. The Ant build executes the following targets to create bindings for Java, Python, and Perl:

```
    <target name="gen-thrift-java">
      <echo>Generating Thrift Java code from ${basedir}/interface/cassandra.thrift
....</echo>
      <exec executable="thrift" dir="${basedir}
/interface">
        <arg line="--gen java" />
        <arg line="-o ${interface.thrift.dir}" />
        <arg line="cassandra.thrift" />
      </exec>
    </target>
    <target name="gen-thrift-py">
      <echo>Generating Thrift Python code from ${basedir}
/interface/cassandra.thrift ....</echo>
      <exec executable="thrift" dir="${basedir}/interface">
        <arg line="--gen py" />
        <arg line="-o ${interface.thrift.dir}" />
        <arg line="cassandra.thrift" />
```

```
        </exec>
      </target>
//etc...
```

These Ant targets call the Thrift program directly, passing arguments to it for each of the different languages. Note that the distribution ships with generated Java API; these targets are not called during a regular build. So if you want to get a Perl or Python interface, you need to execute these targets directly (or modify the build file to include these targets).

 To generate Thrift bindings for other languages, pass it to the `--gen` switch (for example, `thrift --gen php`).

The Ant targets use the *libthrift-r917130.jar* located in Cassandra's *lib* directory. Note that the Thrift JAR version number changes as Cassandra is updated.

Thrift Support for Java

To build Thrift for Java, navigate to the directory *<thrift-home>/lib/java*. Execute the *build.xml* script by typing >`ant` in a terminal.

Exceptions

There are several exceptions that can be thrown from the client interface that you might see on occasion. The following is a list of basic exceptions and explanations of why you might see them, though a couple of them are not in the Thrift definition:

AuthenticationException
> The user has invalid credentials or does not exist.

AuthorizationException
> The user exists but has not been granted access to this keyspace.

ConfigurationException
> This is thrown when the class that loads the database descriptor can't find the configuration file, or if the configuration is invalid. This can happen if you forgot to specify a partitioner or endpoint snitch for your keyspace, used a negative integer for a value that only accepts a positive integer, and so forth. This exception is not thrown from the Thrift interface.

InvalidRequestException
> The user request is improperly formed. This might mean that you've asked for data from a keyspace or column family that doesn't exist, or that you haven't included all required parameters for the given request.

NotFoundException
: The user requested a column that does not exist.

TException
: You might get this when invoking a Thrift method that is no longer valid for the server. This can occur if you mix and match different Thrift versions with server versions. This exception is not thrown from the Thrift interface, but is part of Thrift itself. TExceptions are uncaught, unexpected exceptions that bubble up from the server and terminate the current Thrift call. They are not used as application exceptions, which you must define yourself.

TimedOutException
: The response is taking longer than the configured limit, which by default is 10 seconds. This typically happens because the server is overloaded with requests, the node has failed but this failure has not yet been detected, or a very large amount of data has been requested.

UnavailableException
: Not all of the Cassandra replicas that are required to meet the quorum for a read or write are available. This exception is not thrown from the Thrift interface.

Thrift Summary

If you want to use Thrift directly for your project, there are numerous prerequisites for working on Windows (see *http://wiki.apache.org/thrift/ThriftInstallationWin32*) and many things that can go wrong. Partly because the Thrift project is still nascent, has limitations with transport implementations, and has not received a lot of direct attention since its open source inception, Cassandra is probably switching to Avro.

Avro

The Apache Avro project is a data serialization and RPC system targeted as the replacement for Thrift in Cassandra, starting with version 0.7. Avro was created by Doug Cutting, most famous perhaps for creating Apache Hadoop, the implementation of Google's MapReduce algorithm.

Avro provides many features similar to those of Thrift and other data serialization and RPC mechanisms such as Google's Protocol Buffer, including:

- Robust data structures
- An efficient, small binary format for RPC calls
- Easy integration with dynamically typed languages such as Python, Ruby, Smalltalk, Perl, PHP, and Objective-C

Avro has certain advantages that Thrift doesn't, in particular the fact that static code generation is not required to use RPC for your application, though you can use it for performance optimization for statically typed languages. The project is somewhat more mature (the current release version is 1.3.2) and more active.

When you execute the Cassandra Ant file, the build target calls, among other things, the avro-generate target, which generates the Avro interfaces. These files are in the same *interface* directory where Thrift-generated files are. To find the complete definition of the Avro interface for Cassandra, look in the *cassandra.avpr* file, which contains the JSON defining all the messages and operations that Cassandra clients can use.

```
{
    "namespace":  "org.apache.cassandra.avro",
    "protocol":   "Cassandra",

    "types": [
        {"name": "ColumnPath", "type": "record",
            "fields": [
                {"name": "column_family", "type": "string"},
                {"name": "super_column", "type": ["bytes", "null"]},
                {"name": "column", "type": ["bytes", "null"]}
            ]
        },
        {"name": "Column", "type": "record",
            "fields": [
                {"name": "name", "type": "bytes"},
                {"name": "value", "type": "bytes"},
                {"name": "timestamp", "type": "long"}
            ]
        },
        {"name": "SuperColumn", "type": "record",
            "fields": [
                {"name": "name", "type": "bytes"},
                {"name": "columns", "type": {"type": "array", "items": "Column"}}
            ]
        },
//etc..
        }
    ],

    "messages": {
      "get": {
          "request": [
              {"name": "keyspace", "type": "string"},
              {"name": "key", "type": "string"},
              {"name": "column_path", "type": "ColumnPath"},
              {"name": "consistency_level", "type": "ConsistencyLevel"}
          ],
          "response": "ColumnOrSuperColumn",
          "errors": ["InvalidRequestException", "NotFoundException",
              "UnavailableException", "TimedOutException"]
      },
      "insert": {
          "request": [
              {"name": "keyspace", "type": "string"},
              {"name": "key", "type": "string"},
```

```
          {"name": "column_path", "type": "ColumnPath"},
          {"name": "value", "type": "bytes"},
          {"name": "timestamp", "type": "long"},
          {"name": "consistency_level", "type": "ConsistencyLevel"}
        ],
        "response": "null",
        "errors": ["InvalidRequestException", "UnavailableException",
          "TimedOutException"]
      },
  //etc...
```

The JSON format is concise and easy to read. You can see, for example, that there are at least two kinds of messages, one representing a **get** request and the other representing an **insert** request. The exceptions possible for each type are packaged with their messages.

 The meaning of each exception is discussed earlier in "Thrift" on page 156.

Avro Ant Targets

The Cassandra *build.xml* file defines two Ant targets that are executed when Cassandra is compiled from source, which is made possible by *avro-1.2.0-dev.jar* in the Cassandra *lib* directory. These targets are shown in the following listing:

```
<!--
    Generate avro code
-->
<target name="check-avro-generate">
    <uptodate property="avroUpToDate"
              srcfile="${interface.dir}/cassandra.avpr"
              targetfile="${interface.avro.dir}/org/apache/cassandra/avro/
Cassandra.java" />
    <taskdef name="protocol"
             classname="org.apache.avro.specific.ProtocolTask">
      <classpath refid="cassandra.classpath" />
    </taskdef>
    <taskdef name="schema" classname="org.apache.avro.specific.SchemaTask">
      <classpath refid="cassandra.classpath" />
    </taskdef>
    <taskdef name="paranamer"
        classname="com.thoughtworks.paranamer.ant.ParanamerGeneratorTask">
      <classpath refid="cassandra.classpath" />
    </taskdef>
</target>

<target name="avro-generate" unless="avroUpToDate"
        depends="init,check-avro-generate">
    <echo>Generating avro code...</echo>
    <protocol destdir="${interface.avro.dir}">
```

```
    <fileset dir="${interface.dir}">
      <include name="**/*.avpr" />
    </fileset>
  </protocol>

  <schema destdir="${interface.avro.dir}">
    <fileset dir="${interface.dir}">
      <include name="**/*.avsc" />
    </fileset>
  </schema>
</target>
```

The Ant tasks for Thrift generation directly ran the Thrift executable (as you would on the command line). But the Avro targets are more complex. The `check-avro-generate` target uses a custom property called `avroUpToDate`. The `avro-generate` target does not run if it is determined by the `check-avro-generate` task that all of the files are up to date already. If the generated client API files are not up to date with the current schema, then the *cassandra.avpr* file will be reread and will generate the sources again under *<CASSANDRA_HOME>/interface/avro*. The `org.apache.cassandra.avro.Cassandra` `.java` file represents the runtime Java Avro interface.

The Ant `<taskdef>` tag defines custom extension tasks that subsequent targets can execute. Here we see two: the `SchemaTask` and the `ParanamerGeneratorTask`. The `Schema Task` is part of Avro itself, and is used to generate a Java interface and classes for the described protocol. The ParaNamer library (*paranamer-generator-2.1.jar*) is used to allow the parameter names of nonprivate methods and constructors—which are typically dropped by the compiler—to be accessed at runtime. It reads the source directory of Avro-generated Java classes and outputs to the *build* directory Java classes that maintain the names defined in the source.

Avro Specification

The Avro project defines a specification, so you could theoretically write your own implementation of the Avro spec. Avro supports six kinds of complex types: records, enums, arrays, maps, unions, and fixed.

If you're interested, you can read the complete Avro specification at *http://avro.apache.org/docs/current/spec.html*, though it is definitely not required to work with Cassandra.

Avro definitions are written as schemas, using JavaScript Object Notation (JSON). This is different from in Thrift, however, because the schemas are always present along with the data when it is read. This is an advantage because it means that less type information needs to be sent with the data, so the serialization is compact and efficient. Avro stores data with its schema, which means that any program can process it later, independently of the RPC mechanism.

Avro Summary

As of Cassandra version 0.7, Avro is the RPC and data serialization mechanism for Cassandra. It generates code that remote clients can use to interact with the database. It's well-supported in the community and has the strength of growing out of the larger and very well-known Hadoop project. It should serve Cassandra well for the foreseeable future.

You can read more about Avro at its Apache project page: *http://avro.apache.org*.

A Bit of Git

Cassandra doesn't use Git directly, but understanding at least a bit about Git will help you use a variety of client projects that do use Git. (If you're already familiar with Git, feel free to skip this section.) Many open source projects have started moving to GitHub recently. Git is a relatively new, free source code revision system, written by Linus Torvalds to help him develop the Linux kernel. It includes social features. GitHub is a Git project hosting site, written in Ruby on Rails, that offers free and commercial options.

The following client libraries, which we'll look at individually, all use Git: the Web Console, Hector, Pelops, and other Cassandra-related satellite projects such as Twissandra (as discussed in the example of Twitter implementation using Cassandra).

The simplest way to get the code for a Git project is to find the project's home page on GitHub and click the Download Source button to get either a *.tar* or *.zip* file of the project's trunk.

 If you're on a Linux distribution such as Ubuntu, it couldn't be easier to get Git. At a console, just type >apt-get install git and it will be installed and ready for commands.

If you want to work with the source itself (i.e., to fork it), you'll need a Git client. If you're on Windows, you'll first have to get the Cygwin POSIX emulator and then install Git. Next, go to the GitHub page hosting the project you're interested in and find the project's Git URL. Open a terminal in the directory you want to put the source code into and use the clone command. This will produce output like this:

```
.../gitrep>git clone http://github.com/suguru/cassandra-webconsole.git
Initialized empty Git repository in C:/git/cassandra-webconsole/.git
remote: Counting objects: 604, done.
remote: Compressing objects: 100% (463/463), done.
remote: Total 604 (delta 248), reused 103 (delta 9)
Receiving objects: 100% (604/604), 6.24 MiB | 228 KiB/s, done.
Resolving deltas: 100% (248/248), done.
```

Now we have a subdirectory named after the Git project so that we can build the project and start using it. This is enough to get you started so that you can run the clients. A full discussion of Git is outside the scope of this book, but you can read more about it at GitHub.com. There's a good help section on how to get set up at *http://help.github .com*, and the site *http://gitref.org* offers a really good reference for beginners.

Connecting Client Nodes

Once your cluster is set up, it does not matter which node in the cluster your client connects to. That's because Cassandra nodes are symmetrical, and any node will act as a proxy to a given request, forwarding the request to the node that handles the desired range.

There are a few options here to keep things organized and efficient.

Client List

The most straightforward way to connect to a cluster is to maintain a list of the addresses or hostnames of the servers in the cluster and cycle through them on the client side. You allow clients to choose among them according to some algorithm of your choosing, such as random or sequential. In this way, you're setting up a sort of poor-man's client balancer.

This has the advantage of being the simplest to set up, and requires no intervention from operations. For testing, this is fine, but it ultimately will become difficult to manage.

Round-Robin DNS

Another option is to create a record in DNS that represents the set of servers in the cluster. Using round-robin DNS allows clients to connect simply and cleanly. This has the significant advantage of not requiring any maintenance or logic on the client side for connecting to different nodes, and is the recommended approach.

Load Balancer

The third option is to have operations deploy a load balancer in front of the Cassandra cluster, and then configure clients to connect to it. The load balancer will act as the configuration point.

Cassandra Web Console

There's a web console available from Suguru Namura, who contributed the code as a GitHub project. The console makes it easy to interact with Cassandra to perform a variety of tasks and view information about your cluster. I'm starting with this console before getting into the real clients you will use to interact with the database because it gives you a very user-friendly view into the configuration of your Cassandra instance.

You can download the console, which runs as a WAR, at *http://github.com/suguru/cassandra-webconsole*. If you want to modify the source code, either fork it with Git or just grab one of the binaries from the Downloads page of the project. The console requires Java 6 and Tomcat 6. If you want to compile the project, you'll need Maven 2.

Let's take a brief look at its features:

Keyspaces
> The console allows you to view keyspace properties and add, rename, and drop a keyspace. You can view the configuration information about each keyspace as well, including the column families.

Column families
> You can add or drop column families and view their keys.

Ring
> You can view system information such as uptime and heap usage.

 You will likely need to modify the port on which you start Tomcat if you also have Cassandra running on the same box, because Cassandra will use ports 8080 and 8084 for JMX.

I've started up the console on my local machine at *http://localhost:9999/cassandra-webconsole*. The first time you start the console, you'll be presented with a screen that lets you enter the information required to connect to a particular Cassandra server.

Framed Transport and Buffered Transport

There are two choices for which transport type you want to use to connect to Cassandra: Framed Transport and Buffered Transport. Framed Transport was added to Thrift in order to support asynchronous servers. There's not necessarily a performance difference between the two, but your choice of client language might dictate which one you need to enable. For example, Twisted Python requires using Framed Transport, whereas Haskell, Ocaml, Cocoa, and Smalltalk (as of this writing) do not support Framed Transport.

Because you need to enable this on the Cassandra server, the console asks you to indicate which one you're using.

Once you've connected to a Cassandra server, the web console reads its configuration information and brings you to a screen to start interacting with Cassandra.

Figure 8-1 shows the configuration screen for the console itself. Figure 8-2 shows a screenshot of the keyspace and column family configuration information that the web console lets you view. You can see here that I have four keyspaces. Keyspace1 has been selected to show the column family definitions; the others are system, Test, and Twitter. Using this screen, you can add a column family to the keyspace, rename a keyspace, drop a keyspace entirely, or create a new keyspace.

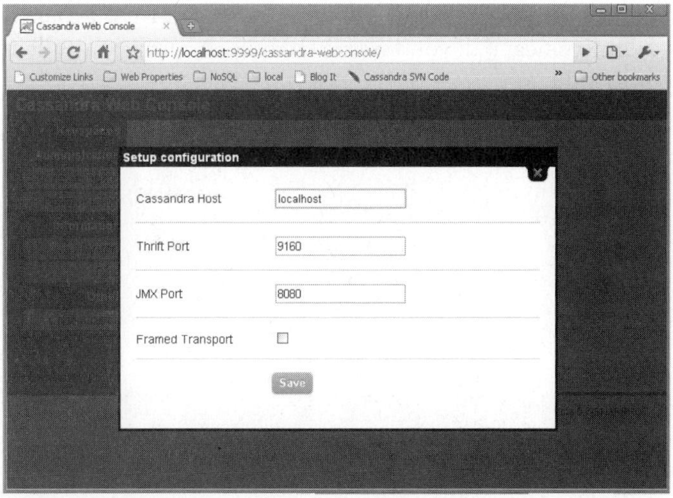

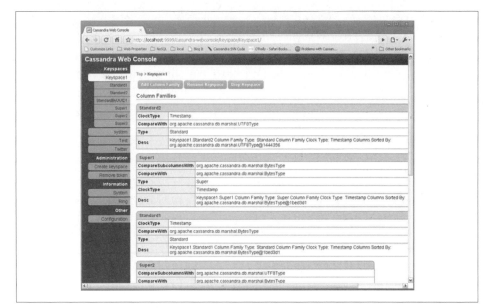

Figure 8-1. The Setup configuration screen for a Cassandra web console

Figure 8-2. Keyspace and column family information in the web console

Adding a column family or super column family is easy, as shown in Figure 8-3. However, the web console doesn't let you add data to your column families, as you might expect.

Figure 8-3. Adding a super column family in the web console

You can determine how long your server has been up, how much memory it's using, and the load by viewing the Ring screen, as shown in Figure 8-4.

Overall, the web console presents an intuitive, attractive interface that makes it easy to perform basic administration tasks for your Cassandra setup.

Hector (Java)

Hector is an open source project written in Java using the MIT license. It was created by Ran Tavory of Outbrain (previously of Google) and is hosted at GitHub. It was one of the early Cassandra clients and is used in production at Outbrain. It wraps Thrift and offers JMX, connection pooling, and failover.

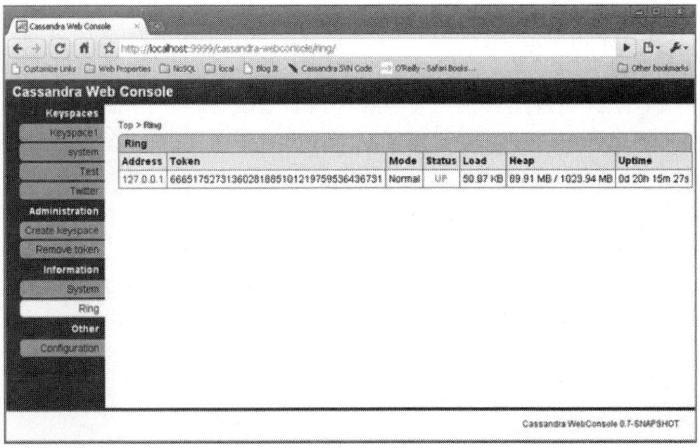

Figure 8-4. The Ring screen shows system usage

> In Greek mythology, Hector was the builder of the city of Troy and was known as an outstanding warrior. He was also Cassandra's brother.

Because Hector was one of the first Cassandra client projects, and because it is used by a wide variety of developers and even has other client projects based on it (see "HectorSharp (C#)" on page 170), we'll write a complete but simple example application using it.

To get Hector, clone it from its GitHub site at *http://github.com/rantav/hector*. Use the `git` command if you want the source, or just download the binary from the Downloads tab.

Features

Hector is a well-supported and full-featured Cassandra client, with many users and an active community. It offers the following:

High-level object-oriented API
> Java developers should find the interfaces that Hector offers, such as Keyspace and Column, very natural to use.

Fail over support
> Thrift does not provide support for failed clients. This is because Cassandra is intended to be used in a highly distributed fashion and has good support for failed nodes in the database ring. But if your client connects to a node that has gone down, it would be nice to have your client *fail over*—to automatically search for another node to use to complete your request. Happily, Hector provides this.

Connection pooling

Cassandra is specifically built for very high scalability, and it therefore also becomes a requirement on the client side to support connection pools so that your application doesn't become a bottleneck that robs you of Cassandra's speed. It's expensive to open and close connections, just as it is in JDBC. Hector's connection pooling uses Apache's `GenericObjectPool`.

JMX support

Cassandra makes liberal use of JMX, which comes in very handy for monitoring. Hector directly supports JMX by exposing metrics such as bad connections, available connections, idle connections, and more.

The Hector API

The following is an example from Ran Tavory's blog (*http://prettyprint.me*) illustrating how Hector simplifies working with Cassandra:

```
// Create a cluster
Cluster c = HFactory.getOrCreateCluster("MyCluster", "cassandra1:9160");
// Choose a keyspace
KeyspaceOperator ko = HFactory.createKeyspaceOperator("Keyspace1", c);
// create an string extractor.
StringExtractor se = StringExtractor.get();
// insert value
Mutator m = HFactory.createMutator(keyspaceOperator);
m.insert("key1", "ColumnFamily1", createColumn("column1", "value1", se, se));

// Now read a value
// Create a query
ColumnQuery<String, String> q = HFactory.createColumnQuery(keyspaceOperator, se, se);
// set key, name, cf and execute
Result<HColumn<String, String>> r = q.setKey("key1").
        setName("column1").
        setColumnFamily("ColumnFamily1").
        execute();
// read value from the result
HColumn<String, String> c = r.get();
String value = c.getValue();
System.out.println(value);
```

HectorSharp (C#)

HectorSharp is a C# port of Ran Tavory's Hector Java client (Tavory is also a committer on the HectorSharp project). Its features are similar to Hector:

- A high-level client with an intuitive, object-oriented interface
- Client-side failover
- Connection pooling
- Load balancing

Let's walk through creating an application using HectorSharp as our interface to Cassandra. This is probably the best way to see how to incorporate it into your projects. We'll create a simple C# console project that reads and writes some data to Cassandra so you can see how it's used.

As of this writing, HectorSharp works with version 0.6 of Cassandra, but not 0.7.

Using Git, download HectorSharp from *http://github.com/mattvv/hectorsharp*. Remember, to easily get source code from Git, open a terminal in the directory you want as the parent, and use the `git clone` command with the *.git* URL, like this:

```
>git clone http://github.com/mattvv/hectorsharp.git
```

Once you have the source, make sure you also have the .NET framework, version 3.5 or better, which you can download for free from Microsoft.com. You can also use the Visual Studio .NET 2010 Express IDE, which is free, uses the .NET 4.0 framework, and makes it very easy to work with C# projects. Download Visual Studio C# Express from *http://www.microsoft.com/express/Downloads*. This may take a while and will require you to restart your computer.

Once Visual Studio is installed, open the HectorSharp project so you can view the source code and add it as a reference to our own project. To open the project, choose File > Open Project... and then select the file *HectorSharp.sln*. The Express version of Visual Studio may complain about not doing Solution files, but don't worry about that.

Build the HectorSharp source by right-clicking the HectorSharp project name in the Solution Explorer window. You should see a notice in the bottom-left corner saying "Build Succeeded". This will produce the HectorSharp *.dll* client that we can use in our own application.

To create our application that wraps HectorSharp, choose File > New Project... > Console Application. Call your new project *ExecuteHector*. You'll be presented with a shell class called *Program.cs* with a main method.

Now let's reference the HectorSharp DLL so we can use its classes. To do this, choose Project > Add Reference. When the dialog window comes up, pick the Browse tab, then navigate to the location where you unpacked HectorSharp. Go to the *bin\ Release* directory and pick the *HectorSharp.dll* file. You should see HectorSharp added as a reference in your Solution Explorer.

I have changed the name of my application to *CassandraProgram.cs*. If you do this too, you'll need to change the executable in the project by choosing Project > ExecuteHector Properties. Choose the Application tab, and then enter your program name in the Startup Object field.

Let's take a quick look at some of the high-level constructs that HectorSharp makes available:

ICassandraClient

> This is the interface used by HectorSharp client objects, whose implementation type is typically a `KeyedCassandraClientFactory` object.

Pool

> HectorSharp pools its connections to Cassandra, so you use a factory method to create a pool, like this: `Pool = new CassandraClientPoolFactory().Create();`. Then, using the pool, you can create a client.

Client

> From the connection pool, you can get a `Client` that is used to connect with Cassandra. This is neat:

```
Client = new KeyedCassandraClientFactory(
            Pool,
            new KeyedCassandraClientFactory.Config { Timeout = 10 })
        .Make( new Endpoint("localhost", 9160) );
```

> You pass the pool into your client factory, then you can specify additional configuration details (such as timeout in seconds), and finally build an endpoint using the host and port you want to connect to. In the preceding example, we specified a new `timeout` value of 10 (the default is 20).

Keyspace

> This represents a Cassandra keyspace, which you obtain from the `Client` object. It allows you to specify the name of the keyspace to connect to and a consistency level to use:

```
Keyspace = Client.GetKeyspace(
            "Keyspace1",
            ConsistencyLevel.ONE,
            new FailoverPolicy(0) { Strategy = FailoverStrategy.FAIL_FAST });
```

> The `FailoverPolicy` class allows you to indicate what HectorSharp should do if it encounters an error in communication (not an application error); that is, if it thinks that a node it's trying to connect to is down. You can retry, retry on increments, or just decide to quit, which is what I've specified here.

ColumnPath

> A `ColumnPath` is a simple wrapper that allows you to easily reference an entire column family, a super column within a particular column family, or a single column within a column family. It consists of nothing but C# properties for each of those three items, plus constructors.

HectorSharp uses the Gang of Four Command pattern for Data Access Objects (DAOs), because that's how Hector works. So you could create a DAO with a **get** method as shown here:

```
/**
 * Get a string value.
 * @return The string value; null if no value exists for the given key.
 */
public String get(String key) {
  return execute(new Command<String>(){
    public String execute(Keyspace ks) {
      try {
        return string(ks.getColumn(key, createColumnPath(COLUMN_NAME)).getValue());
      } catch (NotFoundException e) {
        return null;
      }
    }
  });
}

protected static <T> T execute(Command<T> command) {
  return command.execute(CASSANDRA_HOST, CASSANDRA_PORT, CASSANDRA_KEYSPACE);
}
```

The get command is using the parameterized execute method, as are other sibling commands for insert and delete (not shown in the example). For our sample application, we'll just keep it simple, but this is a reasonable pattern to follow for such a use case.

We're finally ready to write some code. Your application should look like the listing in Example 8-1.

Example 8-1. CassandraProgram.cs

```
using System;
using HectorSharp;
using HectorSharp.Utils;
using HectorSharp.Utils.ObjectPool;

/**
 * Stands in for some C# application that would use HectorSharp
 * as a high-level Cassandra client.
 */
namespace ExecuteHector
{
    class CassandraProgram
    {
        internal ICassandraClient Client;
        internal IKeyspace Keyspace;
        internal IKeyedObjectPool<Endpoint, ICassandraClient> Pool;

        static void Main(string[] args)
        {
            CassandraProgram app = new CassandraProgram();

            Console.WriteLine("Starting HectorSharp...");

            app.Pool = new CassandraClientPoolFactory().Create();
            Console.WriteLine("Set up Pool.");
```

```
app.Client = new KeyedCassandraClientFactory(app.Pool,
    new KeyedCassandraClientFactory.Config { Timeout = 10 })
    .Make(new Endpoint("localhost", 9160));
Console.WriteLine("Created client.");

app.Keyspace = app.Client.GetKeyspace(
    "Keyspace1",
    ConsistencyLevel.ONE,
    new FailoverPolicy(0) { Strategy = FailoverStrategy.FAIL_FAST });
Console.WriteLine("Found keyspace " + app.Keyspace.Name);

//set up column path to use
var cp = new ColumnPath("Standard1", null, "MyColumn");

// write values
Console.WriteLine("\nPerforming write using " + cp.ToString());
for (int i = 0; i < 5; i++)
{
    String keyname = "key" + i;
    String value = "value" + i;
    app.Keyspace.Insert(keyname, cp, value);
    Console.WriteLine("wrote to key: " + keyname  + " with value: " + value);
}

// read values
Console.WriteLine("\nPerforming read.");
for (int i = 0; i < 5; i++)
{
    String keyname = "key" + i;
    var column = app.Keyspace.GetColumn(keyname, cp);
    Console.WriteLine("got value for " + keyname + " = " + column.Value);
}

Console.WriteLine("All done.");
        }
    }
}
```

Compile this code into a console application by choosing Debug > Build Solution.

Now we're ready to test it out. Open a console and start Cassandra as usual: >bin
\cassandra -f. Now open a second console and navigate to the directory where you
have your "ExecuteHector" project, then switch into the *bin\Release* directory. This
directory has our executable in it; to run our program, just enter ExecuteHector.exe
at the prompt. You should see output similar to the following:

```
C:\git\ExecuteHector\bin\Release>ExecuteHector.exe
Starting HectorSharp...
Set up Pool.
Created client.
Found keyspace Keyspace1

Performing write using ColumnPath(family: 'Standard1', super: '', column: 'MyColumn'
wrote to key: key0 with value: value0
```

```
wrote to key: key1 with value: value1
wrote to key: key2 with value: value2
wrote to key: key3 with value: value3
wrote to key: key4 with value: value4

Performing read.
got value for key0 = value0
got value for key1 = value1
got value for key2 = value2
got value for key3 = value3
got value for key4 = value4
All done.

C:\git\ExecuteHector\bin\Release>
```

As you can see, if you're creating a C# application and want to use Cassandra as the backing database, it is very easy to get started with HectorSharp, and its object model is very high-level, intuitive, and easy to use. Just be aware that as of this writing, HectorSharp is still in the nascent stages, so make sure that your requirements are supported before going too far.

You can find out more about HectorSharp at *http://hectorsharp.com*.

Chirper

If you're a .NET developer, you might be interested in Chirper. Chirper is a port of Twissandra to .NET, written by Chaker Nakhli. It's available under the Apache 2.0 license, and the source code is on GitHub at *http://github.com/nakhli/Chirper*. You can read a blog post introducing Chirper at *http://www.javageneration.com/?p=318*.

Chiton (Python)

Chiton is a Cassandra browser written by Brandon Williams that uses the Python GTK framework. You can get it from *http://github.com/driftx/chiton*. It has several prerequisites, so a little setup is required. Before you can use it, make sure you have the following setup:

- Python 2.5 or better.
- Twisted Python (an event-driven networking interface for Python), available at *http://twistedmatrix.com/trac*.
- Thrift (0.2).
- PyGTK 2.14 or later (a graphical user interface kit for Python), available at *http://www.pygtk.org*. This in turn requires GTK+. You likely already have it if you're on Linux; you can download the binary if you're on Windows. Just uncompress the download into a directory and manually add the *bin* subfolder to the system's path environment variable.

Pelops (Java)

Pelops is a free, open source Java client written by Dominic Williams. It is similar to Hector in that it's Java-based, but it was started more recently. This has become a very popular client. Its goals include the following:

- To create a simple, easy-to-use client
- To completely separate concerns for data processing from lower-level items such as connection pooling
- To act as a close follower to Cassandra so that it's readily up to date

And the API is much simpler than using the low-level stuff exposed by Thrift and Avro. To write data, you just need a `Mutator` class; to read data, just use a `Selector`. Here's a brief sample from Williams' website that creates a connection pool to a list of Cassandra servers, then writes multiple subcolumn values to a super column:

```
Pelops.addPool(
    "Main",
    new String[] { "cass1.database.com", "cass2.database.com", "cass3.database.com"},
    9160,
    new Policy());

Mutator mutator = Pelops.createMutator("Main", "SupportTickets");

UuidHelper.newTimeUuidBytes(), // using a UUID value that sorts by time
mutator.newColumnList(
    mutator.newColumn("category", "videoPhone"),
    mutator.newColumn("reportType", "POOR_PICTURE"),
    mutator.newColumn("createdDate", NumberHelper.toBytes(System.currentTimeMillis())),
    mutator.newColumn("capture", jpegBytes),
    mutator.newColumn("comment") ));

mutator.execute(ConsistencyLevel.ONE);
```

Consider how much easier that is than using the API provided out of the box.

You can get the source code from *http://code.google.com/p/pelops*, and you can read some samples and explanations of how to use Pelops at Dominic Williams' site, *http://ria101.wordpress.com*.

If you're using Cassandra from a Java application, I encourage you to give Pelops a try.

Kundera (Java ORM)

Kundera is an object-relational mapping (ORM) implementation for Cassandra written using Java annotations. It's available at *http://kundera.googlecode.com* under an Apache 2.0 license. According to its author, Impetus Labs, the aim of Kundera is:

...to make working with Cassandra drop-dead simple and fun. Kundera does not reinvent the wheel by making another client library; rather it leverages the existing libraries and builds—on top of them—a wrap-around API to help developers do away with unnecessary boiler plate codes, and program a neater-and-cleaner code that reduces code-complexity and improves quality. And above all, improves productivity.

Kundera uses Pelops under the hood. A sample Java entity bean looks like this:

```
@Entity
@ColumnFamily(keyspace = "Keyspace1", family = "Band")
public class Band {
    @Id
    private String id;
    @Column(name = "name")
    private String name;
    @Column(name = "instrument")
    private String instrument;
```

You can perform a JPA query like this:

```
Query query = entityManager.createQuery("SELECT m from Band c where name='george'");
List<SimpleComment> list = query.getResultList();
```

This library is quite new at the time of this writing, so it has yet to be seen how readily it will be adopted. Still, it does appear promising, and it speaks to burgeoning interest in Cassandra among general application developers.

Fauna (Ruby)

Ryan King of Twitter and Evan Weaver created a Ruby client for the Cassandra database called Fauna. If you envision using Cassandra from Ruby, this might fit the bill. To find out more about Fauna, see *http://github.com/fauna/cassandra/blob/master/README .rdoc*.

Summary

You should now have an understanding of the variety of client interfaces available for Cassandra and how to install and use them. There are many Cassandra clients, each with its own strengths and limitations, in different languages and varying degrees of production-readiness. It's not possible to cover all of them here, so I've taken a representative sample from a few different languages. To see a variety of other options that might fit your needs better, see the Cassandra project wiki Client Options page at *http: //wiki.apache.org/cassandra/ClientOptions*.

## CHAPTER 9

Monitoring

This chapter is about using a variety of tools to monitor and understand important events in the life cycle of your Cassandra cluster. We'll look at some simple ways to see what's going on, such as changing the logging levels and understanding the output.

But Cassandra also features built-in support for Java Management Extensions (JMX), which offers a rich way to monitor your Cassandra nodes and their underlying Java environment. With just a little integration work, we can see the health of the database and ongoing events, and even interact with it remotely to tune certain values. JMX is an important part of Cassandra, and we'll spend some time to make sure we know how it works and what exactly Cassandra makes available for monitoring and management with JMX, and we'll even write our own custom MBean to expose a new Cassandra feature. Let's get started!

Logging

The simplest way to get a picture of what's happening in your database is to just change the logging level to make the output more verbose. This is great for development and for learning what Cassandra is doing under the hood.

Cassandra uses Log4J for its logging utility. By default, the Cassandra server log level is set at INFO, which doesn't give you much detail about what work Cassandra is doing at any given time. It just outputs basic status updates, such as the following:

```
INFO 08:49:17,614 Saved Token found: 94408749511599155261361719888434486550
INFO 08:49:17,614 Saved ClusterName found: Test Cluster
INFO 08:49:17,620 Starting up server gossip
INFO 08:49:17,655 Binding thrift service to morpheus/192.168.1.5:9160
INFO 08:49:17,659 Cassandra starting up...
```

When you start Cassandra in a terminal, you keep this output running in the terminal window by passing the program the -f flag (to keep output visible in the foreground of the terminal window). But Cassandra is also writing these logs to physical files for you to examine later.

By changing the logging level to DEBUG, we can see much more clearly what activity the server is working on, instead of seeing only these stage updates.

To change the logging level, open the file *<cassandra-home>/conf/log4j-server .properties* and find the line that looks like this:

```
log4j.rootLogger=INFO,stdout,R
```

Change this line so it looks like this:

```
log4j.rootLogger=DEBUG,stdout,R
```

 Of course, in production you'll want to tune the logging level back up to WARN or ERROR, as the verbose output will slow things down considerably.

Now we can see a lot more activity as Cassandra does its work:

```
 INFO 09:41:54,936 Completed flushing /var/lib/cassandra/data/system/
LocationInfo-8-Data.db
DEBUG 09:41:54,942 Checking to see if compaction of LocationInfo would be useful
DEBUG 09:41:54,942 discard completed log segments for CommitLogContext(file='/var/
lib/cassandra/commitlog/CommitLog-1277397714697.log',...
 INFO 09:41:54,943 Compacting [org.apache.cassandra.io.SSTableReader(path='/var/
lib/cassandra
DEBUG 09:41:54,943 Marking replay position 121 on commit log CommitLogSegment(/var/
lib/cassandra/commitlog/CommitLog-1277397714697.log)...
DEBUG 09:41:54,943 index size for bloom filter calc for file
  : /var/lib/cassandra/data/system/LocationInfo-5-Data.db   : 256
DEBUG 09:41:54,944 index size for bloom filter calc for file
  : /var/lib/cassandra/data/system/LocationInfo-6-Data.db   : 512
DEBUG 09:41:54,944 index size for bloom filter calc for file
  : /var/lib/cassandra/data/system/LocationInfo-7-Data.db   : 768
 INFO 09:41:54,985 Log replay complete
 INFO 09:41:55,009 Saved Token found: 94408749511599155261361719888434486550
 INFO 09:41:55,010 Saved ClusterName found: Test Cluster
 INFO 09:41:55,016 Starting up server gossip
 INFO 09:41:55,048 Binding thrift service to morpheus/192.168.1.5:9160
 INFO 09:41:55,051 Cassandra starting up...
DEBUG 09:41:55,112 Marking /var/lib/cassandra/data/system/LocationInfo-5-Data.db
compacted
//...
DEBUG 09:41:55,117 Estimating compactions for Super1
DEBUG 09:41:55,117 Estimating compactions for Standard2
DEBUG 09:41:55,117 Estimating compactions for Super2
DEBUG 09:41:55,118 Estimating compactions for Standard1
DEBUG 09:41:55,118 Estimating compactions for StandardByUUID1
DEBUG 09:41:55,118 Estimating compactions for LocationInfo
DEBUG 09:41:55,118 Estimating compactions for HintsColumnFamily
DEBUG 09:41:55,118 Checking to see if compaction of Super1 would be useful
DEBUG 09:41:55,119 Checking to see if compaction of Standard2 would be useful
DEBUG 09:41:55,119 Checking to see if compaction of Super2 would be useful
//...
```

```
DEBUG 09:41:56,023 GC for ParNew: 1 ms, 14643776 reclaimed leaving 80756296 used;
max is 1177812992
DEBUG 09:41:56,035 attempting to connect to lucky/192.168.1.2
DEBUG 09:41:57,025 Disseminating load info ...
```

This allows you to see exactly what Cassandra is doing and when, which is very helpful in troubleshooting. But it's also helpful in simply understanding what Cassandra does to maintain itself.

If you want to change the location of the logs directory, just find the following entry in the same *log4j.properties* file and chose a different filename:

```
log4j.appender.R.File=/var/log/cassandra/system.log
```

There's not a different entry for Windows; on Windows systems this will automatically resolve to *C:\\var\log\cassandra\system.log*.

 If you don't see any logfiles in this location, make sure that you are the owner of the directories, or at least that proper read and write permissions are set. Cassandra won't tell you if it can't write the log; it just won't. Same for the datafiles.

Note that this is the location for the log of the activity of the database, and not for Cassandra's internal datafiles. Those are stored in */var/lib/cassandra*.

Tailing

You don't need to start Cassandra using the foreground switch in order to see the rolling log. You can also simply start it without the **-f** option and then tail the logs. Tailing is not specific to Cassandra; it's a small program available in Linux distributions to see new values printed to a console as they are appended to a file.

To tail the logs, start Cassandra like this:

```
>bin/cassandra
```

Then open a second console, enter the **tail** command, and pass it the location of the particular file you want to tail, like this:

```
>tail -f /var/log/cassandra/system.log
```

The **-f** option means "follow," and as Cassandra outputs information to the physical logfile, **tail** will output it to the screen. To stop tailing, just type Ctrl-C.

You can do the same thing if you're using Windows, but Windows doesn't include a tail program natively. So to achieve this, you'll need to download and install Cygwin, which is a Bash shell emulator. Cygwin allows you to have a Linux-style interface and use a variety of Linux tools on Windows. You can get Cygwin for free from *http://www .cygwin.com*.

Then you can start Cassandra regularly and tail the logfile using this command:

```
eben@lucky~$ tail -f C:\\var\\log\\cassandra\\system.log
```

This will show the output in the console in the same way as if it were foregrounded.

General Tips

Following along

Once you're running the server with debug logging enabled, you can see a lot more happening that can help during debugging. For example, here we can see the output when writing and then reading a simple value to the database:

```
DEBUG 12:55:09,778 insert
DEBUG 12:55:09,779 insert writing local key mycol
DEBUG 12:55:36,387 get
DEBUG 12:55:36,390 weakreadlocal reading SliceByNamesReadCommand(
    table='Keyspace1', key='mycol',
    columnParent='QueryPath(columnFamilyName='Standard1',
    superColumnName='null', columnName='null')',
    columns=[6b6579393939,])
```

That's the server output generated by executing this command in the CLI:

```
cassandra> set Keyspace1.Standard1['mycol']['key999']='value999'
Value inserted.
cassandra> get Keyspace1.Standard1['mycol']['key999']
=> (column=6b6579393939, value=value999, timestamp=1277409309778000
```

Notice what's happened here. We've inserted a value in the column family named Standard1. When we perform a get request, the column key key999 is translated to 6b6579393939, because the Standard1 column family is defined as using BytesType as a CompareWith value.

However, if we use the Standard2 column family, we'll see the key column name on the get request as we typed it because that column family is defined as using a Compare With of UTF-8. So again we'll do a set and then a get request for the same value. The CLI output is shown here:

```
cassandra> set Keyspace1.Standard2['mycol']['key888']='value888'
Value inserted.
cassandra> get Keyspace1.Standard2['mycol']['key888']
=> (column=key888, value=value888, timestamp=1277409950795000)
```

The server log records this query as follows:

```
DEBUG 13:06:03,291 get
DEBUG 13:06:03,292 weakreadlocal reading SliceByNamesReadCommand(
    table='Keyspace1', key='mycol',
    columnParent='QueryPath(columnFamilyName='Standard2',
    superColumnName='null', columnName='null')',
    columns=[key888,])
```

This should give you enough information to follow along with what the server's doing as you work.

Warning signs

There are a few things to look out for as you run Cassandra. For example, if you see something like this in the logs with no further update, there's something wrong with the nodes in your ring:

```
DEBUG 12:39:56,312 attempting to connect to mywinbox/192.168.1.3
```

It's OK to attempt to connect, but then it should actually connect. It's possible for this to happen when you mix Windows and Linux boxes in a Cassandra cluster, which is definitely not recommended. If your Linux and Windows boxes can see each other, share resources such as printers, read and write files between them, view web pages the other is serving, and so forth, this might give you the impression that this should work. Don't be tempted to mix and match in a production environment.

Overview of JMX and MBeans

In this section, we explore how Cassandra makes use of Java Management Extensions (JMX) to enable remote management of your servers. JMX started as Java Specification Request (JSR) 160 and has been a core part of Java since version 5.0.

You can read more about the JMX implementation in Java by examining the `java.lang.management` package.

JMX is a Java API that provides management of applications in two key ways. First, JMX allows you to understand your application's health and overall performance in terms of memory, threads, and CPU usage—things that are generally applicable to any Java application. Second, JMX allows you to work with specific aspects of your application that you have instrumented.

Instrumentation refers to putting a wrapper around application code that provides hooks from the application to the JVM in order to allow the JVM to gather data that external tools can use. Such tools include monitoring agents, data analysis tools, profilers, and more. JMX allows you not only to view such data but also, if the application enables it, to manage your application at runtime by updating values.

JMX is commonly used for a variety of application control operations, including:

- Low available memory detection, including the size of each graduation space on the heap
- Thread information such as deadlock detection, peak number of threads, and current live threads
- Verbose classloader tracing

- Log level control
- General information such as application uptime and the active classpath

Many popular Java applications are instrumented using JMX, including the JVM itself, HP Open View, Oracle WebLogic Server, the Glassfish application server, and Cassandra. In these applications, JMX is simply one way of managing the container; JBoss Application Server, on the other hand, uses JMX as the primary way of interacting with the container.

For example, the WebLogic server provides a very wide range of activities via JMX. You can, for example, monitor the number of available JDBC connections in a pool or see the number of stateless session beans loaded in the container in a given state. Not only can you monitor these things, but you can use a graphical console that ships with the Sun (now Oracle) JDK to change their values. Want to increase the size of the pool of message-driven beans? A JMX-enabled container could allow you to manage your resources in this way.

A depiction of the JMX architecture is shown in Figure 9-1.

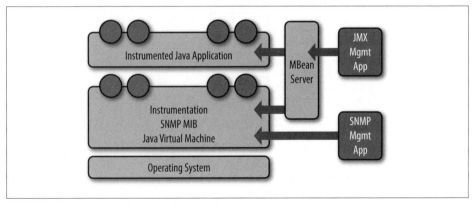

Figure 9-1. The JMX architecture

The JMX architecture is simple. The JVM collects information from the underlying operating system. The JVM itself is instrumented, so many of its features are exposed for management as described earlier. An instrumented Java application (such as Cassandra) runs on top of this, also exposing some of its features as manageable objects. The JDK includes an MBean server that makes the instrumented features available over a remote protocol to a JMX Management Application. The JVM also offers management capabilities to Simple Network Monitoring Protocol (SNMP) agents and works in a similar manner.

But within a given application, you can manage only what the application developers have made available for you to manage. Luckily, the Cassandra developers have instrumented large parts of the database, making management via JMX fairly straightforward.

This instrumentation of a Java application is performed by wrapping the application code that you want JMX to hook into with managed beans.

MBeans

A *managed bean*, or MBean, is a special type of Java bean that represents a single manageable resource inside the JVM. MBeans interact with an MBean server to make their functions remotely available.

The `jconsole` tool ships with the standard Java Development Kit. It provides a graphical user interface client for working with MBeans and can be used for local or remote management. A view of JConsole is shown in Figure 9-2.

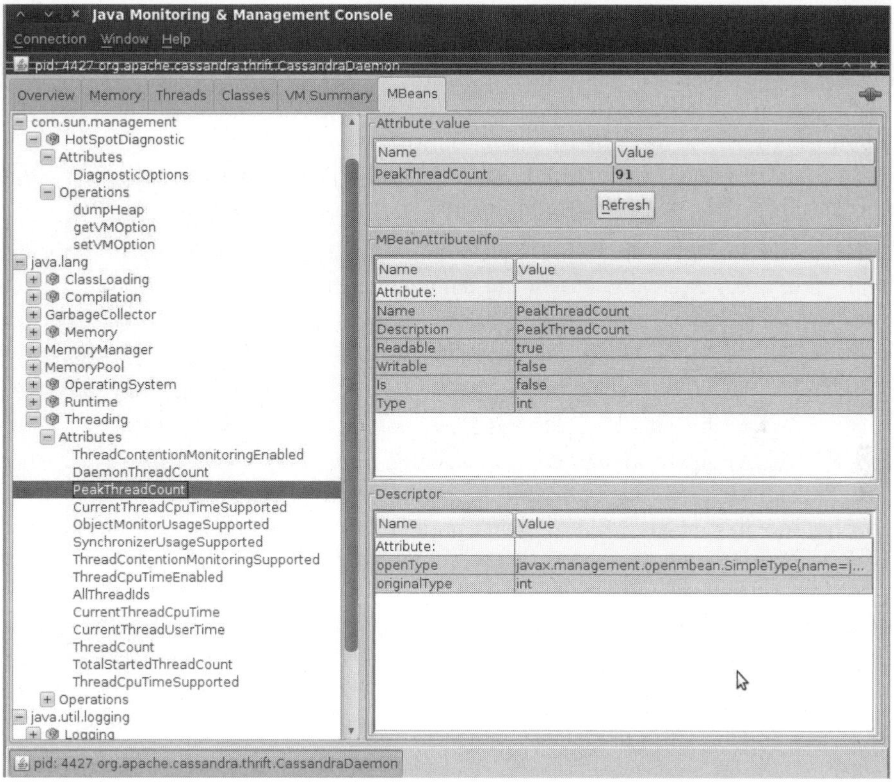

Figure 9-2. JConsole showing the peak thread count for a Cassandra daemon

In this figure, you can see the two kinds of views into your application that JMX offers: the general view about threads, memory, and CPU that every application will have, and a more detailed view that exposes the peak thread count value. You can see that many other instrumented aspects of the application are also available.

JConsole is popular because it's easy to use and ships with the JDK. But this is only one possible JMX client. The JBoss Application Server web console, for example, is itself a JMX client of the JBoss server.

There are many aspects of an application or the JVM that can be instrumented but that may be disabled. Thread Contention is one example of a potentially useful MBean that is turned off by default in the JVM. These aspects can be very useful for debugging, so if you see an MBean that you think might help you hunt down a problem, go ahead and enable it. But keep in mind that nothing comes for free, and it's a good idea to read the JavaDoc on the MBean you want to enable in order to understand the potential impact on performance. `ThreadCPUTime` is another example of a useful, but expensive, MBean.

Some simple values in the application are exposed as *attributes*. An example of this is `Threading > PeakThreadCount`, which just reports the value that the MBean has stored for the greatest number of threads the application used at a single point in time. You can refresh to see the most recent value, but that's pretty much all you can do with it. Because such a value is maintained internally in the JVM, it doesn't make sense to set it externally (it's derived from actual events, and not configurable).

But other MBeans are configurable. They make operations available to the JMX agent that let you get and set values. You can tell whether the MBean will let you set a value by looking at the value for `writable`. If it's false, you will see a label indicating the read-only value; if it's true, you will see a set of one or more fields to add your new value and a button to update it. An example of this is the `java.util.logging.Logger` bean, as shown in Figure 9-3.

Note that the parameter names are not available to the JMX agent; they're just labeled as `p0`, `p1`, etc. That's because the Java compiler "forgot" the parameter names during compilation. So in order to know what parameters to set, you'll need to look at the JavaDoc for the particular MBean you're working with. In the case of `java.util .logging.Logger`, this class implements an interface called `java.util.logging .LoggingMXBean`, which wraps it for instrumentation. To find out what the right parameters are, we examine the JavaDoc for this class and see that `p0` is the name of the logger you want to change, and `p1` is the logging level you want to set that logger to.

 If it's not obvious, setting the logging level for `java.util.logging` won't help you much if that's not what your application is using for logging. It's just used here as a general example because it's easy to understand and serves as a gentle introduction. But Cassandra does not use that logging package.

Some MBeans return an attribute value of `javax.management.openmbean.CompositeData Support`. That means that these are not simple values that can be displayed in a single

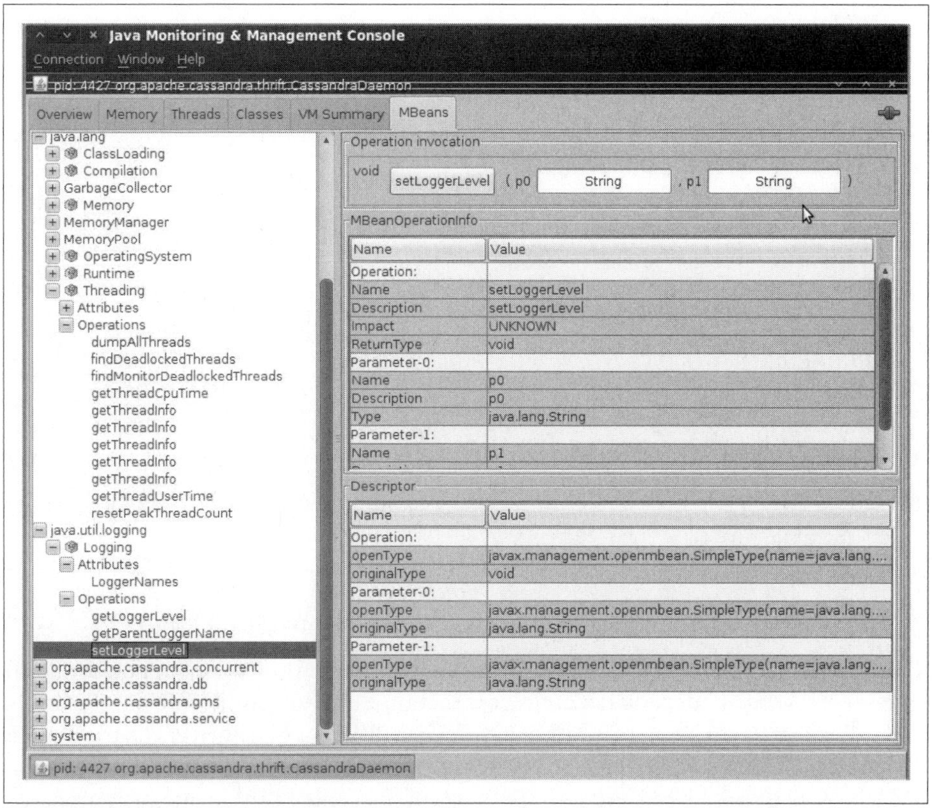

Figure 9-3. The java.util.logging.Logger MBean allows you to set a logger's log level

field, such as `LoadedClassCount`, but are instead multivalued. One example is `Memory >`
`HeapMemoryUsage`, which offers several data points and therefore has its own view.

Another type of MBean operation is one that doesn't simply show a value or allow you
to set a value, but instead lets you execute some useful action. `dumpAllThreads` and
`resetPeakThreadCount` are two such operations.

Now we'll quickly get set up to start monitoring and managing Cassandra specifically.

Integrating JMX

Enabling Cassandra to use JMX is easy, but there are a couple of dependencies. Go to
http://mx4j.sourceforge.net and download version 3.0.1 of the library MX4J. You can
probably use a newer version if one's available, but this version is known to work.

After you've downloaded the library, unzip it and navigate to the *lib* directory. Copy
two JARs from this directory: *mx4j.jar* and *mx4j-tools.jar*. Paste them into your
<cassandra-home>/lib directory and restart Cassandra. Now other Cassandra nodes

can connect via JMX to monitor its health and even to set values for the functions that are exposed as MBeans.

If you've downloaded Cassandra's source code, just drop the two necessary JARs into the *lib* directory and rebuild the source. The next time you start Cassandra, you should see output similar to the following:

```
 INFO 13:37:28,473 Cassandra starting up...
DEBUG 13:37:28,474 Will try to load mx4j now, if it's in the classpath
 INFO 13:37:28,508 mx4j successfuly loaded
HttpAdaptor version 3.0.2 started on port 8081
```

Here, MX4J will act as our JMX server agent, and now we're ready to start getting some benefit from JMX.

Interacting with Cassandra via JMX

Now that JMX is enabled, let's connect to Cassandra on its JMX port. To do so, open a new terminal and type the following:

```
>jconsole
```

When you run `jconsole`, you'll see a login screen similar to that in Figure 9-4.

From here, you can simply double-click on the value `org.apache.cassandra.thrift` `.CassandraDaemon` under the Local Process section if you're monitoring a node on the same machine. If you want to monitor a node on a different machine, check the Remote Process radio button, then enter the host and port you want to connect to. Cassandra JMX by default broadcasts on port 8080, so you can enter a value like the one shown here and then hit Connect:

```
>lucky:8080
```

 If you have trouble with this, make sure that you don't have something else running on port 8080, as that's a popular port for tools such as Apache Tomcat.

Once you've connected to a server, the default view includes four major categories about your server's state, which are updated constantly:

Heap Memory Usage
    This shows the total memory available to the Cassandra program, as well as how much it's using right now.

Threads
    This is the number of live threads Cassandra is using.

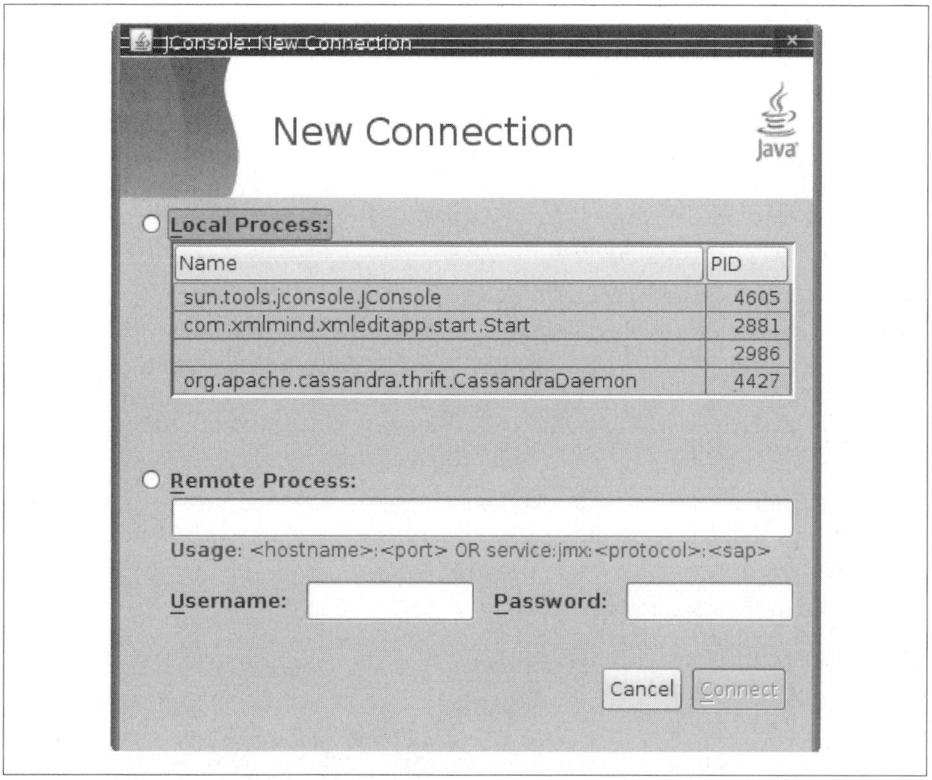

Figure 9-4. The jconsole login

Classes

The number of classes that Cassandra has loaded. This number is relatively small for such a powerful program; Cassandra typically requires around 2,300 classes out of the box. Compare this to a program such as Oracle WebLogic, which typically loads around 24,000 classes.

CPU Usage

This shows the percentage of the processor that the Cassandra program is currently using.

You can use the selector to adjust the time range shown in the charts.

If you want to see a more detailed view of how Cassandra is using the Java heap and nonheap memory, click the Memory tab. By changing the chart value in the drop-down, you can see in detail the graduations in which Cassandra is using its memory. You can also (try to) force a garbage collection if you think it's necessary.

You can connect to more than one JMX agent at once. Just choose File > New Connection… and repeat the steps to connect to another running Cassandra node to view multiple servers at once.

Cassandra's MBeans

Once you've connected with a JMX agent such as JConsole, you can manage Cassandra using the MBeans it exposes. To do so, click the MBeans tab. Other than the standard Java items available to every agent, there are several Cassandra packages that contain manageable beans, organized by their package names, which start with `org.apache.cassandra`. We won't go into detail on all of them here, but there are several of interest that we'll take a look at.

Many classes in Cassandra are exposed as MBeans, which means in practical terms that they implement a custom interface that describes the operations that need to be implemented and for which the JMX agent will provide hooks. The steps are basically the same for getting any MBean to work; I'll use a single key class as an example. If you'd like to JMX-enable something that isn't already enabled, modify the source code following this general outline and you'll be in business.

For this example, we look at Cassandra's `StorageService` and how it uses MBeans. Here's the partial definition of the `StorageServiceMBean` class, with some operations omitted for brevity:

```
public interface StorageServiceMBean
{
    public Set<String> getLiveNodes();

    public Set<String> getUnreachableNodes();

    public void forceTableFlush(String tableName, String... columnFamilies)
        throws IOException;

    public void removeToken(String token);

//...
}
```

As you can see by this MBean interface definition, there's no magic going on. This is just a regular interface defining the set of operations that will be exposed to JMX that the `StorageService` implementation must support. This typically means maintaining additional metadata as the regular operations do their work.

The `StorageService` class implements this interface and must do the work of directly supporting JMX. The consistency manager field has a reference type of `java.util .concurrent.ExecutorService`, but the actual implementation is of type `org.apache .cassandra.concurrent.JMXEnabledThreadPoolExecutor`.

```
private ExecutorService consistencyManager_ =
    new JMXEnabledThreadPoolExecutor(DatabaseDescriptor.getConsistencyThreads(),
        DatabaseDescriptor.getConsistencyThreads(),
        StageManager.KEEPALIVE,
        TimeUnit.SECONDS,
        new LinkedBlockingQueue<Runnable>(),
        new NamedThreadFactory("CONSISTENCY-MANAGER"));
```

The `JMXEnabledThreadPoolExecutor` implements the `JMXEnabledThreadPoolExecutorM`
`Bean` and, by association, `org.apache.cassandra.concurrent.IExecutorMBean`, so that all
the Cassandra classes that use thread pools can expose the same operations to JMX.
It's in the `JMXEnabledThreadPoolExecutor` that we see how Cassandra becomes JMX-
enabled.

The executor pool registers with the platform MBean server in its constructor, as
shown here:

```
public JMXEnabledThreadPoolExecutor(int corePoolSize,
    int maximumPoolSize,
    long keepAliveTime,
    TimeUnit unit,
    BlockingQueue<Runnable> workQueue,
    NamedThreadFactory threadFactory)
{
    super(corePoolSize, maximumPoolSize, keepAliveTime, unit, workQueue,
threadFactory);
    super.prestartAllCoreThreads();

    MBeanServer mbs = ManagementFactory.getPlatformMBeanServer();
    mbeanName = "org.apache.cassandra.concurrent:type=" + threadFactory.id;
    try
    {
        mbs.registerMBean(this, new ObjectName(mbeanName));
    }
    catch (Exception e)
    {
        throw new RuntimeException(e);
    }
}
```

The platform server here is simply the default one embedded in the JDK. The MBean
is named and registered so that the MBean server knows to monitor it and make it
manageable via the agent.

In order to do proper cleanup, when the `JMXEnabledThreadPoolExecutor` is shut down,
the class will also unregister itself from the MBean server:

```
private void unregisterMBean()
{
  try
    {
    ManagementFactory.getPlatformMBeanServer().unregisterMBean
(new ObjectName(mbeanName));
    }
  catch (Exception e)
    {
    throw new RuntimeException(e);
  }
}
```

Likewise, the `StorageService` class itself registers and unregisters with the MBean
server for the JMX properties that it maintains locally. So this implementation does all

of the work that it is intended to do, and then has implementations of the methods that are only necessary for talking to the MBean server. For example, here is the Storage Service implementation of the of the getUnreachableNodes operation:

```
public Set<String> getUnreachableNodes()
{
  return stringify(Gossiper.instance.getUnreachableMembers());
}
```

The Gossiper class is a Singleton that maintains lists of IP addresses of the nodes it has sent and received heartbeat messages from, so when you call the getUnreachable Nodes operation in the JMX agent, it calls the MBean method in StorageService, which delegates the call to the Gossiper, which returns the set of unreachable IP addresses, wrapped in a new set so it can't be modified directly by the caller:

```
/* unreachable member set */
private Set<InetAddress> unreachableEndpoints_ =
    new ConcurrentSkipListSet<InetAddress>(inetcomparator);
//...
public Set<InetAddress> getUnreachableMembers()
{
    return new HashSet<InetAddress>(unreachableEndpoints_);
}
```

So when we open it up in the JMX agent JConsole, we see, happily, that we have no unreachable nodes because the set is empty. If there were unreachable nodes, their IP addresses would appear in the Value field, as shown in Figure 9-5.

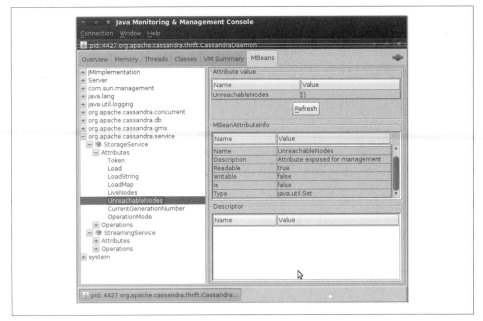

Figure 9-5. The StorageService unreachable nodes attribute

In the following sections, we see what features are available for monitoring and management in this way via JMX, by package.

org.apache.cassandra.concurrent

This package houses Cassandra's threading and streaming functionality. As such, it is the home of the Staged Event-Driven Architecture (SEDA) classes, the gossiper, the balancers, and the classes that flush data in memtables.

Most of these MBeans allow you to view only attributes. If you are suspicious of data writing problems or unbalanced node problems in your Cassandra ring, start here.

Because of the SEDA architecture, each stage in Cassandra is exposed as its own MBean. This means you're able to quickly determine exactly how many objects are in a given stage at a given time. The stages include:

- Anti-Entropy Stage
- Migration Stage
- Response Stage
- Row Mutation Stage (for deletes and updates)
- Row Read Stage
- Stream Stage

For each of these stages you can see the counts for active, completed, and pending tasks. Some of the stages, such as for reading and writing data, maintain their own thread pools, and the MBeans allow you to see the pool size. All of the stage objects expose only attributes and don't allow you to perform any operations.

org.apache.cassandra.db

These are the Cassandra classes related to the core database itself that are exposed as MBeans. They include Caches, Column Family Stores, the Commit Log, and the Compaction Manager.

You can view information about a variety of caches that Cassandra maintains— including the caches for column family key and row hints—for location information of keys, rows, and migrations. The cache information contains attributes for the cache's current size, capacity, number of cache requests, cache hits, and recent cache activity.

Column Family Stores is another set of MBeans, but these give you a richer variety of attribute values, and also allow you to perform some operations. These give you a view into your memtables, SSTables, and Bloom filter usage. You can use the operations provided to force a flush of the memtables, initiate a major compaction by calling the forceMajorCompaction method of the CompactionManager class, or invalidate a row cache.

One useful set of statistics here relates to reading and writing data, included in the ColumnFamilyStores > system > Schema bean:

Total Read Count
> This is the number of reads Cassandra has performed, available from the Read Count attribute.

Recent Read Latency
> You get this number (in microseconds) from the RecentReadLatencyMicros attribute. You can also see the TotalReadLatencyMicros; the total reads multiplied by the read latency gives you that number.

These statistics come in very handy if you are concerned that performance is degrading. But they also are great for showing how fast Cassandra can be. For example, on my eight-core machine, I've recorded write latency at 92 microseconds for simple values in a small database.

This set of MBeans also makes data regarding the Compaction Manager available, including the total bytes that are in the process of being compacted and the total bytes that have been compacted.

org.apache.cassandra.gms

This package has one MBean with three operations: you can dump arrival times or get and set the conviction threshold, which by default is 8.

org.apache.cassandra.service

The service package offers two beans: StorageService and StreamingService. Because these classes are central to Cassandra's operations, they expose the greatest number of operations and give you considerable external control. Let's take a moment to survey some of the key elements.

StorageService

Because Cassandra is a database, it's essentially a very sophisticated storage program; therefore, one of the first places you'll want to look when you encounter problems is the StorageService MBean. This allows you to inspect your OperationMode, which reports normal if everything is going smoothly (other possible states are leaving, joining, decommissioned, and client).

You can also view the current set of live nodes, as well as the set of unreachable nodes in the cluster. If any nodes are unreachable, Cassandra will tell you their IP addresses in the UnreachableNodes attribute. But there are many other standard maintenance operations that this bean affords you, and understanding the operations available here is important to keeping your cluster in good health. I encourage you to check out the bean for yourself, of course, and here I highlight some of the key maintenance operations.

If you want to change Cassandra's log level at runtime without interrupting service (as we saw earlier in the general example), you can invoke the setLog4jLevel(String class Qualifier, String level) method. For example, say that you have set Cassandra's log level to debug because you're troubleshooting an issue. You can use some of the methods described here to try to help fix your problem, then you might want to change the log level to something less trying on the system. To do this, navigate to the StorageSer vice MBean in JConsole. We'll change the value for a particularly chatty class: the LoadDisseminator. The first parameter to this operation is the name of the class you want to set the log level for, and the second parameter is the level you want to set it to. Enter org.apache.cassandra.service.LoadDisseminator and INFO, and click the button labeled setLog4jLevel. You should see the following output in your logs (assuming your level was already debug):

```
DEBUG 17:17:30,515 Disseminating load info ...
 INFO 17:17:42,001 set log level to INFO for classes under
'org.apache.cassandra.service.LoadDisseminator'
(if the level doesn't look like 'INFO' then log4j couldn't parse 'INFO')
```

As you can see from this output, Cassandra was logging a load info statement because the logger was set to debug. After invoking the setLog4jLevel operation, we get the INFO output and no more debug level statements.

To get an understanding of each node's load, you can use the getLoadMap() method, which will return to you a Java Map with keys of IP addresses with values of their corresponding loads.

If you're looking for a certain key, you can use the getNaturalEndpoints(String table, byte[] key) operation. Pass it the table name and the key for which you want to find the endpoint value, and it will return a list of IP addresses that are responsible for storing this key.

You can also use the getRangeToEndpointMap operation to get a map of range to end points describing your ring topology.

If you wish to decommission a server, you can also do that with this MBean. Invoke the decommission() operation, and the current node's data will automatically transfer to another machine and take this node out of service.

If you're feeling brave, you can invoke the truncate operation for a given column family in a given keyspace. If all of the nodes are available, this operation will delete all data from the column family but leave its definition intact.

A good idea for general maintenance is to use the loadBalance() operation if you discover through other MBeans that your nodes have become very unbalanced. This can happen from time to time, where some nodes have an inordinate share of the data. This operation will cause the current node to unload its data onto one of its neighboring nodes, and then it will bootstrap to receive the data of the node in the ring burdened with the most data.

StreamingService

The `org.cassandra.streaming.StreamingServiceMBean` defines the following interface:

```java
public interface StreamingServiceMBean
{
    public Set<InetAddress> getStreamDestinations();

    public List<String> getOutgoingFiles(String host) throws IOException;

    public Set<InetAddress> getStreamSources();

    public List<String> getIncomingFiles(String host) throws IOException;

    public String getStatus();
}
```

There are two basic ideas here: a stream source and a stream destination. Each node can stream its data to another node in order to perform load balancing, and this class supports these operations. The MBean methods give you a necessary view into the data that is moving between nodes in the cluster.

The `getStatus` operation is not an enumeration with some set list of possible statuses. It rather returns a string in the form of `ReceivingFrom: [node] SendingTo: [node]`.

So in conjunction with the `Storage-Service` MBean, if you're concerned that a node is not receiving data as it should, or that a node is unbalanced or even down, these two services working together can give you very rich insight into exactly what's happening in your cluster during a snapshot in time.

Custom Cassandra MBeans

Let's quickly write a very simple MBean so that you can do this kind of work yourself if there's a new feature you'd like to JMX-enable. There's nothing to it.

First, we get the source code and create our MBean interface next to the Cassandra source file it wraps. Our MBean will return the current version of the Cassandra API, which is not currently available in Cassandra. Our MBean looks like this:

```java
package org.apache.cassandra.thrift;

public interface CassandraServerMBean {
    public String getVersion();
}
```

Now we need to open up the source of *CassandraServer.java* and make it implement our MBean interface and hook into the JMX server. Finally, we'll actually implement

---

the method. Thrift generates a version number that is accessible from the CLI, so we'll just reuse that. Our new *CassandraServer.java* class looks like this:

```java
package org.apache.cassandra.thrift;

import javax.management.MBeanServer;
import javax.management.ObjectName;

import org.apache.cassandra.auth.AllowAllAuthenticator;
import org.apache.cassandra.concurrent.StageManager;

//rest of imports...

public class CassandraServer implements Cassandra.Iface, CassandraServerMBean
{
    public static final String MBEAN_OBJECT_NAME =
        "org.apache.cassandra.service:type=CassandraService";

    public CassandraServer()
    {
        storageService = StorageService.instance;

        final MBeanServer mbs = ManagementFactory.getPlatformMBeanServer();
        try
        {
            mbs.registerMBean(this, new ObjectName(MBEAN_OBJECT_NAME));
        }
        catch (Exception e)
        {
            throw new RuntimeException(e);
        }
    }


    //rest of server implementation...

    //our mbean hook method
      public String getVersion() {
        String version = null;
        try {
          version = describe_version();
        } catch(TException e) {
          logger.warn("Cassandra server version unavailable: ", e.getMessage());
          version = "unavailable";
        }
        return version;
      }
}
```

So we have implemented the interface and connected the Cassandra server with the management platform. Now all we need to do is open a terminal, navigate to our *<cassandra-home>* directory using the $ ant command, and start the server. Then, run jconsole and connect to your server instance. You should see your attribute available, as shown in Figure 9-6.

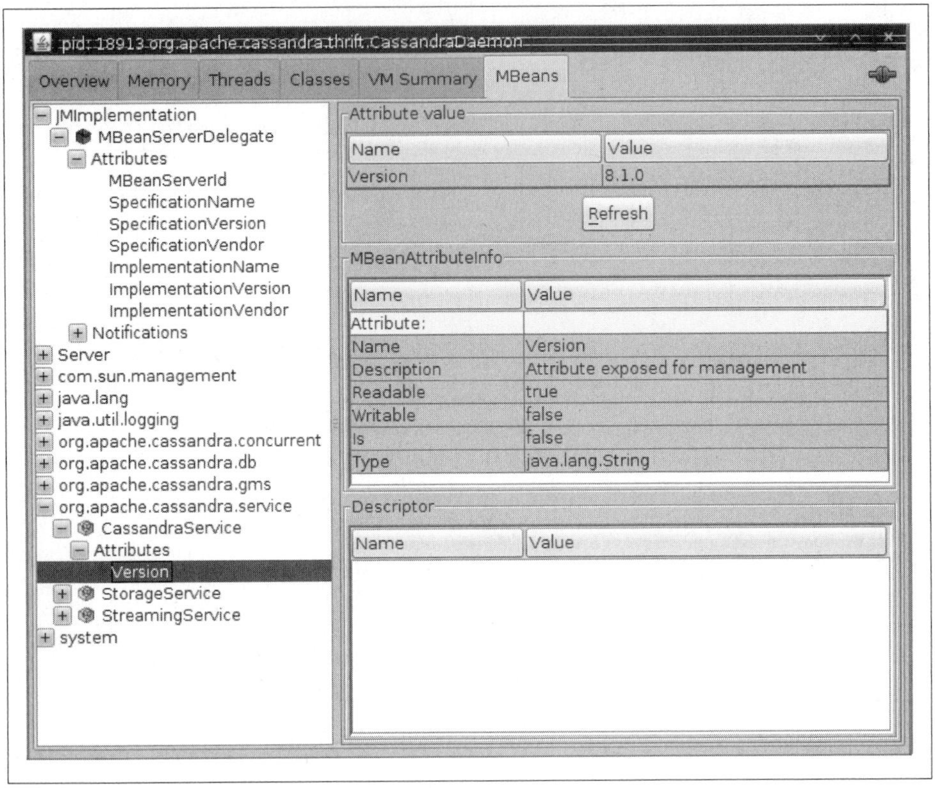

Figure 9-6. Our custom MBean exposing the Cassandra version

Here, version 8.1.0 is the API version information generated as a Thrift constant; it doesn't necessarily correspond to the release version.

> If you are modifying the source and are unsure about what you've changed, you can always use Subversion to check the changes in your local repository against what you checked out. Use the `svn diff` command to see the changes between the two files and dump the result to a new file:

```
eben@morpheus:~$ svn diff
/home/eben/cassandra/dist/trunk-svn-1/src/java/org/apache/cassandra/thrift/
CassandraServer.java
/home/eben/cassandra/dist/trunk-svn-2/src/java/org/apache/cassandra/thrift/
CassandraServer.java
>> /home/eben/CassandraServer.patch
```

Runtime Analysis Tools

We don't need to go into too much more detail about JMX in general here, but to understand Cassandra and manage it, it's good to know what features are exposed with JMX. It's also useful to know what tools Java makes available out of the box to detect and spot the source of a memory leak, analyze a hung process, and so on. Because Cassandra is a Java application, and because it is relatively young, there are no third-party tools specific to Cassandra at this point.

 If you are debugging and you're not sure what commands have been executed against Cassandra with the CLI, look in your home directory for a hidden file called *.cassandra.history*. This acts like your Bash shell history, listing the commands in a plain-text file in the order Cassandra executed them. Nice!

Heap Analysis with JMX and JHAT

As you're debugging your Cassandra application, it's often useful to understand what's happening in your heap. If you're working off of the trunk or are otherwise unsure of your Cassandra build, there are some native Java tools available to you.

Cassandra can use a lot of memory, and garbage collection and major compactions can have a big impact on performance. One helpful program here is called Java Heap Analysis Tool (JHAT). JHAT uses the HPROF binary format to create web pages that allow you to browse all the objects in the heap and see all the references to and from heap objects. You can combine this tool, which ships with the JDK, with some data made available through JMX.

To gain a better understanding of our heap, we'll use the `com.sun.management.HotSpot Diagnostic` bean. It has an operation called `dumpHeap`. Because that's the name of the operation in the MBean, that's the label on the button in the JMX agent. This bean allows you to specify a filename where you want to dump the heap to; then you click the button and it writes the heap information into the file you specified. But the `dump Heap` operation writes the heap's current state to a file that's encoded in the HPROF binary format for heap and CPU profiling. So we can't read it in a text file and will need to use JHAT to view the data.

To get a heap dump, run JConsole and navigate to the `com.sun.management.HotSpot Diagnostic` bean, expand the Operations tree, and click the `dumpHeap` operation. Enter a relative or absolute path naming the file you want to write the heap dump to, as shown in Figure 9-7.

Open a new terminal and start up `jconsole`. You should see a pop-up box indicating that the method was successfully invoked.

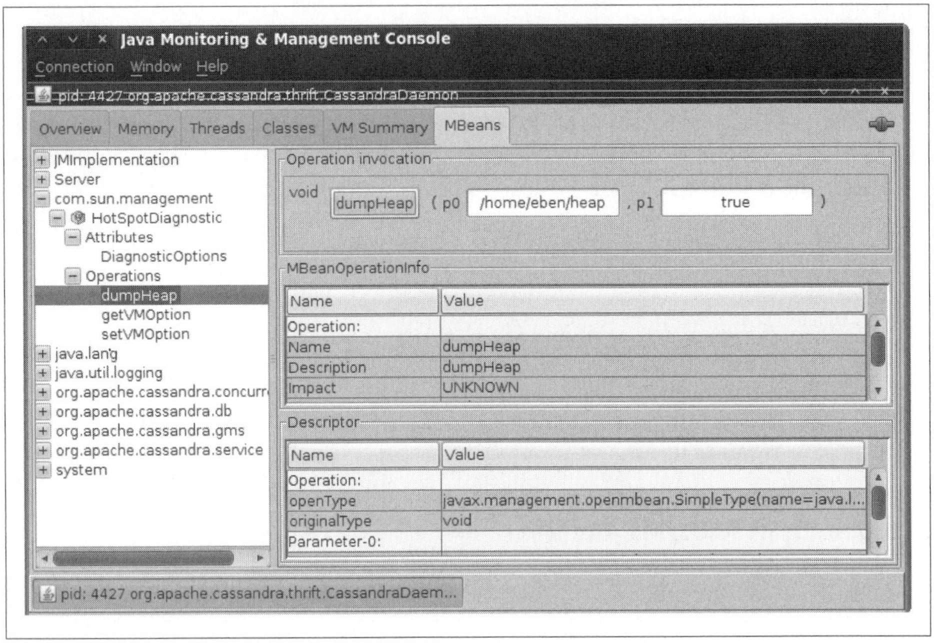

Figure 9-7. *Invoking the dumpHeap operation on our Cassandra node*

You can also get a heap dump file on a running process without the graphical interface using the `jmap` tool that ships with the JDK. First, get your Cassandra instance's process ID. To get the process IDs on a Linux system for programs, use the **ps** command and look for 'java'. Or, if you have many Java processes running, you can find Cassandra more specifically by grepping for the Cassandra daemon.

> You can find Cassandra's process ID on a Linux system by opening a terminal and using the **ps** command as follows:
>
> ```
> $ ps -ef | grep 'CassandraDaemon'
> ```

Once you have the Cassandra process ID, we can use it to specify the heap we want to get a snapshot of with the `jmap` tool. This is useful for finding out what's going on in a hung process, locating the source of a memory leak, and so on.

```
eben@morpheus:~$ jmap -dump:live,format=b,file=/home/eben/jmapdump.bin 4427
Dumping heap to /home/eben/jmapdump.bin ...
Heap dump file created
```

Now that we have captured our heap data, let's use JHAT to check it out. To run JHAT, open a terminal and type something like the following, replacing my heap dump file location with yours:

```
$jhat /home/eben/jmapdump.bin
```

This command will run for a moment and then output something like the following:

```
Chasing references, expect 63 dots................................................
..................
Eliminating duplicate references................................................
...............
Snapshot resolved.
Started HTTP server on port 7000
Server is ready.
```

Now that the server is started, you can open a browser to *http://localhost:7000* to view the file. The heap dump file is also portable, so you can move it to another box after you generate it and view it there in JHAT.

 JHAT will run for a moment and then launch a web server (there's a small HTTP server built into the JDK since version 6) on port 7000, so you might need to close JConsole or some other program to ensure that port can be used, because it's not configurable. To make sure it's open, type >netstat -o -a on Windows or >netstat -o -a | less on Linux.

For more information on how to use JHAT, consult *http://java.sun.com/javase/6/docs/technotes/tools/share/jhat.html* or just type jhat -h for help options.

The generated website offers a variety of options, including limiting your view to only:

- All classes, including Java platform classes
- All classes, excluding Java platform classes
- All members of the rootset
- Instance counts for all classes
- Heap histogram, showing all classes with the number of instances that have been created and their total size
- Classes awaiting finalizer execution

If there's a problem with Cassandra, an *hprof* file will be created, as we can see in the following output:

```
DEBUG 16:13:17,640 Disseminating load info ...
java.lang.OutOfMemoryError: Java heap space
Dumping heap to java_pid21279.hprof ...
Heap dump file created [2766589 bytes in 0.032 secs]
ERROR 16:13:34,369 Fatal exception in thread Thread[pool-1-thread-1,5,main]
java.lang.OutOfMemoryError: Java heap space
 at org.apache.thrift.protocol.TBinaryProtocol.readStringBody(TBinaryProtocol
.java:296)
 at org.apache.thrift.protocol.TBinaryProtocol.readMessageBegin(TBinaryProtocol
.java:203)
 at org.apache.cassandra.thrift.Cassandra$Processor.process(Cassandra.java:1113)
```

The file will be created in <*cassandra-home*>, and you can open it like this:

```
$ jhat java_pid21279.hprof
```

The file will be analyzed, the server will be created, and you can open a browser to see what the state of your objects were at the time of the crash.

Alternatively, you can create your own custom view by executing a query of the heap data in an HTML form. Object Query Language (OQL) is a simple SQL-like syntax for querying the heap dump file to find only objects that meet certain specified properties. The query in Figure 9-8 allows us to filter on only objects that are in Cassandra's `org.apache.cassandra.db` package.

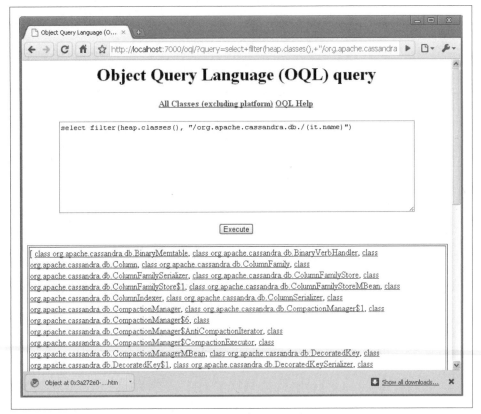

Figure 9-8. Using Object Query Language in JHAT to filter only Cassandra's classes in the db package

Once the query result returns, you can click on the class name to see additional detail about it.

You can execute queries about more specific properties of objects as well. For example, you may want to filter for only objects that have a string longer than 200 characters. Using OQL, you could issue a statement such as this:

```
select s from java.lang.String s where s.count >= 200
```

More detail on the Object Query Language is beyond the scope of this book, but it's not hard to use. There are a few examples included with the tool, and its syntax is very similar to SQL. There are also some good blogs describing how to use it; in particular, check out A. Sundararajan's blog at *http://blogs.sun.com/sundararajan/entry/querying_java_heap_with_oql.*

In this case, we can use the results of the query to see the classpath information held in a string:

```
Object at 0x3a272e0

instance of -ea -Xdebug
-Xrunjdwp:transport=dt_socket,server=y,address=8888,suspend=n
-Xms128m -Xmx1G -XX:TargetSurvivorRatio=90 -XX:+AggressiveOpts
-XX:+UseParNewGC -XX:+UseConcMarkSweepGC -XX:+CMSParallelRemarkEnabled
-XX:+HeapDumpOnOutOfMemoryError
-XX:SurvivorRatio=128 -XX:MaxTenuringThreshold=0
-Dcom.sun.management.jmxremote.port=8080
-Dcom.sun.management.jmxremote.ssl=false
-Dcom.sun.management.jmxremote.authenticate=false -Dcassandra
-Dstorage-config=/opt/apache-cassandra-0.6.2/0.6.2-source/conf
-Dcassandra-foreground=yes (24 bytes)
```

This is a roundabout way to see your classpath switches, but it does give you an idea of how JMap and JHAT can help you find interesting information about your runtime state.

Detecting Thread Problems

If you are seeing slowness or uncontrollable growth in the JConsole, you might want to inspect the current thread behavior. Cassandra makes heavy use of thread pools and the Java concurrency libraries, so understanding their state can be important to debugging efforts.

In the console, click the Threads tab. The window on the left will show you a list of threads and pools, and you can click any of them to see a stack. This view will also show you their current state. If you see any threads in a stuck state, that's a sign that your server is not releasing resources as it should, and you will start to see performance bottlenecks around this thread. If many stuck threads begin to queue up in a stuck state, your server will eventually crash. If you're seeing unusual growth in heap usage where garbage collection is not reclaiming space, you might have an issue with stuck threads, and you can check this area of the console to determine thread state.

In Java, a "stuck" thread is a thread that the application has transitioned to the "stuck" state following a timeout period; that is, the application has decided that after a certain amount of time during which work is not being completed, the thread will never complete its work. This can prevent it from getting returned to the thread pool, which means fewer threads will be available for new work, which means performance will start crumbling.

Finally, you can click the Detect Deadlock button if you're concerned that you might have internal deadlocked threads.

Health Check

There are a few basic things that you'll want to look for to ensure that nodes in your cluster are healthy:

- Check the MBean for `org.apache.cassandra.concurrent.ROW_MUTATION_STAGE`. You're looking to see that the completed task counts are increasing, which means that writes (inserts, updates, and deletes) are coming through and are completing successfully.

- Check the MBean for `org.apache.cassandra.concurrent.ROW_READ_STAGE`. For this, you're also ensuring that the completed task counts are increasing, which means that read operations are coming through and are completing successfully.

- Make sure for both of these MBeans that the number in the `PendingTasks` attribute is not growing too much. Even if it's not a very low number, it should be relatively stable. A growing set of pending tasks means that Cassandra is having trouble keeping up with the load. As is usual with databases, once this problem starts, it will only continue in a downward spiral. Three things that can improve this situation are a decreased load, scaling up (adding more hardware), or scaling out (adding another node and rebalancing).

- As usual, check the logs to make sure that nothing is reporting at `ERROR` level.

Summary

In this chapter we looked at ways you can monitor and manage your Cassandra cluster. In particular, we went into some detail on JMX and learned the rich variety of operations Cassandra makes available to the MBean server. We saw how to use JConsole to view what's happening in your Cassandra cluster, and we performed basic maintenance tasks. Using just a little Java code, we saw how you could easily use MBeans yourself to JMX-enable a new aspect of the source code if you wish.

We also gained some insight into how to use tools that come with the Java Development Kit to help us understand the runtime object graph within Cassandra. Using JMap and the Java Heap Analysis Tool, we took a snapshot of the program's memory and then queried it using Object Query Language to find objects with properties we might be concerned about.

There are a variety of other operations monitoring tools that are more robust, but this will get you started. Your organization might use one already that you can hook into, such as OpenNMS (see *http://www.opennms.org*), which has JMX hooks. Nagios, for example, is open source, free, and rather straightforward. It also has the advantage of readily connecting to JMX, and it's what they use at Mahalo to monitor their Cassandra ring.

 There's an article on Mahalo about how to integrate Nagios with JMX. See *http://www.mahalo.com/how-to-monitor-cassandra-with-nagios*.

You should now be ready to perform routine maintenance, understand your Cassandra cluster better, and know how to perform some general and fine-grained tuning tasks to keep Cassandra healthy.

## CHAPTER 10

Maintenance

In this chapter, we look at some things you can do to keep Cassandra healthy. So put your operations hat on, and let's get started.

The Nodetool ships with Cassandra and can be found in *<cassandra-home>/bin*. This is a command-line program that offers a rich array of ways to look at your cluster, understand its activity, and modify it. Nodetool lets you get limited statistics about the cluster, see the ranges each node maintains, move data from one node to another, decommission a node, and even repair a node that's having trouble.

 Many of the tasks in Nodetool overlap with functions available in the JMX interface. This is because, behind the scenes, Nodetool is invoking JMX using a helper class called `NodeProbe`. So JMX is doing the real work, the `NodeProbe` class is used to connect to the JMX agent and sort out the data, and the `NodeCmd` class is used to present it in an interactive command-line interface.

To use Nodetool, you need to have the same environment as Cassandra itself; that is, it requires the same classpath and logging files.

 The command-line Nodetool is a wrapper around `org.apache.cassandra` `.tools.NodeCmd`. Take a look at the source for that class if you need to know more about exactly what it's doing.

Starting Nodetool is a breeze. Just open a terminal, navigate to *<cassandra-home>*, and enter the following command:

```
$bin/nodetool
```

Running it this way will error out, but you also cause the program to print a list of available commands, which are covered next.

Getting Ring Information

There is a variety of information you can get about the ring and its nodes, which we look at in this section. You can get basic information on an individual node or on all the nodes participating in a ring.

Info

The most straightforward command to issue is the info command. It tells Nodetool to connect with a single node and get some basic data about its current state. Just pass it the address of the node you want info for:

```
$ bin/nodetool -h 192.168.1.5 info
13443958511545321511233195266486163581
Load            : 3.93 MB
Generation No   : 1277663698
Uptime (seconds) : 19639
Heap Memory (MB) : 36.60 / 1011.25
```

The only item here that might not be entirely obvious is the "Generation No" field. This is a heartbeat state associated with every endpoint. It's maintained by the Gossiper using a timestamp.

Ring

To determine what nodes are in your ring and what state they're in, use the host and ring switches on Nodetool, like this:

```
$ bin/nodetool -host 192.168.1.5 ring
```

This will give you a result like this one:

```
Address       Status    Load      Range                                             Ring
                                   41654880048427970483049687892424207188
192.168.1.5   Up        1.71 KB   20846671262289044293293447172905883342    |<--|
192.168.1.7   Up        2.93 KB   41654880048427970483049687892424207188    |-->|
```

Here we see the IP addresses of all the nodes in the ring. In this case we have two nodes, one at 1.5 and one at 1.7, both of which are up (currently available and ready for queries). The load column represents the byte count of the data each node is holding.

Range Tokens

Keyspaces divide their data into ranges. Cassandra assigns each node in the cluster a unique token, called the Range Token, which determines what keys that node will be the primary replica for. The range column shown using the ring switch indicates the token each node is responsible for.

There is a special range called the "wrapping range." The node with the lowest token value gets assigned all the keys that are less than that token, as well as all the keys greater than the range of the largest token; i.e., it wraps from the largest back around to the lowest.

Getting Statistics

Nodetool also lets you gather statistics about the state of your server down to the data level. This is much more detailed information about your data than is gathered by the info switch. There are two basic commands: cfstats and tpstats, both of which we examine now.

Using cfstats

To see an overview of each column family, you can use the cfstats switch. This gives you cluster metrics. To view column family statistics, execute Nodetool as follows (replacing the IP address with one in your cluster, of course):

```
$ bin/nodetool -host 192.168.1.5 cfstats
```

This will generate output like the following:

```
Keyspace: Keyspace1
    Read Count: 13
    Read Latency: 0.3252307692307692 ms.
    Write Count: 3
    Write Latency: 0.13266666666666665 ms.
    Pending Tasks: 0
        Column Family: StandardByUUID1
        SSTable count: 0
        Space used (live): 0
        Space used (total): 0
        Memtable Columns Count: 0
        Memtable Data Size: 0
        Memtable Switch Count: 0
        Read Count: 0
        Read Latency: NaN ms.
        Write Count: 0
        Write Latency: NaN ms.
        Pending Tasks: 0
        Key cache capacity: 200000
        Key cache size: 0
        Key cache hit rate: NaN
        Row cache: disabled
        Compacted row minimum size: 0
        Compacted row maximum size: 0
        Compacted row mean size: 0

        Column Family: Standard2
        SSTable count: 1
        Space used (live): 379
```

```
Space used (total): 379
Memtable Columns Count: 0
Memtable Data Size: 0
Memtable Switch Count: 1
Read Count: 13
Read Latency: 0.325 ms.
Write Count: 3
Write Latency: 0.133 ms.
Pending Tasks: 0
Key cache capacity: 1
Key cache size: 0
Key cache hit rate: NaN
Row cache: disabled
Compacted row minimum size: 0
Compacted row maximum size: 0
Compacted row mean size: 0
```

Here I have omitted lots of the output for brevity; the same statistics are generated for each column family. We can see the latency on reads and writes, the total number of reads and writes, the cache hit ratio, and the number of tasks that are not yet complete in the Pending Tasks count.

 Look out for a large number of pending tasks, and especially a growing number of pending tasks. This could mean that Cassandra is running out of resources and cannot keep up. If Nodetool reveals a large number of pending tasks, check with JMX (as shown in Chapter 9) or execute the tpstats command (as we'll see next) to see what stage different tasks are in. For example, a large number of tasks in the ROW-MUTATION-STAGE (writes) might mean that inserts, updates, or deletes are coming in faster than Cassandra can execute them.

One thing that the statistics here show is how fast Cassandra is. Admittedly, there's very little load on this box, but writes are executed in 1/10 of a millisecond.

Using tpstats

The tpstats tool gives us information on the thread pools that Cassandra maintains. Cassandra is highly concurrent, and optimized for multiprocessor/multicore machines. Moreover, Cassandra employs a Staged Event-Driven Architecture (SEDA) internally, so understanding the behavior and health of the thread pools is important to good Cassandra maintenance.

To find statistics on the thread pools, execute Nodetool with the tpstats switch, like this:

```
$ bin/nodetool -host 192.168.1.5 tpstats
```

This will generate ASCII output representing the thread pool data on the specified node:

Pool Name	Active	Pending	Completed
FILEUTILS-DELETE-POOL	0	0	101
MESSAGING-SERVICE-POOL	2	4	71594081
STREAM-STAGE	0	0	2
RESPONSE-STAGE	0	0	38154433
ROW-READ-STAGE	0	0	12542
LB-OPERATIONS	0	0	0
COMMITLOG	1	0	65070187
GMFD	0	0	1002891
MESSAGE-DESERIALIZER-POOL	0	0	105025414
LB-TARGET	0	0	0
CONSISTENCY-MANAGER	0	0	2079
ROW-MUTATION-STAGE	1	1	52419722
MESSAGE-STREAMING-POOL	0	0	121
LOAD-BALANCER-STAGE	0	0	0
FLUSH-SORTER-POOL	0	0	115
MEMTABLE-POST-FLUSHER	0	0	115
COMPACTION-POOL	0	0	364
FLUSH-WRITER-POOL	0	0	115
HINTED-HANDOFF-POOL	0	0	154

You can see directly how many operations are in what stage, and whether they are active, pending, or completed. This output was captured during a write operation, and therefore shows that there is an active task in the ROW-MUTATION-STAGE.

Seeing lots of zeroes in the output means that you either have very little activity on the server or that Cassandra is doing an exceptional job of keeping up with the load.

Basic Maintenance

There are a few tasks that you'll need to perform before or after more impactful tasks. For example, it makes sense to take a snapshot only after you've performed a flush. So in this section we look at some of these basic maintenance tasks: repair, snapshot, and cleanup.

Repair

Running nodetool repair causes Cassandra to execute a major compaction. A Merkle tree of the data on the target node is computed, and the Merkle tree is compared with those of other replicas. This step makes sure that any data that might be out of sync with other nodes isn't forgotten.

During a major compaction (see "Compaction" in the Glossary), the server initiates a TreeRequest/TreeReponse conversation to exchange Merkle trees with neighboring nodes. The Merkle tree is a hash representing the data in that column family. If the trees from the different nodes don't match, they have to be reconciled (or "repaired") in order to determine the latest data values they should all be set to. This tree comparison validation is the responsibility of the org.apache.cassandra.service.AntiEntropy Service class. AntiEntropyService implements the Singleton pattern and defines the static `Differencer` class as well, which is used to compare two trees. If it finds any differences, it launches a repair for the ranges that don't agree.

So although Cassandra takes care of such matters automatically on occasion, you can run it yourself as well.

 Anti-entropy is used in Amazon's Dynamo, and Cassandra's implementation is modeled on that (see Section 4.7 of the Dynamo paper if you have an academic interest).

The `repair` command, unlike other Nodetool commands, requires passing the name of the particular keyspace you want to repair:

```
$ bin/nodetool repair Keyspace1 -h 192.168.1.7
```

After running the tool, you'll see some moderate output in your server logs, similar to this:

```
DEBUG 13:34:59,683 Started deliverAllHints
 INFO 13:34:59,684 Compacting []
DEBUG 13:34:59,684 Expected bloom filter size : 128
DEBUG 13:34:59,685 Finished deliverAllHints
```

What's a Merkle tree?

A Merkle tree, named for its inventor, Ralph Merkle, is also known as a "hash tree." It's a data structure represented as a binary tree, and it's useful because it summarizes in short form the data in a larger data set. In a hash tree, the leaves are the data blocks (typically files on a filesystem) to be summarized. Every parent node in the tree is a hash of its direct child node, which tightly compacts the summary.

In Cassandra, the Merkle tree is implemented in the `org.apache.cassandra.utils` `.MerkleTree` class.

Merkle trees are used in Cassandra to ensure that the peer-to-peer network of nodes receives data blocks unaltered and unharmed. They are also used in cryptography to verify the contents of files and transmissions, and are used in the Google Wave product as well.

 Because major compaction is a complex and sensitive operation, it's a good idea to run it only infrequently (not every day) and during low-traffic periods.

Flush

Data is stored in a memtable. To force a write of the data from the memtable to the SSTable on the filesystem, you can use the `flush` command on Nodetool, like this:

```
bin/nodetool flush -h 192.168.1.1 -p 9160
```

If you check the server logs, you'll see output similar to this:

```
DEBUG 15:16:33,945 Forcing binary flush on keyspace Keyspace1, CF Standard2
DEBUG 15:16:33,945 Forcing flush on keyspace Keyspace1, CF Standard2
INFO 15:16:33,945 Standard2 has reached its threshold;
 switching in a fresh Memtable at
 CommitLogContext(file='/var/lib/cassandra/commitlog/CommitLog-1277663698134.log',
 position=1390)
//etc
INFO 15:16:34,104 Completed flushing /var/lib/cassandra/data/Keyspace1/
Standard2-3-Data.db
```

Cleanup

Say that you've had a cluster running for some time, and you want to change the replication factor or the replication strategy. That's possible, but with two caveats. First, these are not intended to be performed on a live cluster, and therefore will likely require you to bring nodes down and then back up, even if you've reloaded the configuration dynamically. Second, you will want to run a Nodetool cleanup afterward to make sure that everything is OK.

You can execute Nodetool with the `cleanup` argument and the node you want to clean:

```
$ bin/nodetool cleanup -h 192.168.1.7
```

This will execute and then immediately return control to the terminal. Essentially this will run an anti-compaction on the specified node.

Snapshots

The purpose of a snapshot is to make a copy of some or all of the keyspaces in a node and save it to what is essentially a separate database file. This means that you can back up the keyspaces elsewhere or leave them where they are in case you need to restore them later.

Taking a Snapshot

When you take a snapshot of one or more keyspaces, Cassandra delegates the call to the `Table` class, which then calls the snapshot method on every column family. This just uses Java's file facilities to create a copy of the SSTables. Note the implication here: if data exists only in the commit log, it will *not* be part of the snapshot. Only data that has been previously flushed will be part of the snapshot, because the storage service basically performs a direct file copy.

 To perform a flush before taking a snapshot, see "Flush" on page 213.

Taking a snapshot is straightforward:

```
$ bin/nodetool -h 192.168.1.5 snapshot
```

This will print out in the server logs an indication that a snapshot has been taken:

```
DEBUG 14:25:15,385 Snapshot for Keyspace1 table data file
/var/lib/cassandra/data/Keyspace1/Standard2-1-Filter.db
created as /var/lib/cassandra/data/Keyspace1/snapshots/1277673915365/
Standard2-1-Filter.db

DEBUG 14:25:15,424 Snapshot for system table data file
/var/lib/cassandra/data/system/LocationInfo-9-Filter.db
created as /var/lib/cassandra/data/system/snapshots/1277673915389/
LocationInfo-9-Filter.d
```

Notice that the snapshot has been placed in a folder named for the timestamp at which it was taken, in its own datafile ending with a *.db* extension, like Cassandra's regular data tables. Here, a snapshot has been taken for all of the keyspaces on the server, including Cassandra's internal keyspace system.

If you want to specify only a single keyspace to take a snapshot of, you can pass it as an additional argument:

```
$ bin/nodetool -h 192.168.1.5 snapshot Keyspace1
```

 You don't have to move the snapshots somewhere else for backups. In case a node's datafile gets corrupted, it will be much easier to restore if you leave them where Cassandra writes them.

If you want to restore a snapshot that you have previously taken, there are a few simple steps to follow. Simply shut down the node and remove the old SSTables and commit logs. Then, copy all the files from the snapshot directory into the regular data directory.

Clearing a Snapshot

You can also delete any snapshots you've made, say, after you've backed them up to permanent storage elsewhere. To clear your snapshots, use the clearsnapshot switch on Nodetool.

You'll see output on the server like this:

```
DEBUG 14:45:00,490 Disseminating load info ...
DEBUG 14:45:11,797 Removing snapshot directory
  /var/lib/cassandra/data/Keyspace1/snapshots
DEBUG 14:45:11,798 Deleting Standard2-1-Index.db
DEBUG 14:54:45,727 Deleting 1277675283388-Keyspace1

//...clearing out other data files

DEBUG 14:54:45,728 Deleting snapshots
DEBUG 14:45:11,806 Cleared out all snapshot directories
```

Note the behavior here: all snapshots are cleared, including those stored with the system table for this keyspace.

Load-Balancing the Cluster

If you find that your cluster is becoming unbalanced, perhaps because many keys were inserted within a certain range, you can redistribute data in order to balance out your cluster.

loadbalance and streams

Executing Nodetool with the loadbalance switch will decommission a node, sending its tokens to other nodes, and then bootstrap it again. The loadbalance command is essentially a convenience wrapper around performing two separate tasks: decommis sion and boostrap.

You can monitor your load-balancing operation, which can take some time if you have a lot of data, by issuing the stream switch to Nodetool.

Here we issue the loadbalance argument to Nodetool to start sending data from 1.5 to other nodes:

```
$ bin/nodetool -host 192.168.1.5 loadbalance
```

This will begin the load-balancing process. While that's happening, we can check the status by using the streams argument with the host we want to check out, and then make sure that our other node is still OK:

```
eben@morpheus$ bin/nodetool streams -h 192.168.1.5
Mode: Leaving: streaming data to other nodes
Not sending any streams.
Not receiving any streams.

eben@morpheus$ bin/nodetool streams -h 192.168.1.7
Mode: Normal
Not sending any streams.
Not receiving any streams.
```

Once the load balancing is complete, we can check the logs to see what happened during the balancing.

Here we can see that the node on 1.5 started leaving the cluster after we load balanced, sending its data to the other node, then bootstrapped itself, and then started accepting data again. This has the effect of load balancing.

```
DEBUG 10:46:58,727 Leaving: old token was 20846671262228904429329344717290588342
DEBUG 10:46:58,746 Pending ranges:
/192.168.1.7:
(41654880048427970483049687892424207188,
20846671262228904429329344717290588342]

 INFO 10:46:58,746 Leaving: sleeping 30000 for pending range setup
DEBUG 10:46:59,323 Disseminating load info ...
DEBUG 10:47:28,748 Node /192.168.1.5 ranges
[(41654880048427970483049687892424207188,20846671262228904429329344717290588342]]
DEBUG 10:47:28,749 Range
(41654880048427970483049687892424207188,20846671262228904429329344717290588342]
will be responsibility of /192.168.1.7
DEBUG 10:47:28,750 Ranges needing transfer are
[(41654880048427970483049687892424207188,20846671262228904429329344717290588342]]
 INFO 10:47:28,750 Leaving: streaming data to other nodes
DEBUG 10:47:28,753 Beginning transfer process to /192.168.1.7 for ranges
(41654880048427970483049687892424207188,20846671262228904429329344717290588342]
 INFO 10:47:28,753 Flushing memtables for Keyspace1...
 INFO 10:47:28,753 Performing anticompaction ...
DEBUG 10:47:28,754 waiting for stream aks.
 INFO 10:47:28,754 AntiCompacting [org.apache.cassandra.io.SSTableReader(
path='/var/lib/cassandra/data/Keyspace1/Standard2-1-Data.db')]
DEBUG 10:47:28,755 index size for bloom filter calc for file  :
/var/lib/cassandra/data/Keyspace1/Standard2-1-Data.db   : 256
DEBUG 10:47:28,755 Expected bloom filter size : 128
 INFO 10:47:28,886 AntiCompacted to /var/lib/cassandra/data/Keyspace1/stream/
Standard2-2-Data.db.
239/239 bytes for 1 keys.  Time: 131ms.
 INFO 10:47:28,887 AntiCompacting []
DEBUG 10:47:28,887 Expected bloom filter size : 128
 INFO 10:47:28,888 AntiCompacting []
 INFO 10:47:28,892 Stream context metadata /var/lib/cassandra/data/Keyspace1/stream/
Standard2-2-Index.db:55,
1 sstables./var/lib/cassandra/data/Keyspace1/stream/Standard2-2-Filter.db:325,
1 sstables./var/lib/cassandra/data/Keyspace1/stream/Standard2-2-Data.db:239
DEBUG 10:47:28,893 Adding file /var/lib/cassandra/data/Keyspace1/stream/
Standard2-2-Index.db to be streamed.
DEBUG 10:47:28,893 Adding file /var/lib/cassandra/data/Keyspace1/stream/
Standard2-2-Filter.db to be streamed.
DEBUG 10:47:28,893 Adding file /var/lib/cassandra/data/Keyspace1/stream/
Standard2-2-Data.db to be streamed.
 INFO 10:47:28,895 Sending a stream initiate message to /192.168.1.7 ...
DEBUG 10:47:28,895 attempting to connect to /192.168.1.7
 INFO 10:47:28,895 Waiting for transfer to /192.168.1.7 to complete
DEBUG 10:47:29,309 Running  on default stage
DEBUG 10:47:29,310 Received a stream initiate done message ...
DEBUG 10:47:29,310 Streaming 55 length file /var/lib/cassandra/data/Keyspace1/stream/
```

```
Standard2-2-Index.db ...
DEBUG 10:47:29,316 Bytes transferred 55
DEBUG 10:47:29,316 Done streaming /var/lib/cassandra/data/Keyspace1/stream/
Standard2-2-Index.db
DEBUG 10:47:29,331 Running  on default stage
DEBUG 10:47:29,332 Deleting file /var/lib/cassandra/data/Keyspace1/stream/
Standard2-2-Index.db after streaming
55/619 bytes.
DEBUG 10:47:29,332 Streaming 325 length file /var/lib/cassandra/data/Keyspace1/stream/
Standard2-2-Filter.db ...
DEBUG 10:47:29,335 Bytes transferred 325
DEBUG 10:47:29,335 Done streaming /var/lib/cassandra/data/Keyspace1/stream/
Standard2-2-Filter.db
DEBUG 10:47:29,345 Running  on default stage
DEBUG 10:47:29,345 Deleting file /var/lib/cassandra/data/Keyspace1/stream/
Standard2-2-Filter.db after streaming
325/619 bytes.
DEBUG 10:47:29,345 Streaming 239 length file /var/lib/cassandra/data/Keyspace1/
stream/Standard2-2-Data.db ...
DEBUG 10:47:29,347 Bytes transferred 239
DEBUG 10:47:29,347 Done streaming /var/lib/cassandra/data/Keyspace1/stream/
Standard2-2-Data.db
DEBUG 10:47:29,389 Running  on default stage
DEBUG 10:47:29,390 Deleting file /var/lib/cassandra/data/Keyspace1/stream/
Standard2-2-Data.db after streaming
239/619 bytes.
DEBUG 10:47:29,390 Signalling that streaming is done for /192.168.1.7
 INFO 10:47:29,390 Done with transfer to /192.168.1.7
DEBUG 10:47:29,391 stream acks all received.
DEBUG 10:47:29,392 No bootstrapping or leaving nodes -> empty pending ranges
for Keyspace1
DEBUG 10:48:59,322 Disseminating load info ...
DEBUG 10:49:01,406 Processing response on a callback from 191997@/192.168.1.7
 INFO 10:49:01,406 New token will be 134439585115453215112331952664863163581 to
assume load from /192.168.1.7
 INFO 10:49:01,407 re-bootstrapping to new token
134439585115453215112331952664863163581
 INFO 10:49:01,407 Joining: sleeping 30000 for pending range setup
 INFO 10:49:31,408 Bootstrapping
DEBUG 10:49:31,408 Beginning bootstrap process
DEBUG 10:49:31,413 Added /192.168.1.7/Keyspace1 as a bootstrap source
DEBUG 10:49:31,414 Requesting from /192.168.1.7 ranges
(41654880048427970483049687892424207188,134439585115453215112331952664863163581]
DEBUG 10:49:32,097 Running  on default stage
DEBUG 10:49:32,098 StreamInitiateVerbeHandler.doVerb STREAM_INITIATE 10579
```

Let's look a little more closely at the steps Cassandra goes through to achieve the load
balancing. We see several things happen in this output. First, Cassandra inspects the
cluster nodes available and the token ranges on each. It then creates a list of the database
files on the 1.5 server that need to be streamed. Because the `Standard2` column family
has data, it will move its Index, Data, and Filter file values to another node (in this case,
the 1.7 node). The 1.5 node then sends a `stream initiate` message to the 1.7 node to
indicate that it's going to start streaming its data to that node. The bytes are then
transferred, and once 1.7 acknowledges receipt of the data, the local files are deleted

from 1.5 and the server is decommissioned for a moment. Immediately, the 1.5 node returns, and gossip indicates to the cluster that it's available to start receiving data. New range tokens are assigned, and the 1.5 node starts assuming some of the load from the 1.7 server.

If we now execute Nodetool with the `ring` argument, we see that new ranges have been assigned to the nodes, and they both have roughly the same amount of data:

```
Address         Status    Load     Range                                          Ring
                                   134439585115453215112331952664863163581
192.168.1.7     Up        3.53 KB  41654880048427970483049687892424207188         |<--|
192.168.1.5     Up        2.95 KB  134439585115453215112331952664863163581        |-->|
```

Decommissioning a Node

Decommissioning a node means pulling it out of service. When you call `decommission` on Nodetool, you're calling the decommission operation on Cassandra's `Storage Service` class.

Say that we have two nodes in the ring:

```
eben@morpheus$ bin/nodetool -host 192.168.1.5 ring
Address         Status    Load     Range                                          Ring
                                   134439585115453215112331952664863163581
192.168.1.7     Up        4.17 KB  41654880048427970483049687892424207188         |<--|
192.168.1.5     Up        3.59 KB  134439585115453215112331952664863163581        |-->|
```

Now we want to decommission the 1.7 node. You can issue the `decommission` argument to Nodetool to pull one of the nodes out of service, as shown here:

```
$ bin/nodetool decommission -h 192.168.1.7
```

After issuing this command, it will wait for some time, as configured. By default, this is 30 seconds. Nodetool won't print anything further, but the server logs will. On our 1.5 node—the node that we're keeping—we see the following output after issuing the `decommission` command:

```
DEBUG 13:59:00,488 Disseminating load info ...
DEBUG 13:59:40,010 Node /192.168.1.7 state leaving, token
41654880048427970483049687892424207188
DEBUG 13:59:40,022 Pending ranges:
/192.168.1.5:
(134439585115453215112331952664863163581,41654880048427970483049687892424207188]

DEBUG 14:00:00,488 Disseminating load info ...
DEBUG 14:00:10,184 Running  on default stage
DEBUG 14:00:10,184 StreamInitiateVerbeHandler.doVerb STREAM_INITIATE 4084
DEBUG 14:00:10,187 no data needed from /192.168.1.7
DEBUG 14:00:10,551 Node /192.168.1.7 state left, token
41654880048427970483049687892424207188
DEBUG 14:00:10,552 No bootstrapping or leaving nodes -> empty pending ranges for
Keyspace1
  INFO 14:00:18,049 InetAddress /192.168.1.7 is now dead.
```

The gossiper tells 1.5 that it's in a leaving state. In this particular case, it didn't need to stream data from 1.7 because it was already balanced, and then 1.5 is given the news: 1.7 is dead. If we run `nodetool -h <ip> ring` at this point, our 1.7 node has indeed fallen off the list.

Meanwhile, in the server logs for the node we decommissioned, we see the following output:

```
INFO 13:37:36,299 InetAddress /192.168.1.5 is now UP
INFO 13:59:40,929 Leaving: sleeping 30000 for pending range setup
INFO 14:00:11,286 Leaving: streaming data to other nodes
INFO 14:00:11,318 Flushing memtables for Keyspace1...
INFO 14:00:11,318 Performing anticompaction ...
INFO 14:00:11,333 AntiCompacting [org.apache.cassandra.io.SSTableReader(path='c
:\var\lib\cassandra\data\Keyspace1\Standard2-2-Data.db'),org.apache.cassandra.io
.SSTableReader(path='c:\var\lib\cassandra\data\Keyspace1\Standard2-1-Data.db')]
INFO 14:00:11,349 AntiCompacting []
INFO 14:00:11,364 AntiCompacting []
INFO 14:00:11,411 Stream context metadata
INFO 14:00:11,427 Sending a stream initiate message to /192.168.1.5 ...
INFO 14:00:13,455 Shutting down MessageService...
INFO 14:00:13,455 Shutdown complete (no further commands will be processed)
INFO 14:00:13,470 Decommissioned
INFO 14:00:13,470 MessagingService shutting down server thread.
```

The node starts out aware of 1.5, then receives the `decommission` command. It enters the leaving state and sleeps for 30 seconds to make sure it has enough time to gather all the necessary range information. The memtables are flushed from memory to disk in the SSTables, and an anti-compaction is performed on the data. It then initiates a stream to transfer its data to the 1.5 node as necessary. Finally, it shuts down.

If you call `decommission` on a node that can't be decommissioned (i.e., one that isn't part of the ring yet, or on the only node available), you'll see an error message to that effect. The basic steps that are executed during a decommission are:

1. The gossiper is shut down so it doesn't receive more data.
2. The messaging service is shut down for this node.
3. The SEDA stage manager is shut down, because it won't accept more work to move through a stage.
4. The mode is set to "decommissioned".
5. The storage service determines what available nodes can receive data appropriate for the ranges that need transferring. The data is streamed to other nodes.
6. Once the receiving node acknowledges successful transfer of the data and has no more to transfer, the server can leave the ring.

 Be warned that data is not automatically removed from a decommissioned node. If you decide that you want to reintroduce a previously decommissioned node into the ring with a different range, you'll need to manually delete its data first.

Updating Nodes

Removing Tokens

If you wish to remove a token, you can do so with Nodetool.

Simply execute the command like this, where the argument to the removetoken command is the actual token you want to remove:

```
$ bin/nodetool -h 127.0.0.1 removetoken 42218023250148343019074760608074740927
```

The client will return without comment on success. Note that you cannot remove a node's own token, as that would destroy the node's integrity. You can connect to node 1 and use it to remove a given token, wherever it is on the ring.

Compaction Threshold

The compaction threshold refers to the number of SSTables that are in the queue to be compacted before a minor compaction is actually kicked off. By default, the minimum number is 4 and the maximum is 32. You don't want this number to be too small, or Cassandra will spend time fighting with clients for resources to perform many frequent, unnecessary compactions. You also don't want this number to be too large, or Cassandra could spend a lot of resources performing many compactions at once, and therefore will have fewer resources available for clients.

To find out the compaction threshold on a given node, invoke Nodetool with the getcompactionthreshold command:

```
eben@morpheus$ bin/nodetool -h 192.168.1.5 getcompactionthreshold
Current compaction threshold: Min=4, Max=32
```

Changing Column Families in a Working Cluster

If you need to, you can add, remove, or rename column families in a live Cassandra cluster. Here are the steps to follow:

1. Using Nodetool, run *drain* to empty the commit log.
2. Shut down Cassandra and make sure that there's no remaining data in the commit log.
3. Delete the SSTable files. These files are in your data directory and are named *<cf>-Data.db*, *<cf>-Index.db*, and *<cf>-Filter.db*, looking only for the files prefixed with the name of the column family you want to change. Rename these files in a corresponding fashion.

Summary

In this chapter we looked at some of the ways you can interact with Cassandra to perform routine operational maintenance tasks. We saw how to get statistics, how to rebalance lopsided nodes, how to take a snapshot of your database for backup purposes, how to decommission nodes, and more.

## CHAPTER 11

Performance Tuning

In this chapter, we look at how to tune Cassandra to improve performance. A variety of settings in the configuration file help us do this, and we present a few pointers on hardware selection and configuration. There are several isolated settings that you can update in Cassandra's configuration file; although the defaults are often appropriate, there might be circumstances in which you need to change them. In this chapter, we look at several of those settings.

As a general rule, it's important to note that simply adding nodes to a cluster will not improve performance on its own. You need to replicate the data appropriately, then send traffic to all the nodes from your clients. If you aren't distributing client requests, the new nodes could just stand by somewhat idle.

We also see how to use the Python stress test tool that ships with Cassandra to run a reasonable load against Cassandra and quickly see how it behaves under stress test circumstances. We can then tune Cassandra appropriately and feel confident that we're ready to launch in a staging environment.

Data Storage

There are two sets of files that Cassandra writes to as part of handling update operations: the commit log and the datafile. Their different purposes need to be considered in order to understand how to treat them during configuration.

The *commit log* can be thought of as short-term storage. As Cassandra receives updates, every write value is written immediately to the commit log in the form of raw sequential file appends. If you shut down the database or it crashes unexpectedly, the commit log can ensure that data is not lost. That's because the next time you start the node, the commit log gets replayed. In fact, that's the only time the commit log is read; clients never read from it. But the normal write operation to the commit log blocks, so it would damage performance to require clients to wait for the write to finish.

The *datafile* represents the Sorted String Tables (SSTables). Unlike the commit log, data is written to this file asynchronously. The SSTables are periodically merged during major compactions to free up space. To do this, Cassandra will merge keys, combine columns, and delete tombstones.

Read operations can refer to the in-memory cache and in this case don't need to go directly to the datafiles on disk. If you can allow Cassandra a few gigabytes of memory, you can improve performance dramatically when the row cache and the key cache are hit.

The commit logs are periodically removed, following a successful flush of all their appended data to the dedicated datafiles. For this reason, the commit logs will not grow to anywhere near the size of the datafiles, so the disks don't need to be as large; this is something to consider during hardware selection. For example, if Cassandra runs a flush, you'll see something in the server logs like this:

```
INFO 18:26:11,497 Enqueuing flush of Memtable-LocationInfo@26830618(52 bytes, 2
operations)
INFO 18:26:11,497 Writing Memtable-LocationInfo@26830618(52 bytes, 2 operations)
INFO 18:26:11,732 Completed flushing /var/lib/cassandra/data/system/
LocationInfo-2-Data.db
INFO 18:26:11,732 Discarding obsolete commit log:
   CommitLogSegment(/var/lib/cassandra/commitlog/CommitLog-1278894011530.log)
```

Then, if you check the commit log directory, that file has been deleted.

By default, the commit log and the datafile are stored in the following locations:

```
<CommitLogDirectory>/var/lib/cassandra/commitlog</CommitLogDirectory>

<DataFileDirectories>
   <DataFileDirectory>/var/lib/cassandra/data</DataFileDirectory>
</DataFileDirectories>
```

You can change these values to store the datafiles or commit log in different locations. You can specify multiple datafile directories if you wish.

 You don't need to update these values for Windows, even if you leave them in the default location, because Windows will automatically adjust the path separator and place them under *C:*. Of course, in a real environment, it's a good idea to specify them separately, as indicated.

For testing, you might not see a need to change these locations. However, it's recommended that you store the datafiles and the commit logs on separate hard disks for maximum performance. Cassandra, like many databases, is particularly dependent on the speed of the hard disk and the speed of the CPUs (it's best to have four or eight cores, to take advantage of Cassandra's highly concurrent construction). So make sure for QA and production environments to get the fastest disks you can, and get at least two separate ones so that the commit logfiles and the datafiles are not competing for

I/O time. It's more important to have several processing cores than one or two very fast ones.

Reply Timeout

The reply timeout is a setting that indicates how long Cassandra will wait for other nodes to respond before deciding that the request is a failure. This is a common setting in relational databases and messaging systems. This value is set by the `RpcTimeoutIn Millis` element (`rpc_timeout_in_ms` in YAML). By default, this is 5,000, or five seconds.

Commit Logs

You can set the value for how large the commit log is allowed to grow before it stops appending new writes to a file and creates a new one. This is similar to setting log rotation on Log4J.

This value is set with the `CommitLogRotationThresholdInMB` element (`commitlog_rota tion_threshold_in_mb` in YAML). By default, the value is 128MB.

Another setting related to commit logs is the sync operation, represented by the `commitlog_sync` element. There are two possible settings for this: `periodic` and `batch`. `periodic` is the default, and it means that the server will make writes durable only at specified intervals. When the server is set to make writes durable periodically, you can potentially lose the data that has not yet been synced to disk from the write-behind cache.

In order to guarantee durability for your Cassandra cluster, you may want to examine this setting.

If your commit log is set to `batch`, it will block until the write is synced to disk (Cassandra will not acknowledge write operations until the commit log has been completely synced to disk). This clearly will have a negative impact on performance.

You can change the value of the configuration attribute from `periodic` to `batch` to specify that Cassandra must flush to disk before it acknowledges a write. Changing this value will require taking some performance metrics, as there is a necessary trade-off here: forcing Cassandra to write more immediately constrains its freedom to manage its own resources. If you do set `commitlog_sync` to `batch`, you need to provide a suitable value for `CommitLogSyncBatchWindowInMS`, where MS is the number of milliseconds between each sync effort. Moreover, this is not generally needed in a multinode cluster when using write replication, because replication by definition means that the write isn't acknowledged until another node has it.

If you decide to use `batch` mode, you will probably want to split the commit log onto a separate device to mitigate the performance impact. It's a good idea to split it out onto a separate disk from the SSTables (data) anyway, even if you don't do this.

Memtables

Each column family has a single memtable associated with it. There are a few settings around the treatment of memtables. The size that the memtable can grow to before it is flushed to disk as an SSTable is specified with the `MemtableSizeInMB` element (`binary_memtable_throughput_in_mb` in YAML). Note that this value is based on the size of the memtable itself in memory, and not heap usage, which will be larger because of the overhead associated with column indexing.

You'll want to balance this setting with `MemtableObjectCountInMillions`, which sets a threshold for the number of column values that will be stored in a memtable before it is flushed.

A related configurable setting is `memtable_throughput_in_mb`. This refers to the maximum number of columns that will be stored in a single memtable before the memtable is flushed to disk as an SSTable. The default value is 0.3, which is approximately 333,000 columns.

You can also configure how long to keep memtables in memory after they've been flushed to disk. This value can be set with the `memtable_flush_after_mins` element. When the flush is performed, it will write to a flush buffer, and you can configure the size of that buffer with `flush_data_buffer_size_in_mb`.

Another element related to tuning the memtables is `memtable_flush_writers`. This setting, which is 1 by default, indicates the number of threads used to write out the memtables when it becomes necessary. If you have a very large heap, it can improve performance to set this count higher, as these threads are blocked during disk I/O.

Concurrency

Cassandra differs from many data stores in that it offers much faster write performance than read performance. There are two settings related to how many threads can perform read and write operations: `concurrent_reads` and `concurrent_writes`. In general, the defaults provided by Cassandra out of the box are very good. But you might want to update the `concurrent_reads` setting immediately before you start your server. That's because the `concurrent_reads` setting is optimal at two threads per processor core. By default, this setting is 8, assuming a four-core box. If that's what you have, you're in business. If you have an eight-core box, tune it up to 16.

The `concurrent_writes` setting behaves somewhat differently. This should match the number of clients that will write concurrently to the server. If Cassandra is backing a web application server, you can tune this setting from its default of 32 to match the number of threads the application server has available to connect to Cassandra. It is common in Java application servers such as WebLogic to prefer database connection pools no larger than 20 or 30, but if you're using several application servers in a cluster, you'll need to factor that in as well.

Caching

There are several settings related to caching, both within Cassandra and at the operating system level. Caches can use considerable memory, and it's a good idea to tune them carefully once you understand your usage patterns.

There are two primary caches built into Cassandra: a row cache and a key cache. The row cache caches complete rows (all of their columns), so it is a superset of the key cache. If you are using a row cache for a given column family, you will not need to use a key cache on it as well.

Your caching strategy should therefore be tuned in accordance with a few factors:

- Consider your queries, and use the cache type that best fits your queries.
- Consider the ratio of your heap size to your cache size, and do not allow the cache to overwhelm your heap.
- Consider the size of your rows against the size of your keys. Typically keys will be much smaller than entire rows.

The `keys_cached` setting indicates the number of key locations—not key values—that will be saved in memory. This can be specified as a fractional value (a number between 0 and 1) or as an integer. If you use a fraction, you're indicating a percentage of keys to cache, and an integer value indicates an absolute number of keys whose locations will be cached.

 The `keys_cached` setting is a per-column family setting, so different column families can have different numbers of key locations cached if some are used more frequently than others.

This setting will consume considerable memory, but can be a good trade-off if your locations are not hot already.

The purpose of `disk_access_mode` is to enable memory mapped files so that the operating system can cache reads, thus reducing the load on Cassandra's internal caches. This sounds great, but in practice, `disk_access_mode` is one of the less-useful settings, and at this point doesn't work exactly as was originally envisioned. This may be improved in the future, but it is just as likely that the setting will be removed. Certainly feel free to play around with it, but you might not see much difference.

You can also populate the row cache when the server starts up. To do this, use the `preload_row_cache` element. The default setting for this is false, but you will want to set it to true to improve performance. The cost is that bootstrapping can take longer if there is considerable data in the column family to preload.

The `rows_cached` setting specifies the number of rows that will be cached. By default, this value is set to `0`, meaning that no rows will be cached, so it's a good idea to turn this on. If you use a fraction, you're indicating a percentage of everything to cache, and an integer value indicates an absolute number of rows whose locations will be cached. You'll want to use this setting carefully, however, as this can easily get out of hand. If your column family gets far more reads than writes, then setting this number very high will needlessly consume considerable server resources. If your column family has a lower ratio of reads to writes, but has rows with lots of data in them (hundreds of columns), then you'll need to do some math before setting this number very high. And unless you have certain rows that get hit a lot and others that get hit very little, you're not going to see much of a boost here.

Buffer Sizes

The buffer sizes represent the memory allocation when performing certain operations. The following is a quick overview of these settings:

flush_data_buffer_size_in_mb
> By default, this is set to 32 megabytes and indicates the size of the buffer to use when memtables get flushed to disk.

flush_index_buffer_size_in_mb
> By default, this is set to 8 megabytes. If each key defines only a few columns, then it's a good idea to increase the index buffer size. Alternatively, if your rows have many columns, then you'll want to decrease the size of the buffer.

sliced_buffer_size_in_kb
> Depending on how variable your queries are, this setting is unlikely to be very useful. It allows you to specify the size, in kilobytes, of the buffer to use when executing slices of adjacent columns. If there is a certain slice query that you perform far more than others, or if your data is laid out with a relatively consistent number of columns per family, then this setting could be moderately helpful on read operations. But note that this setting is defined globally.

Using the Python Stress Test

Cassandra ships with a popular utility called py_stress that you can use to run a stress test on your Cassandra cluster. To run py_stress, navigate to the *<cassandra-home>/ contrib* directory. You might want to check out the *README.txt* file, as it will have the list of dependencies required to run the tool.

There are a few steps we need to go through before we can run the tool. First, make sure that you still have the default keyspace (Keyspace1) in your configuration and have it loaded, as the tool will run against the default column family definitions.

Then, you need to build the Python Thrift interface, which may require a few steps.

Generating the Python Thrift Interfaces

Before we can run the stress tool, we need to make sure that we have the Thrift interfaces for Python available to it (because it's a Python script). You'll know that you haven't done this step yet, or have done it incorrectly, if you see an error like this after running the command:

```
No module named thrift.transport
```

Make sure that you have Python installed on your system. To do this, open a terminal and type **$python**; you should see output similar to this:

```
eben@morpheus$ python
Python 2.6.5 (r265:79063, Apr 16 2010, 13:09:56)
[GCC 4.4.3] on linux2
Type "help", "copyright", "credits" or "license" for more information
```

Make sure that you have Python 2.6 or better installed so that you can take advantage of the newest multithreading capabilities it offers, which come in handy with the stress test.

Getting Thrift

To get Thrift, download it from *http://incubator.apache.org/thrift*. This will give you a file like *thrift-0.2.0-incubating.tar.gz*, which you can decompress. Then, in the directory where you decompressed it, execute the following command on Linux to establish some dependencies:

```
$ sudo apt-get install -y libboost-dev libevent-dev python-dev automake pkg-config
libtool flex bison
```

Thrift might not run on your system if you don't have the C++ Boost libraries properly installed. Get Boost from *http://www.boost.org*. Then, in the Boost home directory, run these commands:

```
$ ./bootstrap.sh
$ ./bjam
```

This should compile and install Boost. Now, to build Thrift, run a series of commands as root from the Thrift home directory:

```
$ ./bootstrap.sh
$ ./configure
$ ./make
$ ./make install
$ cd lib/py
$ ./make
```

Now run the command *$which thrift*. This will tell you where Thrift installed. On my system, this is */usr/local/bin/thrift*.

On Ubuntu Linux, you might see an error such as "autoscan: not found" when trying to install Thrift. Autoscan is also not available via yum or apt-get. In order to get autoscan, which the Thrift bootstrap needs, you'll have to run this command: **$ sudo apt-get install automake**. You can tell whether you have autoscan installed by executing the command **$which autoscan**. If it returns nothing, you don't have it.

If Thrift is installed properly, you should be able to run the Thrift program and see help output:

```
$ thrift -version
Thrift version 0.2.0-exported
```

Put your *site-packages* directory on the Python path:

```
$ export PYTHONPATH=/usr/lib/python2.6/site-packages/
```

Now you can navigate to the *<cassandra-home>* directory. Run the following command to generate the Thrift interfaces for Python:

```
$ ant gen-thrift-py
```

You should see a successful build message. Now you'll have the Cassandra Thrift interfaces for Python generated in the directory *<cassandra-home>/interfaces/thrift/gen-py*. Copy this directory to *<cassandra-home>/contrib/py_stress*. Now just make sure that your Cassandra server is started, and you're ready to run the Python stress test.

Running the Python Stress Test

Now that we're all set up, we can run the stress test. Navigate to the *<cassandra-home>/contrib/py_stress* directory. In a terminal, type **stress.py** to run the test against local host.

If you see a message indicating that the stress test cannot connect to `localhost:9160`, you have a couple of options. First, make sure that your Cassandra server is actually started and listening on that address and port. If you configured Cassandra to listen on your IP or hostname instead of localhost, you can change the script to point where your server is, change your config to listen on localhost, or, probably best, just pass the script the -d option to indicate which node you want to connect to. Here we go:

```
$ stress.py -d 192.168.1.5
```

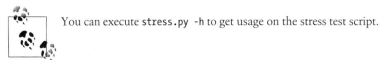 You can execute stress.py -h to get usage on the stress test script.

The test will run until it inserts one million values, and then stop. I ran this test on a single regular workstation with an Intel I7 processor (which is similar to eight cores) with 4GB of RAM available and a lot of other processes running. Here was my output:

```
eben@morpheus$ ./stress.py -d 192.168.1.5 -o insert
total,interval_op_rate,avg_latency,elapsed_time
196499,19649,0.0024959407711,10
370589,17409,0.00282591440216,20
510076,13948,0.00295883878841,30
640813,13073,0.00438663874102,40
798070,15725,0.00312562838215,50
950489,15241,0.0029109908417,60
1000000,4951,0.00444872583334,70
```

Let's unpack this a bit. What we've done is generated and inserted one million values into a completely untuned single node Cassandra server in about 70 seconds. You can see that in the first 10 seconds we inserted 196,499 randomly generated values. The average latency per operation is 0.0025 seconds, or 2.5 milliseconds. But this is using the defaults, and is on a Cassandra server that already has 1GB of data in the database to manage before running the test. Let's give the test more threads to see if we can squeeze a little better performance out of it:

```
eben@morpheus$ ./stress.py -d 192.168.1.5 -o insert -t 10
total,interval_op_rate,avg_latency,elapsed_time
219217,21921,0.000410911544945,10
427199,20798,0.000430060066223,20
629062,20186,0.000443717396772,30
832964,20390,0.000437958271074,40
1000000,16703,0.000463042383339,50
```

What we've done here is used the -t flag to use 10 threads at once. This means that in 50 seconds, we wrote 1,000,000 records—about 2 milliseconds latency per write, with a totally untuned database that is already managing 1.5GB of data.

You should run the test several times to get an idea of the right number of threads given your hardware setup. Depending on the number of cores on your system, you're going to see worse—not better—performance if you set the number of threads arbitrarily high, because the processor will devote more time to managing the threads than doing your work. You want this to be a rough match between the number of threads and the number of cores available to get a reasonable test.

Now that we have all of this data in the database, let's use the test to read some values too:

```
$ ./stress.py -d 192.168.1.5 -o read
total,interval_op_rate,avg_latency,elapsed_time
103960,10396,0.00478858081549,10
225999,12203,0.00406984714627,20
355129,12913,0.00384438665076,30
485728,13059,0.00379976526221,40
617036,13130,0.00378045491559,50
749154,13211,0.003756200621777,60
```

```
880605,13145,0.00377542658007,70
1000000,11939,0.00374060139004,80
```

As you can see, Cassandra doesn't read nearly as fast as it writes; it takes about 80 seconds to read one million values. Remember, though, that this is out of the box, untuned, single-threaded, on a regular workstation running other programs, and the database is 2GB in size. Regardless, this is a great tool to help you do performance tuning for your environment and to get a set of numbers that indicates what to expect in your cluster.

Startup and JVM Settings

Cassandra allows you to configure a variety of options for how the server should start up, how much Java memory should be allocated, and so forth. In this section we look at how to tune the startup.

If you're using Windows, the startup script is called *cassandra.bat*, and on Linux it's *cassandra.sh*. You can start the server by simply executing this file, which sets several defaults. But there's another file in the *bin* directory that allows you to configure a variety of settings related to how Cassandra starts. This file is called *cassandra.in.sh* and it separates certain options, such as the JVM settings, into a different file to make it easier to update.

Tuning the JVM

Try tuning the options passed to the JVM at startup for better performance. The key JVM options included in *cassandra.in.sh* and guidelines for how you might tweak them are illustrated in Table 11-1. If you want to change any of these values, simply open the *cassandra.in.sh* file in a text editor, change the values, and restart.

Table 11-1. Java performance tuning options

Java option	Setting guidelines
Heap Min and Max	By default, these are set to 256MB and 1GB, respectively. To tune these, set them higher (see following note) and to the same value.
Assertions	By default, the JVM is passed the -ea option to enable assertions. Changing this option from -ea to -da (disable assertions) can have a positive effect on performance.
Survivor Ratio	The Java heap is broadly divided into two object spaces: young and old. The young space is subdivided into one for new object allocation (called "eden space") and another for new objects that are still in use. Older objects still have some reference, and have therefore survived a few garbage collections, so the Survivor Ratio is the ratio of eden space to survivor space in the young object part of the heap. Increasing the ratio makes sense for applications with lots of new object creation and low object preservation; decreasing it makes sense for applications with longer-living objects. Cassandra sets this value to 8 by default, meaning that the ratio of eden to survivor space is 1:8 (each survivor space will be 1/8 the size of eden). This is fairly low, because the objects are living longer in the memtables. Tune this setting along with MaxTenuringThreshold.

Java option	Setting guidelines
MaxTenuring Threshold	Every Java object has an age field in its header, indicating how many times it has been copied within the young generation space. They're copied (into a new space) when they survive a young generation garbage collection, and this copying has a cost. Because long-living objects may be copied many times, tuning this value can improve performance. By default, Cassandra has this value set at 1. Set it to 0 to immediately move an object that survives a young generation collection to the tenured generation.
UseConcMarkS weepGC	This instructs the JVM on what garbage collection (GC) strategy to use; specifically, it enables the ConcurrentMarkSweep algorithm. This setting uses more RAM, and uses more CPU power to do frequent garbage collections while the application is running in order to keep the GC pause time to a minimum. When using this strategy, it's important to set the heap min and max values to the same value, in order to prevent the JVM from having to spend a lot of time growing the heap initially. It is possible to tune this to -XX:+UseParallelGC, which also takes advantage of multiprocessor machines; this will give you peak application performance, but with occasional pauses. Do not use the Serial GC with Cassandra.

The majority of options in the include configuration file surround the Java settings. For example, the default setting for the maximum size of the Java heap memory usage is 1GB. If you're on a machine capable of using more, you may want to tune this setting. Try setting the -Xmx and -Xms options to the same value to keep Java from having to manage heap growth.

 The maximum theoretical heap size for a 32-bit JVM is 4GB. However, do not simply set your JVM to use as much memory as you have available up to 4GB. There are many factors involved here, such as the amount of swap space and memory fragmentation. Simply increasing the size of the heap using -Xmx will not help if you don't have any swap available. Typically it is possible to get approximately 1.6GB of heap on a 32-bit JVM on Windows and closer to 2GB on Solaris. Using a 64-bit JVM on a 64-bit system will allow more space. See *http://java.sun.com/docs/hot spot/HotSpotFAQ.html* for more information.

Tuning some of these options will make stress tests perform better. For example, I saw a 15% performance improvement using the following settings over the defaults:

```
JVM_OPTS=" \
        -da \
        -Xms1024M \
        -Xmx1024M \
        -XX:+UseParallelGC \
        -XX:+CMSParallelRemarkEnabled \
        -XX:SurvivorRatio=4 \
        -XX:MaxTenuringThreshold=0
```

When performance tuning, it's a good idea to set only the heap min and max options, and nothing else at first. Only after real-world usage in your environment and some performance benchmarking with the aid of heap analysis tools and observation of your specific application's behavior should you dive into tuning the more advanced JVM settings. If you tune your JVM options and see some success using a load-testing tool or something like the Python stress test in *contrib*, don't get too excited. You need to test under real-world conditions; don't simply copy these settings.

 For more information on Java 6 performance tuning (Java 6 operates differently than previous versions), see *http://java.sun.com/javase/tech nologies/hotspot/gc/gc_tuning_6.html*.

In general, you'll probably want to make sure that you've instructed the heap to dump its state if it hits an out of memory error. This is just good practice if you've been getting out of memory errors. You can also instruct the heap to print garbage-collection details. Also, if you have a lot of data in Cassandra and you're noticing that garbage collection is causing long pauses, you can attempt to cause garbage collection to run when the heap has filled up less memory than it otherwise would take as a threshold to initialize a garbage collection. All of these parameters are shown here:

```
-XX:CMSInitiatingOccupancyFraction=88 \
-XX:+HeapDumpOnOutOfMemoryError \
-XX:+PrintGCDetails -XX:+PrintGCTimeStamps -verbose:gc \
```

Summary

In this chapter we looked at the settings available in Cassandra to aid in performance tuning, including caching settings, memory settings, and hardware concerns. We also set up and used the Python stress test tool to write and then read one million rows of data.

If you're somewhat new to Linux systems and you want to run Cassandra on Linux (which is recommended), you may want to check out Jonathan Ellis's blog entry on using a variety of Linux performance monitoring tools to help you understand the performance of your underlying platform so that you can troubleshoot in the right place. You can find that entry at *http://spyced.blogspot.com/2010/01/linux-performance -basics.html*.

Ultimately, you want to have lots of memory available, and as many processors and cores as you can afford.

## CHAPTER 12

Integrating Hadoop

Jeremy Hanna

As companies and organizations adopt technologies like Cassandra, they look for tools that can be used to perform analytics and queries against their data. The built-in ways to query can do much, along with custom layers atop that. However, there are distributed tools in the community that can be fitted to work with Cassandra as well.

Hadoop seems to be the elephant in the room when it comes to open source big data frameworks. There we find tools such as an open source MapReduce implementation and higher-level analytics engines built on top of that, such as Pig and Hive. Thanks to members of both the Cassandra and Hadoop communities, Cassandra has gained some significant integration points with Hadoop and its analytics tools.

In this chapter, we explore how Cassandra and Hadoop fit together. First, we give a brief history of the Apache Hadoop project and go into how one can write MapReduce programs against data in Cassandra. From there, we cover integration with higher-level tools built on top of Hadoop: Pig and Hive. Once we have an understanding of these tools, we cover how a Cassandra cluster can be configured to run these analytics in a distributed way. Finally, we share a couple of use cases where Cassandra is being used alongside Hadoop to solve real-world problems.

What Is Hadoop?

If you're already familiar with Hadoop, you can safely skip this section. If you haven't had the pleasure, Hadoop (*http://hadoop.apache.org*) is a set of open source projects that deal with large amounts of data in a distributed way. Its Hadoop distributed filesystem (HDFS) and MapReduce subprojects are open source implementations of Google's GFS and MapReduce.

Google found that several internal groups had been implementing similar functionality in order to solve problems in a distributed way. They saw that it was common to have two phases of operations over distributed data: a map phase and a reduce phase. A map function operates over raw data and produces intermediate values. A reduce function distills those intermediate values in some way, producing the final output for that MapReduce computation. By standardizing on a common framework, they could build more solutions to problems rather than new models of the same wheel.

Doug Cutting decided to write open source implementations of the Google File System (*http://labs.google.com/papers/gfs.html*) and MapReduce (*http://labs.google.com/papers/mapreduce.html*), and thus, Hadoop was born. Since then, it has blossomed into myriad tools, all dealing with solutions for big data problems. Today, Hadoop is widely used, by Yahoo!, Facebook, LinkedIn, Twitter, IBM, Rackspace, and many other companies. There is a vibrant community and a growing ecosystem.

Cassandra has built-in support for the Hadoop implementation of MapReduce (*http://hadoop.apache.org/mapreduce*).

Working with MapReduce

This section covers details on how to write a simple MapReduce job over data stored in Cassandra using the Java language. We also briefly cover how to output data into Cassandra and discuss ongoing progress with using Cassandra with Hadoop Streaming for languages beyond Java.

> The word count example given in this section is also found in the Cassandra source download in its *contrib* module. It can be compiled and run using instructions found there. It is best to run with that code, as the current version might have minor modifications. However, the principles remain the same.

For convenience, the word count MapReduce example can be run locally against a single Cassandra node. However, for more information on how to configure Cassandra and Hadoop to run MapReduce in a more distributed fashion, see the section "Cluster Configuration" on page 241.

Cassandra Hadoop Source Package

Cassandra has a Java source package for Hadoop integration code, called `org.apache.cassandra.hadoop`. There we find:

ColumnFamilyInputFormat
    The main class we'll use to interact with data stored in Cassandra from Hadoop. It's an extension of Hadoop's `InputFormat` abstract class.

ConfigHelper
    A helper class to configure Cassandra-specific information such as the server node to point to, the port, and information specific to your MapReduce job.

ColumnFamilySplit

>The extension of Hadoop's `InputSplit` abstract class that creates splits over our Cassandra data. It also provides Hadoop with the location of the data, so that it may prefer running tasks on nodes where the data is stored.

ColumnFamilyRecordReader

>The layer at which individual records from Cassandra are read. It's an extension of Hadoop's `RecordReader` abstract class.

There are similar classes for outputting data to Cassandra in the Hadoop package, but at the time of this writing, those classes are still being finalized.

Running the Word Count Example

Word count is one of the examples given in the MapReduce paper and is the starting point for many who are new to the framework. It takes a body of text and counts the occurrences of each distinct word. Here we provide some code to perform a word count over data contained in Cassandra. A working example of word count is also included in the Cassandra source download.

First we need a `Mapper` class, shown in Example 12-1.

Example 12-1. The TokenizerMapper.java class

```java
public static class TokenizerMapper extends Mapper<byte[],
    SortedMap<byte[], IColumn>, Text, IntWritable> {

  private final static IntWritable one = new IntWritable(1);
  private Text word = new Text();
  private String columnName;

  public void map(byte[] key, SortedMap<byte[], IColumn> columns, Context context)
    throws IOException, InterruptedException {

    IColumn column = columns.get(columnName.getBytes());
    String value = new String(column.value());
    StringTokenizer itr = new StringTokenizer(value);

    while (itr.hasMoreTokens()) {
      word.set(itr.nextToken());
      context.write(word, one);
    }
  }

  protected void setup(Context context)
    throws IOException, InterruptedException {

    this.columnName = context.getConfiguration().get("column_name");
  }
}
```

Readers familiar with MapReduce programs will notice how familiar this mapper looks. In this case, the inputs to the mapper are row keys and associated row values from Cassandra. Row values in the world of Cassandra are simply maps containing the column information. In addition to the word count code itself, we override the setup method to set the column name we are looking for. The rest of the mapper code is generic to any word count implementation.

 When iterating over super columns in your mapper, each `IColumn` would need to be cast to a `SuperColumn`, and it would contain nested column information.

Next, let's look at a `Reducer` implementation for our word count, shown in Example 12-2.

Example 12-2. The Reducer implementation

```
public static class IntSumReducer extends
  Reducer<Text, IntWritable, Text, IntWritable> {

  private IntWritable result = new IntWritable();

  public void reduce(Text key, Iterable<IntWritable> values, Context context)
    throws IOException, InterruptedException {

    int sum = 0;
    for (IntWritable val : values) {
      sum += val.get();
    }
    result.set(sum);
    context.write(key, result);
  }
}
```

There should be nothing surprising in this reducer; nothing is Cassandra-specific.

Finally, we get to the class that runs our MapReduce program, shown in Example 12-3.

Example 12-3. The WordCount class runs the MapReduce program

```
public class WordCount extends Configured implements Tool {

  public int run(String[] args) throws Exception {
    Job job = new Job(getConf(), "wordcount");
    job.setJarByClass(WordCount.class);
    job.setMapperClass(TokenizerMapper.class);
    job.setCombinerClass(IntSumReducer.class);
    job.setReducerClass(IntSumReducer.class);
    job.setOutputKeyClass(Text.class);
    job.setOutputValueClass(IntWritable.class);
    job.setInputFormatClass(ColumnFamilyInputFormat.class);
```

```
    FileOutputFormat.setOutputPath(job, new Path("/tmp/word_count"));
    ConfigHelper.setThriftContact(job.getConfiguration(), "localhost", 9160);
    ConfigHelper.setInputColumnFamily(
        job.getConfiguration(), "Keyspace1", "Standard1");

    SlicePredicate predicate = new SlicePredicate().setColumn_names(
        Arrays.asList(columnName.getBytes()));

    ConfigHelper.setInputSlicePredicate(job.getConfiguration(), predicate);
    job.waitForCompletion(true);

    return 0;
  }
}
```

There are a few things to note about the WordCount class that go beyond a boilerplate word count. We need to set the InputFormat to Cassandra's ColumnFamilyInputFormat, along with the column name that our mapper is looking for. Cassandra includes something called a ConfigHelper that provides a way to set properties we'll need, such as the Thrift contact information (server and port), the keyspace, and the column family. It also allows us to set our slice predicate.

Outputting Data to Cassandra

Our example reducer used a FileOutputFormat to output its results. As its name suggests, FileOutputFormat writes the results out to a filesystem. As of 0.7, there will be a Cassandra-based OutputFormat implementation. As of this writing, some of the implementation details are still being finalized. For updates on the built-in output format, see *http://wiki.apache.org/cassandra/HadoopSupport*.

It is possible, however, to write directly to Cassandra via Thrift (or a higher-level client) in the Reducer step. In the previous example, this means that instead of writing to the context, one could write its key and value to Cassandra directly.

Hadoop Streaming

Our word count MapReduce example was written in Java. Hadoop Streaming is the Hadoop way to allow languages besides Java to run MapReduce jobs using Standard In and Standard Out. As of this writing, Hadoop Streaming is not supported in Cassandra's MapReduce integration. However, work is being done to support it in the near future. For details about the current status, see the wiki.

Tools Above MapReduce

MapReduce is a great abstraction for developers so that they can worry less about the details of distributed computing and more about the problems they are trying to solve. Over time, an even more abstracted toolset has emerged. Pig and Hive operate at a level above MapReduce and allow developers to perform more complex analytics more easily. Both of these frameworks can operate against data in Cassandra.

Pig

Pig (*http://hadoop.apache.org/pig*) is a platform for data analytics developed at Yahoo!. Included in the platform is a high-level language called Pig Latin and a compiler that translates programs written in Pig Latin into sequences of MapReduce jobs.

Along with the direct Hadoop integration for running MapReduce jobs over data in Cassandra, there has also been work done to provide integration for Pig. With its grunt shell prompt and the Pig Latin scripting language, Pig provides a way to simplify writing analytics code. To write our word count example using Pig Latin:

```
LOAD 'cassandra://Keyspace1/Standard1' USING CassandraStorage() \
as (key:chararray, cols:bag{col:tuple(name:bytearray, value:bytearray)});
cols = FOREACH rows GENERATE flatten(cols) as (name, value);
words = FOREACH cols GENERATE flatten(TOKENIZE((chararray) value)) as word;
grouped = GROUP words BY word;
counts = FOREACH grouped GENERATE group, COUNT(words) as count;
ordered = ORDER counts BY count DESC;
topten = LIMIT ordered 10;
dump topten;
```

This alternative word count is only eight lines long. Line 1 gets all the data in the Standard1 column family, describing that data with aliases and data types. We extract the name/value pairs in each of the rows. In line 3, we have to cast the value to a character array in order to tokenize it with the built-in TOKENIZE function. We next group by and count each word instance. Finally, we order our data by count and output the top 10 words found.

 It is trivial to operate over super columns with Pig. It is simply another nested level of data that we can flatten in order to get its values.

To some, coding MapReduce programs is tedious and filled with boilerplate code. Pig provides an abstraction that makes our code significantly more concise. Pig also allows programmers to express operations such as joins much more simply than by using MapReduce alone.

The Pig integration code (a LoadFunc implementation) is found in the *contrib* section of Cassandra's source download. It can be compiled and run using instructions found there, and it also includes instructions on how to configure Cassandra-specific configuration options. In a moment, we'll see how to configure a Cassandra cluster to run Pig jobs (compiled down to MapReduce) in a distributed way.

Hive

Like Pig, Hive (*http://hadoop.apache.org/hive*) is a platform for data analytics. Instead of a scripting language, queries are written in a query language similar to the familiar SQL called Hive-QL. Hive was developed by Facebook to allow large data sets to be abstracted into a common structure.

As of this writing, work on a Hive storage handler for Cassandra is being finalized. For updates and documentation on its usage with Cassandra, see the wiki.

Cluster Configuration

MapReduce and other tools can run in a nondistributed way for trying things out or troubleshooting a problem. However, in order to run in a production environment, you'll want to install Hadoop in your Cassandra cluster as well. Although a comprehensive discussion of Hadoop installation and configuration is outside the scope of this chapter, we do go over how to configure Cassandra alongside Hadoop for best performance. Readers can find more about Hadoop configuration at *http://hadoop.apache .org* or in Tom White's excellent reference, *Hadoop: The Definitive Guide* (O'Reilly).

Because Hadoop has some unfamiliar terminology, here are some useful definitions:

HDFS
: Hadoop distributed filesystem.

Namenode
: The master node for HDFS. It has locations of data blocks stored in several datanodes and often runs on the same server as the jobtracker in smaller clusters.

Datanode
: Nodes for storing data blocks for HDFS. Datanodes run on the same servers as tasktrackers.

Jobtracker
: The master process for scheduling MapReduce jobs. The jobtracker accepts new jobs, breaks them into map and reduce tasks, and assigns those tasks to tasktrackers in the cluster. It is responsible for job completion. It often runs on the same server as the namenode in smaller clusters.

Tasktracker
: The process responsible for running map or reduce tasks from the jobtracker. Tasktrackers run on the same servers as datanodes.

Like Cassandra, Hadoop is a distributed system. The MapReduce jobtracker spreads tasks across the cluster, preferably near the data it needs. When a jobtracker initiates tasks, it looks to HDFS to provide it with information about where that data is stored. Similarly, Cassandra's built-in Hadoop integration provides the jobtracker with data locality information so that tasks can be close to the data.

In order to achieve this data locality, Cassandra nodes must also be part of a Hadoop cluster. The namenode and jobtracker can reside on a server outside your Cassandra cluster. Cassandra nodes will need to be part of the cluster by running a tasktracker process on each node. Then, when a MapReduce job is initiated, the jobtracker can query Cassandra for locality of the data when it splits up the map and reduce tasks.

A four-node Cassandra cluster with tasktracker processes running on each Cassandra node is shown in Figure 12-1. At least one node in the cluster needs to be running the datanode process. There is a light dependency on HDFS for small amounts of data (the distributed cache), and a single datanode should suffice. External to the cluster is the server running the Hadoop namenode and jobtracker.

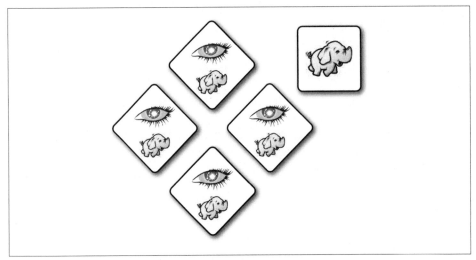

Figure 12-1. Four-node Cassandra cluster with an external namenode/jobtracker

When a job is initiated from a client machine, it goes to the jobtracker. The jobtracker receives information about the data source from when the job is submitted, via the configuration options mentioned earlier. At that point, it can use Cassandra's `Column FamilyRecordReader` and `ColumnFamilySplit` to get the physical locations of different segments of data in the cluster. Then, it can use that location to split up the tasks among the nodes in the cluster, preferring to run tasks on nodes where the associated data resides.

Finally, when creating jobs for MapReduce to execute (either directly or via Pig), the Hadoop configuration needs to point to the namenode/jobtracker (in the Hadoop configuration files) and the Cassandra configuration options. The cluster will be able to handle the integration from there.

Use Cases

To help you understand why Cassandra/Hadoop integration is interesting and useful, here we include a couple of use cases from out in the Cassandra community.

Raptr.com: Keith Thornhill

Raptr is a service that allows gamers to communicate and share their gaming statistics and achievements. Keith Thornhill works as a Senior Software Engineer at Raptr and saw a need to take their storage and analytics backend to the next level. Their legacy storage solution and analytics were home grown, and they were outgrowing them. Doing queries across the entire dataset was tedious and could take hours to run.

Keith saw Cassandra as a promising storage solution for the following reasons:

- Built-in scaling instead of scaffolded on
- Single view of read/write access (no masters or slaves)
- A hands-off style of operations that under normal cases (node failures, adding new nodes, etc.) "just works" and requires very little micromanagement

Keith also watched as the Cassandra/Hadoop integration evolved and saw Pig as an analytics solution he could use. Initially he wanted to look for ways to use PHP or Python to use MapReduce. However, after becoming familiar with Pig, he didn't see a need. He noted that the turnaround time from idea to execution with Pig was very quick. The query runtime was also a nice surprise. He could traverse all of the data in 10–15, minutes rather than hours. As a result, Raptr is able to explore new possibilities in analyzing their data.

As far as configuration, Keith has a separate namenode/jobtracker and installed the datanode/tasktracker on each of his Cassandra nodes. He notes that a nice side effect of this is that the analytics engine scales with the data.

Imagini: Dave Gardner

Imagini provides publishers with tools to profile all their site visitors through "visual quizzes" and an inference engine. Behind the scenes, this involves processing large amounts of behavioral data and then making the results available for real-time access.

After looking at several alternatives, Imagini went with Cassandra because of its fault tolerance, decentralized architecture (no single point of failure), and large write capacity.

Dave Gardner, a senior Imagini developer, writes, "We use Cassandra to store our real-time data, including information on roughly 100 million users, which is expected to grow substantially over the coming year. This is nearly all accessed via simple key lookup."

Currently Imagini aggregates data from a variety of sources into Hadoop's distributed filesystem, HDFS. Using Hadoop Streaming, they use PHP to MapReduce over their data and output directly to Cassandra via Thrift in their reducers. The results reside in Cassandra to provide real-time access to the data.

Looking forward, Imagini hopes to simplify their workflow once Hadoop Streaming becomes available with Cassandra. They're planning on storing even raw data in Cassandra, MapReduce over that data, and then output the result into Cassandra.

Summary

In this chapter, we examined Hadoop, the open source implementation of the Google MapReduce algorithm. We took a brief look at Hadoop basics and how to integrate it with Cassandra by running the word count example that ships with Cassandra, and also saw how to use Pig, a simple and concise language to express MapReduce jobs.

Finally, we got a picture of how a few different companies are using Hadoop and Cassandra together.

The Nonrelational Landscape

Cassandra is one of many new nonrelational database projects that have sprung up recently, and in order to understand their goals and the designs that have been shaped by those goals, it may prove useful to take a step back and understand what these different projects are about.

 We've lately become familiar with the term "NoSQL" to describe a set of databases that don't use SQL. I have been using the term "nonrelational" in acknowledgment that these databases are frequently grouped together in the popular imagination. But part of the point of this appendix is to illustrate that we probably should stop talking this way. It is specious to compare NoSQL databases to relational databases; as you'll see, none of the so-called "NoSQL" databases have the same implementation, goals, features, advantages, and disadvantages. So comparing "NoSQL" to "relational" is really a shell game.

So in this appendix we review a variety of popular nonrelational databases. Cassandra does certain things very, very well. It does other things less well. So my aim here is to help you understand Cassandra's place in the constellation of competing nonrelational databases so that you are best armed to make the right choice of database for your needs. If you already know that you want to employ Cassandra, this survey should still prove useful in understanding some of the design decisions and trade-offs made in Cassandra.

Nonrelational Databases

Of course the world is full of popular databases that have never employed anything like a relational model. These include object databases, XML native databases, document-oriented databases, graph databases, and key-value stores. Some of these represent products that have been around for many years, and some are just starting to see production use. I examine a few of these nonrelational databases here.

There are several other nonrelational databases that I don't discuss, generally because they are less popular, are specialized projects, or are not yet very far along in their implementation and production use. One of these is the "semi-relational" database Drizzle, which is based on MySQL. Microsoft's cloud database platform based on SQL Server is called SQL Server Data Services (SDS). Yahoo!'s PNUTS is definitely worth taking a look at. You can read the PNUTS paper at *http://research.yahoo.com/files/pnuts.pdf*. For a more comprehensive list, visit Alex Popescu's wonderful site MyNoSQL at *http://nosql.mypopescu.com*.

You might be reading this book because you have already selected Cassandra for a database project. But perhaps you've simply heard of its use at popular web properties such as Twitter and Facebook and want to gain a better understanding of what it is. If that's the case, it may prove helpful to understand some of the competing products so you can see what they emphasize, where they differ, and how Cassandra compares in this context.

So let's take a brief look at some of these alternatives to help you see how they differ from what you might already be familiar with. I have tried to characterize each database in terms of the same general categories in order to make the comparison clear.

In general, these databases are distributed, which means that their design allows for more than one node of the database that contains copies of the data, and they handle the replication automatically for you. (There are some exceptions, however, such as Amazon's SimpleDB.) They have a variety of features to help handle massive scale, which is important for many new web applications.

On the negative side, however, what these databases generally share is a lack of great tooling and framework support. Many of the solutions here are new, which means that the developers are focusing on the core product and that you'll have to forego, at least for the time being, tools such as graphical consoles, which we've become used to in the RDBMS world. To employ any of these solutions, including Cassandra, you'll need to feel comfortable working with a command-line interface, simple shell tools, and getting your hands dirty with some plumbing. Because many of these databases are becoming more popular and widely understood, you can expect such conveniences to be available in the near future.

Object Databases

The purpose of an object database is to avoid the object-relational impedance mismatch that occurs when trying to use a relational database under an application written in an object-oriented programming language. Object databases store data not in terms of relations and columns and rows, but in terms of the objects themselves, making it straightforward to use the database from an object-oriented application. This allows you to avoid writing extensive SQL code or stored procedures to map from application objects to database tables and avoid having to use an object-relational mapping (ORM) layer. ORM layers can be cumbersome, add complexity to your overall application, and slow down data operations.

Because you don't have to translate data from application objects into the relational model, applications with object databases can be very fast. You also don't need relational keys to help you join data to fulfill queries, because data is findable in the database as it is in your application: by following pointers.

Object databases have been with us since the mid-1970s and 1980s. They never really caught on for widespread business application use, but have found some success in niche areas such as computer-aided design (CAD) applications, spatial applications, telecommunications, and embedded systems.

InterSystems' object database Caché is probably the best known commercial product, though Persistent Objects and Extended database Technology (POET), which is now the Versant Object Database, is also used for Java, .NET, and C++ applications.

There are some disadvantages to using object-oriented (OO) databases. Although there is often a performance boost to be realized from using an OO database, typically it also tightly couples your data store to your application, but the trade-off may be worth it, depending on your needs. Also, object databases typically will only deserialize objects into the same programming language used to serialize them, which can severely limit your architecture's flexibility by introducing even tighter coupling.

In recent years, there has been less interest and movement in object databases than the other types of data stores discussed here, so I won't go into more detail.

XML Databases

XML databases are a special form of document databases, optimized specifically for working with XML. The first working draft of XML was developed in 1996, and version 1.0 was published as a W3C standard in February of 1998. XML quickly enjoyed widespread use, as web applications found it expressive and easy to use as a transfer format across a wide variety of languages. So-called "XML native" databases soon sprang up, one of the first being Tamino from Software AG. They are now employed in a variety of use cases, such as content management and supply chain systems, document management, publishing, and support of SOA initiatives.

XRX Architecture

In addition to the other uses just mentioned, XML databases are central to what is termed an "XRX Web Application Architecture," which has grown in popularity in recent years. This architecture is called "symmetrical" or sometimes "zero-translation" because it uses XML in every tier of an application. "XRX" stands for XForms, REST, and XQuery.

On the client side, XRX uses XForms, which is a W3C-recommendation XML format distinct from HTML forms; XForms is capable of expressing the kinds of controls required in forms, but it does not dictate the final presentation form. That is, XForms can be rendered in web pages, but also in other applications, such as Open Office and Lotus documents. It accomplishes this flexibility by using a Model View Controller (MVC) design, which allows advanced features such as form validation against an XML schema document, and in-page data refreshes. Currently, no browser natively supports XForms, though plug-ins are available for Firefox, and libraries exist to allow server-side translation of XForms into XHTML.

In the middle tier, XRX uses RESTful services, sometimes only as a facade around the database; on the backend, XRX employs a native XML database to store and query documents using XQuery, and frequently these databases expose a RESTful interface.

XML databases have proven useful in part because they allow developers to work with XML using specifications aimed at XML documents. Working directly with XML in the data tier can be a relief to developers facing the notorious "impedance mismatch" between object-oriented application languages and relational databases.

XML databases have one core function: to allow you to store and query XML documents. Although they are often not stored directly in their "native" format, developers can work with the documents using APIs as if they were. These include:

- Use of XML-friendly query mechanisms such as XPath and XQuery. XPath is the mechanism to address the variety of data items in a document, such as elements and attributes. XQuery affords a robust querying mechanism in the form of FLOWR queries (so named because they allow you to use statements such as "For", "Let", "Where", "Order," and "Return").

- Performance improvements when you're using XML directly within your application. Some applications that work with XML will map these documents to a relational database, but there are a variety of advantages to skipping this step and using an XML database instead. For example, XML documents typically represent hierarchical data structures, which may map poorly to a relational model.

- Flexibility for accessing your data. XML databases frequently allow you to work with data in DOM, JDOM, SAX APIs, and SOAP. Each of these has its own strengths, and you're not limited to the single query mechanism of SQL.

- Responsive full-text searches.

- Features that are familiar from working with relational databases, such as joins across document collections, user-defined functions, search support for metadata as well as data, and more.

- Flexible use of XML throughout the stack, such as when using XForms in the presentation tier.

- Other features, such as storage of non-XML documents (for example, full plain-text [unstructured] documents).

If you're not familiar with XPath as a means to find data in an XML document, consider the following example XML document:

```
<catalog>
  <plays>
    <play name='Hamlet'><price>5.95</price></play>
    <play name='King Lear'><price>6.95</price></play>
  </plays>
</catalog>
```

Given this XML document, the following XPath expression will give us the value "6.95", which is the result of navigating to the value of the price element inside the play element whose value for the name attribute is "King Lear":

```
//catalog/plays/play/[@name='King Lear']/price
```

There are a variety of XML databases in open source projects and commercial offerings. They typically employ one of two data storage mechanisms: text-based or model-based. Text-based XML databases typically will store their data as large text files, character large objects (CLOBs), or even as a binary large object (BLOB) in an underlying relational database, performing the translation for you. Model-based XML databases don't directly store the text of the XML document; instead, they parse documents into an internal proprietary object model that appears to the developer as an XML document. Often this boils down to breaking down the various parts of an XML document (elements, attributes, etc.) and storing them as fragments within a relational database.

The following sections offer a quick overview of some of the popular XML databases.

SoftwareAG Tamino

Tamino was one of the earliest XML-native databases. It's a mature commercial offering that supports a wide variety of the kinds of functions you'd expect in an "enterprise-ready" database, such as high availability.

eXist

The eXist XML database started as a personal project of Wolfgang Meier in 2000 and continues to be actively developed today. It is an open source XML database written in Java. It features rich support for XPath and XQuery, as well as XInclude, WebDAV (Distributed Authoring and Versioning), XML Access Control Markup Language (XACML) for security, SOAP, REST, and XML-RPC. It also comes with an easy-to-use, web-based console to execute queries.

Oracle Berkeley XML DB

Berkeley XML DB is an open source database written in Java that started as a research project at Harvard and is now supported by Oracle. Berkeley XML DB is embeddable, so it can run as a JAR within your application. It supports C++, Java, XQuery, high availability, and transactions. The Berkeley database is specifically geared toward developers rather than DBAs, as the only way to interact with the database is to write code; it has no standalone server and no graphical tool such as SQL Server Management Studio. You can use Berkeley XML DB to store a mixture of XML documents and less-structured documents.

MarkLogic Server

MarkLogic is a server backed by an XML database that supports XQuery for Create, Read, Update, and Delete (CRUD) operations; full-text searching; XML searching; and transactions. It supports REST using XML or JavaScript Object Notation (JSON). Although MarkLogic is a commercial product, there is a free community license available for small projects and nonprofit organizations.

Apache Xindice

The Apache Xindice project was one of the early XML databases, with work beginning in 2001. It was designed for working only with small and medium-sized documents. Since its last release—version 1.1—in 2007, it has not been actively maintained, and version 1.2 has been a work in progress for years now.

Summary

There are many other XML databases, including TigerLogic, MonetDB, Sedna, and more. The importance of XML databases in this context is that some of this work serves as a predecessor to the more recent document-oriented databases, which we explore in a moment. More to the point, however, is that these databases highlight some of the advantages that can be realized by considering how your database maps to the specific needs of your application architecture, rather than simply assuming that a relational database is a one-size-fits-all solution.

Of course, if you are storing only small XML documents and your application doesn't require document collections, then you are not likely to find any performance benefit in an XML database.

Document-Oriented Databases

In a relational database, data is stored in terms of tables, requiring data that might otherwise be repeated to be "broken apart" in order to use relational keys. You then can employ complex queries written to pull your relational data back together for a single query result that captures the data in a two-dimensional grid of rows and columns.

There are several advantages to document-oriented databases in general:

- The basic unit of storage in a document database is a complete document itself. A document can store any number of fields of any length, and each field can store multiple values. This differs from a relational database, which requires all fields to be present for every record.
- In a document-oriented database, you don't need to store "empty" fields for which you have no data, as is required in RDBMS. This can save space in the database.
- They are very free-form in that they do not require a schema.
- Security can be assigned at the individual document level.
- They typically include full-text search capabilities. This is sometimes provided as a special feature of RDBMS and is common in XML databases.

So what is meant by a "document"? It could be text, written and stored as JSON (see "What's JSON?"); it could be XML, though there is a separate discussion around that specialized form of document database; it could be a YAML document (most JSON documents can be parsed by a YAML parser); and it could also be a different format, as there are a variety of alternatives. The technical implementations from one document database to another are not the same. For instance, CouchDB stores data as JSON, and Lotus Notes, which has been around much longer, uses its own internal format.

What's JSON?

JSON, which stands for JavaScript Object Notation, is a data exchange format that serves as an alternative to XML. A basic JSON document for a contact in an address book might look like this:

```
{
  "contact": {
    "fname": "Alison",
    "lname": "Brown",
    "address": {"street": "301 Park Ave", "city": "New York", "state": "NY",
"zip": "10022"},
    "phone": [
          { "type": "mobile", "number": "480-555-5555" },
          { "type": "home", "number": "212-444-4444" }
      ]
  }
}
```

That JSON data would likely be expressed in XML like this:

```
<contact>
    <fname>Alison</fname><lname>Brown</lname>
    <address>
      <street>301 Park Ave</street><city>New York</city>
      <state>NY</state><zip>10022</zip>
    </address>
    <phone type="mobile">480-555-5555</phone>
    <phone type="home">212-444-4444</phone>
</contact>
```

JSON supports just a few data types, as opposed to the many offered by XML. These are number, Unicode string, boolean, array, object, and null.

In the preceding JSON document, you can see we have a `contact` object with a few attributes. The first and last name are defined as strings. The `address` attribute has an object value, as the address defines its own set of attributes. Finally the `phone` attribute has an array value, which is denoted by the surrounding square brackets and the fact that the `type` attribute is repeated. JSON documents have an associated Internet media type of `application/json`.

JSON has been around since 1999, but has grown dramatically in popularity in recent years as developers have become tired of what is perceived as bloated XML documents and difficult tooling and APIs. The simple facts that a typical JSON document contains around 30% fewer characters than the corresponding XML document and that Google started offering JSON as a format for its GData protocol in 2006 probably have had a lot to do with the surge in popularity.

JSON documents are leaner and lighter than XML documents capturing the same data, and although XML enjoys widespread tooling support on a variety of platforms, JSON documents are very simple and require less tooling to interact with in the first place. One potential disadvantage to JSON, depending on your use case, is that JSON can't be validated directly against a schema as XML can.

JSON is highlighted here because of its frequent use in representing data directly or in examples for document databases and distributed hash tables; we see a lot more of it throughout this book.

You can think of document-oriented databases as collections of key-value collections, making them a kind of predecessor to the key-value stores discussed later in "Key-Value Stores and Distributed Hashtables" on page 261. Although that's easy to envision, consider a JSON document such as the one shown here:

```
{
"title": "I Heart LolCatz",
"author: "Inigo Montoya",
"ts": Date("31-Dec-99 11:59"),
"comments": [{
  "author": "Robert Zimmerman",
  "comment: "I'm just a song and dance man"}, {
  "author": "Rogers Nelson",
  "comment: "I'm just a song and dance man"}
  ]
}
```

Consider the tables that might be required to represent even this very simple data structure in a relational database and what the queries might look like. With a document-oriented database, you store exactly that document, and queries are simple one-liners.

IBM Lotus

Lotus, first released in 1989, was perhaps the inspiration for all the other kinds of document-oriented databases, such as CouchDB and MongoDB. Lotus represents a family of products for collaboration, including Lotus Notes and Domino for email, discussion, and calendar; Lotus Sametime for messaging; and others.

- **Website**: *http://www.ibm.com/software/lotus*
- **Orientation**: Document
- **Created**: Lotus was first released in 1989. The most recent version as of this writing is version 8.5, released in March 2010.
- **Schema**: There is no required schema. Documents ("notes") are stored in a native format called a Notes Storage File (NSF), but can be thought of for modeling purposes as JSON documents.
- **Client**: The most recent versions of the Lotus client for end users have been created around Eclipse. To interact with a Domino database, you can access APIs provided in C, C++, or Java. Notes databases are not relational, but you can use a SQL driver with them, and the Domino XML Language provides XML views of all data so you can use these processing tools.
- **CAP**: Lotus can be clustered and performs replication.
- **Production use**: Lotus is used as an end-user collaboration tool throughout many enterprises.

Apache CouchDB

As a database, CouchDB is perhaps most similar to Lotus Notes. This is not entirely surprising, as its creator, Damien Katz, worked on Lotus Notes at IBM before deciding to embark on this project, with the idea that it would be a database "*of* the Web." The documents stored by CouchDB do not need to share the same schema, and query capabilities are made available via views, which are constructed as JavaScript functions.

CouchDB is interesting in part for what it terms Multi-Version Concurrency Control (MVCC). MVCC means that readers will not block writers and writers will not block readers. In order to support this, all writes occur as appends to the document store, making it much harder to corrupt datafiles. This implementation is somewhat similar to Cassandra; using an append-only model means that files can grow very large very quickly, requiring a background process to run compactions.

 If you'd like to read more about CouchDB, check out the O'Reilly book *CouchDB: The Definitive Guide,* by J. Chris Anderson, Jan Lehnardt, and Noah Slater.

- **Website**: *http://couchdb.apache.org*
- **Orientation**: Document
- **Created**: Work was begun in 2005. In 2008, it became an Apache Incubator project.

- **Implementation language**: Erlang
- **Distributed**: Yes. Data can be read and updated by users and the server while disconnected, and any changes can then be replicated bidirectionally later.
- **Schema**: There is no required schema. Documents are stored in their entirety using JSON. Each document is assigned a unique ID.
- **Client**: RESTful JSON API that allows access from any language capable of making HTTP requests.
- **CAP**: Eventually consistent. Replication is used to synchronize multiple copies of data on different nodes. CouchDB features ACID semantics similar to many relational database systems.
- **Production use**: CouchDB is not yet in a 1.0 release as of this writing, but it is used in production in a variety of social websites and software applications. See *http://bit.ly/dn73DY* for a list of specific production instances.
- **Additional features**: MapReduce, incremental replication, and fault-tolerance are all supported. Comes with a web console.

MongoDB

MongoDB is perhaps most similar to CouchDB. It purports to combine the best of key-value stores, document databases, object databases, and RDBMS. That is, it shards automatically as with a key-value store, allows JSON-based dynamic schema documents, and offers a rich query language in the manner of a relational database.

 If you'd like to read more about MongoDB, check out the O'Reilly book *MongoDB: The Definitive Guide,* by Kristina Chodorow and Michael Dirolf.

- **Website**: *http://www.mongodb.org*
- **Orientation**: Document
- **Created**: Developed at 10gen by Geir Magnusson and Dwight Merriman
- **Implementation language**: C++
- **Distributed**: Yes
- **Schema**: JSON-style documents are stored, and you can use dynamic schemas.
- **CAP**: MongoDB uses a single master for any shard, making it completely consistent.
- **Production use**: MongoDB is used in production at SourceForge, Bit.ly, Foursquare, GitHub, Shutterfly, Evite, The New York Times, Etsy, and many more.

- **Additional features**: MapReduce is supported. There's a very neat web interface that lets you try MongoDB in your browser using a JavaScript shell. Check it out at *http://try.mongodb.org*.

Riak

Riak is a hybrid database based on Amazon Dynamo that acts as a document-oriented database and also a distributed key-value store. It's fault-tolerant and scales linearly, and it's intended for use in web applications. It is similar to Cassandra in that it does not have a central controller, and therefore no single point of failure.

The design of Riak includes three basic elements: buckets, keys, and values. Data is organized into buckets, which are little more than flat namespaces for logically grouping key-value pairs. This much is similar in design and terminology to the Google Storage system.

Basho Technologies, the maker of Riak, offers both a commercial version and an open source version.

Riak runs on most Unix-based systems, but is not supported on Windows.

- **Website**: *http://wiki.basho.com*
- **Orientation**: Document and key-value store
- **Created**: Basho Technologies in Cambridge, Massachusetts. This company was formed in 2008 by architects from Akamai.
- **Implementation language**: Primarily Erlang, with some C and JavaScript
- **Distributed**: Yes
- **Replication**: Replication can be set at the bucket level.
- **Schema**: Riak is schema-less and doesn't use specific data types. The values associated with keys are objects. All data is stored as opaque BLOBs, so you can store just about any kind of data in Riak.
- **Client**: Riak offers three primary ways of interacting with it: via a JSON over HTTP interface; drivers for Erlang, Python, Java, PHP, JavaScript, and Ruby; and, finally, a Protocol Buffers client interface. Protocol Buffers is a Google project that they use internally for very fast RPC, and is available at *http://code.google.com/p/protobuf/*.
- **CAP**: Riak is similar to Cassandra in that the database allows for "tuneability" for desired levels of consistency, availability, and partition tolerance.

- **Production use**: Customers include Comcast and Mochi Media.
- **Additional features**: Easy integration with MapReduce/Hadoop. The commercial version, called Enterprise DS, also supports replication across data centers (the open source version supports replication only within a single data center), a web console, and Simple Network Management Protocol (SNMP) support.

Graph Databases

Graph databases present another alternative to the relational data model. You can think of a graph as a network. Instead of storing data in tables or columns, graph databases use three basic constructs to represent data: nodes, edges, and properties. In the graph database world, a *node* is a standalone, independent object that doesn't depend on anything else. An *edge* is an object that depends on the existence of two nodes. *Properties* are straightforward: they're the attributes of a node. For example, a person node might have a name property and an email property. Both nodes and edges can have associated properties.

Figure A-1 shows a graph database with five nodes and five edges. The edges describe a variety of relationships, but in this example, each has only a single property of the edge name. We can see that one of the edges is bidirectional. Each node in this example has a single property ("name"), but they could all have a variety of additional properties. One nice thing about a graph database is that it's "whiteboard friendly"; that is, the data model looks like how we often think when mapping things out at the whiteboard, and we don't need additional translation steps to make the data fit our database's constraints.

Graph databases differ from other nonrelational offerings such as key-value stores in that they represent the edges as first-class citizens, and not just the nodes. That is to say that whereas many programming languages and databases we're used to allow us to infer a relationship, the relationship itself is only indirectly represented (say, via a foreign key relation or a pointer). In graph databases, the relationships are given equal status with the nodes, as the relationship between the nodes is considered central to certain use cases. For example, graph databases have become more popular in recent years because they readily map to the social web domain and perform very well for the kinds of queries required in Web 2.0 social networking applications, where the relationships are really the point of the whole endeavor. A second important and growing use case for graph databases is the Semantic Web, where predicates are given equal status to subjects and objects in a triple.

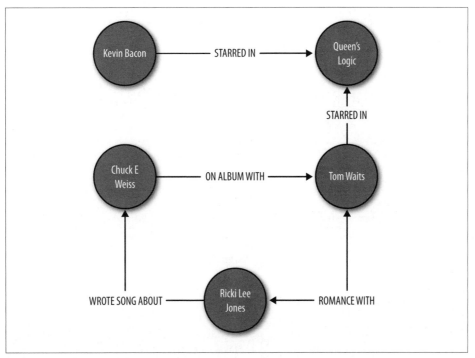

Figure A-1. A graph modeling relationships

Two key trends over the last 15 years have precipitated the rise of graph databases as an important form of data store. The first is a rise in the sheer volume of data, and the second is a rise in the interconnectedness of that data; both of these trends make graph databases an attractive choice.

Consider for example the rough time line shown in Figure A-2. Starting in the early 1990s, text documents and basic linked hypermedia represented the bulk of content on the Web. Such documents were straightforward to store and easy to generate using relational databases. Then, in the early part of this century, RSS feeds, blogs, and wikis started cropping up, adding automation and linking of reference data in new ways that stretched the relational model. As 2005 gave rise to the idea of Web 2.0 (or the Age of Participation, as it was termed by Jonathan Schwartz at Sun), we began to see folk-sonomies, tag clouds, and taxonomies, all optimized for machine consumption and inference as much as for direct human consumption. We started to shift away from thinking of the Web as a bunch of "pages" like those in a magazine whose content can be dynamically generated by pulling together entries in a relational database; we started thinking instead in terms of ways to represent that data so that it can be linked in terms of the ideas represented. The large-scale availability of the high-speed Internet infrastructure allowed social networking sites to blossom. Many more people were suddenly connected, and the Web was offering new ways for them to interact, rather than just read.

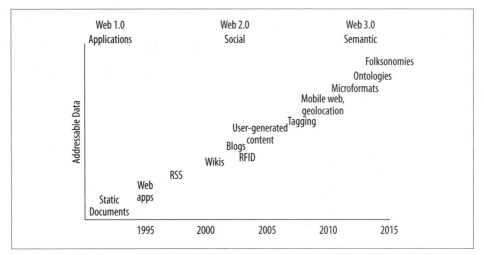

Figure A-2. The need to manage data on a very large scale is increasing, and will continue to do so

It is at this point where the Web starts to employ that important second layer of semantics, accompanied by the explosion in volume of data, and where the largest web properties are forced to start looking at alternatives to the relational database. Some semantic web researchers and enthusiasts have recently suggested that we are entering a new era, Web 3.0, where RDF, microformats, and ontologies will support a super-connected "web of data" culminating in a gigantic graph of the world's knowledge base some years from now. As such, the usefulness of graph databases, which directly support the idea of a semantic relationship between two nodes, becomes more immediately apparent.

Like many document-oriented databases, graph databases typically allow for free-form schemas, allowing your application to evolve easily as your data set grows and changes. Because there is no relational model, joins are not necessary, which can offer more efficient queries as your data set grows.

The primary advantage of a graph database over RDBMS is that there's no impedance mismatch; you can store your objects just as you would use them in your application and just as you would draw them on a whiteboard, which makes for straightforward, readily understandable, and quick modeling. As with key-value stores and document-oriented databases, graph databases allow you to represent semistructured data and naturally evolve your schemas according to newfound relationships and properties.

If you're interested in exploring graph databases for a social web or Semantic Web application, you might want to check out the variety of other graph databases not explored here, including Dex, HypergraphDB, Infogrid, and VertexDB. I encourage you also to take a look at the Gremlin project at *http://wiki.github.com/tinkerpop/grem lin*. Gremlin is an open source programming language designed specifically for performing queries, graph analysis, and manipulation in graph databases. Gremlin can be invoked from a Java Virtual Machine via its implementation in accordance with JSR 223.

We look at only a couple of graph databases here, but if you're a regular Hadoop user you might also check out the Hama project, which is in Incubator status as of this writing. Hama is a package on top of Hadoop that adds support for massive matrix and graph data. See *http://incubator.apache.org/hama*. There is also a Google project called Pregel, which they've been using internally for a couple of years and which they might open source. You can read Google's announcement on Pregel at *http://googleresearch .blogspot.com/2009/06/large-scale-graph-computing-at-google.html*.

FlockDB

In April 2010, Twitter announced that they were open-sourcing to GitHub their new graph database called FlockDB. They created FlockDB to store the adjacency lists for followers on Twitter, so they could readily understand who follows whom and who blocks whom. It scales horizontally and is designed for online, low-latency, high-throughput environments. The Twitter FlockDB cluster stores 13+ billion edges and sustains peak traffic of 20,000 writes per second and 100,000 reads per second.

- **Website**: *http://github.com/twitter/flockdb*
- **Orientation**: Graph
- **Created**: Created in 2010 by Twitter
- **Implementation language**: Scala
- **License**: Apache License v2
- **Distributed**: Yes
- **Schema**: The schema is very straightforward, as FlockDB does not attempt to solve every database problem, but only those relating to the set of problems Twitter faces with their relationship graphs and the size of their dataset. The graph contains entries with four attributes: a source ID, a destination ID, a position, and a state.
- **Client**: FlockDB uses the Thrift 0.2 client, and Twitter has also written a Ruby frontend that offers a richer interface.
- **Replication**: Yes
- **Storage**: MySQL
- **Production use**: Twitter
- **Additional features**: FlockDB allows you to quickly page through result sets that contain millions of entries and to archive and later restore previously archived graph edges. It uses Kestrel as a loosely coupled, reliable message queue that picks a server at random to write to, so there is no cross-server communication (no clustering, no multicast, etc.).

Neo4J

Neo4J is an ACID-compliant graph database optimized for very fast graph traversals. It's transactional, supporting JTA/JTS, two-phase commit, deadlock detection, and MVCC. It has been in production use since 2003, making it one of the older data stores presented here, and is capable of scaling to billions of entities (nodes, edges, properties) in a single JVM.

Neo4J can be embedded as a small JAR file, so it's easy to get up and running and use in a flexible way in your applications.

- **Website**: *http://neo4j.org*
- **Orientation**: Graph
- **Created**: Created and used in production since 2003 by Neo Technologies. Version 1.0 was released in February 2010.
- **Implementation language**: Java
- **License**: Apache GPLv3, with commercial licensing available for advanced features.
- **Distributed**: Neo4J is partially distributed using RMI. Note that the free version of Neo4J is not distributable to multiple machines.
- **Schema**: Schema-less graph of nodes, edges, and optional properties
- **Client**: There are a few options here. You can run Neo4J as a REST server so that you can use simple HTTP operations with JSON; Neo4J has a shell client interface as well. There are language bindings available for Java, Python, Ruby, Clojure, Scala, and PHP. See Neo4j.py for the Jython and CPython interfaces, and Neo4jrb for the JRuby bindings. Neoclipse is a plug-in to the Eclipse IDE that offers a graphical representation of your graph and an interface with Grails.
- **Replication**: As of this writing, Neo4J replication is still in the works. It uses a master/slave replication design based on the one used in MySQL, where you can write to any slave instance, and lock coordination and change distribution are handled by the master. You can tune the consistency level desired, so you can achieve strong consistency by having Neo4J write synchronously to the write master and slave, or you can improve performance using eventual consistency by propagating writes to slaves asynchronously.
- **Storage**: Custom disk-based storage
- **Production use**: Box.net, ThoughtWorks
- **Additional features**: Because it is a graph database, Neo4J can be used to good advantage with semantic web applications. It allows you to execute SPARQL Protocol and RDF Query Language (SPARQL) queries for interacting with Resource Description Framework (RDF) and acts as a partial Web Ontology Language (OWL) store.

Integration with Apache Lucene/Solr is available to store external indexes and perform fast global searches. An index in distributed databases can be thought of like a dictionary—a direct pointer from a key to a value.

As of version 1.1, Neo4J features an event framework.

Key-Value Stores and Distributed Hashtables

In a relational model, we tend to first consider the tables that our domain requires, then think of how we can normalize the tables to avoid duplicate data. The tables with their defined columns and the relationships between the tables become our schema.

In a key-value store, however, typically you don't define a schema as such. Your domain rather becomes a bucket into which you can drop data items; the data items are keys that have a set of attributes. All data relevant to that key is therefore stored with the key, resulting in a sharp contrast to the normalized model prized in relational databases: data is frequently duplicated. There are some variations here, though, and some conceptual overlap results with the columnar databases.

Another contrast is one of modeling. When working with relational databases, we tend to think hard about the schema, trusting that any question we want to ask the database will be answerable. Because the questions—the queries—are secondary in this model, they can become very complex. You've surely seen elaborate SQL statements that use several joins, subqueries, aggregate functions, temporary tables, and so forth. In the columnar model, however, we tend to think of the query first, and the queries we'll execute help dictate the design of the buckets we'll need. The assumption in columnar databases that supports this is that we want replication in order for the database to be available, and that data duplication is OK because disk space is inexpensive.

Data integrity is another point of difference. Data integrity is the extent to which the data in an application is complete and consistent. Relational databases have some built-in capabilities to help ensure data integrity, such as primary keys (which ensure entity integrity) and foreign key constraints (which ensure referential integrity). In a key-value store, however, the responsibility for data integrity resides entirely with the application.

Consider an example: your database might include Customers and Orders. In a relational database, referential keys must be defined in the database to allow you to join these tables and see, for example, all the orders a particular customer has placed. Although you could do this in a key-value store, typically you don't define any relationships in the data model itself; your application is responsible for maintaining data integrity if, for example, you decide to delete a customer record.

One criticism of key-value stores is that they are terrific if you need to scale to billions of records, but that this use case is a concern only for very large, social-based web properties. The suggestion is that key-value stores mean by definition that your application will see the database as a single, enormous, globally accessible hashtable, which is difficult to maintain and hard on programmer productivity.

There are many key-value stores in the wild today, including Tokyo Cabinet, Amazon's SimpleDB, and Microsoft's Dynomite.

Amazon Dynamo

Dynamo is Amazon's proprietary key-value storage system. Though it's not usable by developers, it's still important to discuss because it, along with Google Bigtable, inspired many of the design decisions in Apache Cassandra.

In October of 2007, Werner Vogels, CTO of Amazon, published a white paper for the Association of Computing Machinery (ACM) called "Dynamo: Amazon's Highly Available Key-value Store." This paper continues to be publicly available on his blog "All Things Distributed" at *http://www.allthingsdistributed.com/files/amazon-dynamo -sosp2007.pdf*. The paper is rather technical, but it is clear, concise, and very well written. I will just summarize the main points here.

Dynamo was born, as were many of the systems described in this chapter, from the need to honor strict requirements for realizing high performance under continuous growth, meeting service-level agreements (SLAs), remaining available under strenuous load and failures, gracefully handling those failures, and allowing horizontal scale. Therefore, with respect to the CAP theorem, Dynamo, like Cassandra, is highly available and eventually consistent. Failure handling in both of these systems is regarded as a "normal case without impacting availability or performance." This is achievable because of the trade-off Dynamo makes with consistency.

Dynamo is used for Amazon's shopping cart, and of course consistency is important to Amazon. For a service such as a web-based shopping cart, which does not have competing readers, it is more than worth the trade-offs and will not be problematic. Although consistency is not the main focus of this system, it is a "tuneable" property, such that "eventual" is perhaps a misnomer.

As in Cassandra, consistency in Dynamo works where a configurable property allows the user to decide what number of replicas must successfully respond before it can be determined that an operation was successful. To achieve this, communication between replicas is based on a peer-to-peer (P2P) communication protocol called "gossip," which we'll examine further in terms of Cassandra inherits.

The requirements for the Dynamo architecture were clear. In order to support a highly available model, the team decided to tune down the consistency "knob." Again, this is perfectly acceptable for their given use case. They also wanted a very easy-to-use query model, so the data is referenced using unique keys and stored simply as byte arrays. This eliminates the need for any sophisticated schema design and allows Amazon to put effort toward low-latency and high-throughput performance optimizations and their other primary goals.

To achieve an acceptable level of consistency, Dynamo must support some sort of versioning mechanism so that replicas can know which node has the most recent (valid) copy of written data. So it employs something called a vector clock, in which each process maintains a numeric reference to the most recent event it's aware of. Another facet of the architecture that Cassandra shares with Dynamo is the hinted handoff.

This section has summarized the basic points of the Amazon Dynamo paper in order to help you understand its architectural goals and features. Although I very much encourage you to read the Dynamo paper, be aware that Cassandra does diverge in its own ways, so don't take for granted that something described there will necessarily apply to Cassandra. In short, Cassandra derives its design around consistency and partition tolerance from Dynamo, and its data model is based on Bigtable.

Project Voldemort

Voldemort was started as a project within LinkedIn when they encountered problems with simple data partitioning to meet their scalability needs, similar to how Cassandra was started within Facebook. Voldemort is a distributed, very simple key-value store, based on Amazon's Dynamo and Memcached.

Performance numbers suggested by Jay Kreps of LinkedIn indicate approximately 20,000 reads and 17,000 writes per second with one client and one server.

- **Website**: *http://project-voldemort.com*
- **Orientation**: Key-value store
- **Created**: Created in 2008 by LinkedIn's Data and Analytics team for application to real-time problems
- **Implementation language**: Java
- **Distributed**: Yes
- **Schema**: The primary aims of Voldemort are high performance and availability. As a result, the database supports only the most minimal schema. The following are essentially the only supported queries: value = store.get(key), store.put(key, value), and store.delete(key). Because Voldemort allows you to specify your schema with JSON, it supports all the data types that JSON supports.
- **Client**: Like Cassandra, Voldemort allows for pluggable interfaces. According to the Voldemort website, it supports pluggable serialization and integrates with Thrift, Avro, and Google Protocol Buffers.
- **Replication**: Data is automatically replicated over multiple servers; this is configurable.
- **Storage**: Voldemort allows for pluggable storage on disk using BerkeleyDB or MySQL.
- **Production use**: LinkedIn
- **Additional features**: Can be used in conjunction with Hadoop.

Redis

Redis is not a "plain" key-value store, as it supports a variety of values in different data structures such as binary-safe strings (strings that don't contain a space or newline character), lists and sets of binary-safe strings, and sorted sets, which contain a floating-number score.

In March of 2010, VMWare took over as project sponsor of Redis.

- **Website**: *http://code.google.com/p/redis*
- **Orientation**: Key-value store
- **Created**: Created in 2009
- **Implementation language**: ANSI C
- **Distributed**: No distribution or fault tolerance.
- **Schema**: Key-value store, using `server:key-name` to store and retrieve values.
- **Clients**: Redis supports a wide array of clients, typically through contributed libraries, including Ruby, Python, Twisted Python, Erlang, Tcl, Perl, Lua, Java, Scala, Clojure, C#, C, Haskell, and Google's new Go language.
- **CAP**: Eventually consistent
- **Open source**: Yes. Hosted in Google projects. There's a neat web page that offers a Redis tutorial (based on the MongoDB tutorial) that allows you to try Redis directly from your browser using JavaScript. Give it a try at *http://try.redis-db.com*.

Columnar Databases

A columnar database simply means a data store that organizes data around columns instead of rows. This slight shift in focus optimizes the workload for certain kinds of problems—in particular, data warehouses and analytics applications that require computing aggregate values over very large sets of similar data. Columnar (or "column-oriented") databases are well-suited to online analytical processing (OLAP) work, where queries are executed over a broad dataset.

Data storage works a little differently with columnar databases, in order to optimize disk space and the amount of time spent in IO. For example, columnar databases allow you to write a record containing a value for only one out of a large number of possible columns, and only that single column value will be stored and take up space. This is different from RDBMS, in which nulls are not stored for free. It can be useful to think of RDBMS tables like spreadsheets, in which all columns are of the same size for each row, and null values are maintained to keep the grid-like shape of the data structure. This model doesn't work for columnar databases, though, because null values are not present. It's more helpful to think of columnar data as tags: values can be of arbitrary length, and the names and widths of columns are not preset.

Columnar databases often require the data to be of a uniform type, which presents an opportunity for data compression.

Columnar databases have been around since the early 1970s. Sybase IQ, for example, is one of these, and was for many years the only commercial columnar database.

But of the recent (mostly open source) projects that are part of the NoSQL conversation, there are a few databases that are an evolution of basic key-value stores in that they feature a richer data model. You can think of these columnar databases as multidimensional key-value stores or distributed hash tables that, instead of supporting merely straight key-value pairs, allow for arrangements called column families to help organize columns and provide a richer model. These are Google's Bigtable, HBase, Hypertable, and Cassandra.

Google's Bigtable is really the parent of the modern columnar databases. It is proprietary, but there are a few published papers on its design, and each of the other columnar databases discussed are implementations that closely follow Bigtable's design or, as in the case of Cassandra, take certain key ideas from Bigtable.

Google Bigtable

Bigtable is Google's internally used custom database, designed to scale into the petabyte range. Bigtable is described in the paper published by Google in 2006 called "Bigtable: A Distributed Storage System for Structured Data." The goals of the project are stated in that paper: "wide applicability, scalability, high performance, and high availability." Bigtable is used extensively within Google as the underlying data store, supporting more than 60 projects, including Gmail, YouTube, Google Analytics, Google Finance, Orkut, Personalized Search, and Google Earth. Bigtable runs on top of the Google File System (GFS).

It is useful to understand Bigtable, at least to a certain degree, because many of its attributes and design decisions are explicitly copied in Cassandra. Although Cassandra gets its design for consistency and partition tolerance from Amazon Dynamo, Cassandra's data model is based more closely on Bigtable's. For example, Cassandra borrows from Bigtable (sometimes with modification) the implementation of SSTables, memtables, Bloom filters, and compactions (see the Glossary for definitions of these terms; they are explored in detail elsewhere in this book as appropriate). In this way, Cassandra supports a somewhat richer data model than Dynamo, something more flexible and layered than a simple key-value store, as it supports sparse, semistructured data.

I very much encourage you to read the Google Bigtable paper; it's an excellent read. However, keep in mind that although Cassandra borrows many key ideas from Bigtable, it is not generally a 1:1 correspondence in ideas or implementation. For example, Bigtable defines master and slave nodes, and while Cassandra's data model and storage mechanism are based on Bigtable and use the same terminology in many places, it's not always the case. For example, Bigtable reads and writes are close but not identical to their Cassandra implementations; Bigtable defines a Tablet structure that is not strictly present in Cassandra; and so on. You can read the paper at *http://labs.google.com/papers/bigtable .html*.

Cassandra does contrast with Bigtable in several areas, however, not least of which is that Cassandra maintains a decentralized model. In Bigtable there is a master server that controls operations using the Chubby persistent distributed locking mechanism; in Cassandra, all the nodes are on even par with no centralized control, and they communicate using a gossip model.

Bigtable relies on a distributed lock service called Chubby for several different things: ensuring that there is at most a single master replica at any given time; managing server bootstrapping, discovery, and death; and storing the schema information.

- **Website**: None, but you might be interested in a related project called Google Fusion Tables, which is available at *http://tables.googlelabs.com*.

- **Orientation**: Columnar

- **Created**: By Google, Inc. Development started in 2004, with the paper published in 2006.

- **Implementation language**: C++

- **Distributed**: Yes

- **Storage**: Google File System (GFS). Files are divided into 64-megabyte chunks, and a typical write operation will only ever append to the files in order to provide maximum throughput. GFS has as a driving principle that the filesystem must run on banks of inexpensive commodity servers, which can be prone to failure, and therefore it must be able to manage availability in such a scenario. Bigtable features two server types: one master node and many chunkservers. The chunkservers store the data chunk files, and the master node stores all of the metadata about the chunks, such as the location of some particular piece of data. This is a clear point where Cassandra diverges from Bigtable's design, as Cassandra nodes are all the same and there is no master server centrally controlling the ring.

- **Schema**: The data model in Bigtable is a sparse, distributed, multidimensional sorted map. It allows you to store data in a richer way than, say, Amazon SimpleDB, as you can use list types. The map is indexed using a row key, a column key, and a timestamp; the values themselves are uninterpreted byte arrays.

- **Client**: C++. Queries are also sometimes written in a scripting language developed at Google called Sawzall. Initially, the Sawzall API did not support writing values to the database, but did allow data filtering, transformation, and summarizing. MapReduce is typically used as both an input source and an output source.
- **Open source**: No
- **Additional features**: While Bigtable itself is not directly available for your own use, you can use it indirectly if you build an application with Google App Engine. Bigtable was designed with use of the MapReduce algorithm in mind. There are a few clones of Bigtable, and Hadoop is an open source implementation of MapReduce.

HBase

HBase is a clone of Google's Bigtable, originally created for use with Hadoop (it's actually a subproject of the Apache Hadoop project). In the way that Google's Bigtable uses the Google File System (GFS), HBase provides database capabilities for Hadoop, allowing you to use it as a source or sink for MapReduce jobs. Unlike some other columnar databases that provide eventual consistency, HBase is strongly consistent.

Perhaps it is interesting to note that Microsoft is a contributor to HBase, following their acquisition of Powerset.

- **Website**: *http://hbase.apache.org*
- **Orientation**: Columnar
- **Created**: HBase was created at Powerset in 2007 and later donated to Apache.
- **Implementation language**: Java
- **Distributed**: Yes. You can run HBase in standalone, pseudodistributed, or fully distributed mode. Pseudodistributed mode means that you have several instances of HBase, but they're all running on the same host.
- **Storage**: HBase provides Bigtable-like capabilities on top of the Hadoop File System.
- **Schema**: HBase supports unstructured and partially structured data. To do so, data is organized into column families (a term that appears in discussions of Apache Cassandra). You address an individual record, called a "cell" in HBase, with a combination of row key, column family, cell qualifier, and timestamp. As opposed to RDBMS, in which you must define your table well in advance, with HBase you can simply name a column family and then allow the cell qualifiers to be determined at runtime. This lets you be very flexible and supports an agile approach to development.
- **Client**: You can interact with HBase via Thrift, a RESTful service gateway, Protobuf (see "Additional Features" below), or an extensible JRuby shell.
- **Open source**: Yes (Apache License)

- **Production use**: HBase has been used at Adobe since 2008. It is also used at Twitter, Mahalo, StumbleUpon, Ning, Hulu, World Lingo, Detikcom in Indonesia, and Yahoo!.
- **Additional features**: Because HBase is part of the Hadoop project, it features tight integration with Hadoop. There is a set of convenience classes that allow you to easily execute MapReduce jobs using HBase as the backing data store.

HBase requires Zookeeper to run. Zookeeper, also part of the Hadoop project, is a centralized service for maintaining configuration information and distributed synchronization across nodes in a cluster. Although this does add an external dependency, it makes maintaining the cluster easier and helps simplify the HBase core.

HBase allows you to use Google's Protobuf (Protocol Buffer) API as an alternative to XML. Protobuf is a very efficient way of serializing data. It has the advantage of compacting the same data two to three times smaller than XML, and of being 20–100 times faster to parse than XML because of the way the protocol buffer encodes bytes on the wire. This can make working with HBase very fast. Protobuf is used extensively within Google; they incorporate nearly 50,000 different message types into Protobuf across a wide variety of systems. Check out the Protobuf Google code project at *http://code .google.com/p/protobuf*.

The database comes with a web console user interface to monitor and manage region servers and master servers.

Hypertable

Hypertable is a Google Bigtable clone, very similar to HBase. It is used at Zvents, where the project originated, to write more than one billion cells per day. It can run on a distributed filesystem such as HFS or the Kosmos File System. Hypertable uses Multi-Version Concurrency Control (MVCC) to allow user transactions to execute in a private memory space, which are readable by other clients only once the transaction has committed.

Like Cassandra and other Bigtable derivatives, it uses Bloom filters and commit logs to minimize disk access and improve performance.

Hypertable is well-suited for analytics applications and processing. Unlike many of the other nonrelational solutions, it is not used frequently to back websites.

- **Website**: *http://www.hypertable.org*
- **Orientation**: Columnar
- **Created**: Hypertable was started in February of 2007 at Zvents.
- **Implementation language**: C
- **Distributed**: Yes
- **Open Source**: Yes

- **Schema**: Hypertable stores data as a multidimensional table represented as a flat, sorted list of key-value pairs. The key is essentially the concatenation of four dimension keys (row, column family, column qualifier, and timestamp).

- **Clients**: The primary Thrift API (also used by Cassandra before being replaced by Avro) is C++, with bindings for Java, Python, Ruby, PHP, Perl, Erlang, Haskell, C#, Perl, and Ocaml.

- **Additional features**: Hypertable has its own query language called Hypertable Query Language (HQL). HQL is modeled on SQL, so you can express queries in a familiar manner, such as `select * from QueryLogByTimestamp WHERE ROW =^ '2010-03-27 17:05';`. The query here looks a lot like SQL, but includes a modified syntax. For example, the `^=` operator means "starts with."

Like Voldemort and Cassandra (before Avro, at least), Hypertable uses the Thrift API for client serialization.

Polyglot Persistence

The different styles of persistence that we've toured in this chapter highlight one fact: each of them is good at solving a particular problem, or has particular strengths where the others don't. You may have heard the term "polyglot programming," which is largely credited to Neal Ford. The idea with polyglot programming is that different programming languages are good at different things, and that you can combine programming languages in a single solution in order to realize the maximum benefit. Dean Wampler of *http://polyglotprogramming.com* offers the overwhelming success of Emacs as an example of how polyglot programming can be helpful: Emacs uses C for its kernel, which made it fast, and a scripting dialect of Lisp called Emacs Lisp (ELisp), which made it easy to extend. Polyglot programming as a concept has been enabled by a variety of advances in the last few years, including the ability of the Java Virtual Machine to run a variety of languages. We more frequently hear of large web applications that have parts that are implemented in Scala, Ruby, and PHP. For example, the most recent iteration of the eBay architecture is mostly Java, but the search engine is in C++.

I submit that we may see a similar trend in persistence. The NoSQL conversation has challenged the status quo—that RDBMS is the right tool for every job because it's the tool we have. Some proponents of NoSQL suggest that RDBMS will be replaced with one or more of these solutions. I rather think it's more likely that we'll see *polyglot persistence*, or the use of a variety of data stores performing different tasks within an application. In this vision, relational databases will live side by side with nonrelational databases, and they will operate together within modular, service-oriented applications, each optimized to perform the tasks they do best.

Summary

In the previous sections, we took a whirlwind tour of a variety of nonrelational databases in order to properly contextualize Cassandra in light of the overall NoSQL movement. The purpose was to shed some light on how the industry has been thinking about data over the last few years and to compare and contrast some of these systems in order to understand their broader theoretical underpinnings.

We also took a tour of the many so-called NoSQL offerings in order to understand the alternatives to relational databases that have sprung up in recent years. These databases, in their variety of forms, are different ways of trying to respond to the growing need for handling data at massive "web scale." Another purpose of this tour was to illustrate that NoSQL databases exist for a reason, though some pundits and industry experts may object. They are being used by many large companies with strenuous data requirements and cannot be dismissed as newfangled "art projects." They are strongly rooted in important ideas surrounding data scalability from some of the best minds in the industry, sometimes going back decades. And, though it's true that they have (very public) problems at times, that's also the case with relational databases.

So my purpose in this book has not been to convince you to throw away all your relational databases and replace them with the new flavor of the month. It's been to help you understand the advantages and disadvantages of alternatives to relational databases, and to understand Cassandra in-depth, so that when you're presented with your next data problem, you're ready to take a step back and select not just the default tool, but the best tool for the job.

Glossary

This glossary provides definitions of some of the terms that are important to understand when working with Apache Cassandra. There's some really good material at *http://wiki .apache.org/cassandra*, but reading it for the first time can be tricky, as each new term seems to be explained only with other new terms. Many of these concepts are daunting to beginning or even intermediate web developers or database administrators, so they're presented here in an easy reference. Much of the information in this glossary is repeated and expanded upon in relevant sections throughout this book.

Anti-Entropy

Anti-entropy, or *replica synchronization*, is the mechanism in Cassandra for ensuring that data on different nodes is updated to the newest version.

Here's how it works. During a major compaction (see Compaction), the server initiates a TreeRequest/TreeResponse conversation to exchange Merkle trees with neighboring nodes. The Merkle tree is a hash representing the data in that column family. If the trees from the different nodes don't match, then they have to be reconciled (or "repaired") in order to determine the latest data values they should all be set to. This tree comparison validation is the responsibility of the `org.apache.cassandra.service.AntiEntropy Service` class. `AntiEntropyService` implements the Singleton pattern and defines the static `Differencer` class as well. This class is used to compare two trees, and if it finds any differences, it launches a repair for the ranges that don't agree.

Anti-entropy is used in Amazon's Dynamo, and Cassandra's implementation is modeled on that (see Section 4.7 of the Dynamo paper).

In Dynamo, they use a Merkle tree for anti-entropy (see Merkle Tree). Cassandra does too, but the implementation is a little different. In Cassandra, each column family has its own Merkle tree; the tree is created as a snapshot during a major compaction operation, and it is kept only as long as is required to send it to the neighboring nodes on the ring. The advantage of this implementation is that it reduces disk I/O.

See Read Repair for more information on how these repairs occur.

Async Write

Sometimes called "async writes" in documentation and user lists, this simply means "asynchronous writes" and refers to the fact that Cassandra makes heavy use of `java.util.concurrent` library components such as `ExecutorService` and `Future<T>` for writing data to buffers.

Avro

Avro is (probably) replacing Thrift as the RPC client for interacting with Cassandra. Avro is a subproject of the Apache Hadoop project, created by Doug Cutting (creator of Hadoop and Lucene). It provides functionality similar to Thrift, but is a dynamic data serialization library that has an advantage over Thrift in that it does not require static code generation. Another reason that the project is migrating to Avro is that Thrift was originally created by Facebook and then donated to Apache, but since that time has received little active development attention.

This means that the Cassandra server will be ported from `org.apache.cassandra.thrift.CassandraServer` to `org.apache.cassandra.avro.CassandraServer`. As of this writing, this is underway but not yet complete.

You can find out more about Avro at its project page, *http://avro.apache.org*.

Bigtable

Bigtable is a distributed database created at Google in 2006 as a high-performance columnar database on top of Google File System (GFS). Bigtable and Amazon's Dynamo database are the direct parents of Cassandra. Cassandra inherits these aspects from Bigtable: sparse array data and disk storage using an SSTable.

Yahoo!'s HBase is a Bigtable clone.

You can read the complete Google Bigtable paper at *http://labs.google.com/papers/bigtable.html*.

Bloom Filter

In simple terms, a Bloom filter is a very fast, nondeterministic algorithm for testing whether an element is a member of a set. These algorithms are nondeterministic because it is possible to get a false-positive read but not a false-negative. Bloom filters work by mapping the values in a dataset into a bit array and condensing a larger dataset into a digest string. The digest, by definition, uses a much smaller amount of memory than the original data would.

Cassandra uses Bloom filters to reduce disk access, which can be expensive, on key lookups. Every SSTable has an associated Bloom filter; when a query is performed, the Bloom filter is checked first before accessing disk. Because false-negatives are not possible, if the filter indicates that the element does not exist in the set, it certainly doesn't; if the filter thinks that the element is in the set, the disk is accessed to make sure.

Although it is a disadvantage that false-positives are possible with Bloom filters, their advantage is that they can be very fast because they use space efficiently, due to the fact that (unlike simple arrays, hashtables, or linked lists) they do not store their elements completely. Instead, Bloom filters make heavy use of memory and reduce disk access. One result is that the number of false-positives increases as the number of elements increases.

Bloom filters are used by Apache Hadoop, Google Bigtable, and Squid Proxy Cache. They are named for their inventor, Burton Bloom.

Cassandra

In Greek mythology, Cassandra was the daughter of King Priam and Queen Hecuba of Troy. She was so beautiful that the god Apollo gave her the ability to see the future. But when she refused his amorous advances, he cursed her such that she would accurately predict everything that would happen, yet no one would believe her. Cassandra foresaw the destruction of her city of Troy, but was powerless to stop it. The Cassandra distributed database is named for her.

The data store itself is an Apache project available at *http://cassandra.apache.org*. It started in incubator status in January of 2009. It has the following key properties: it is decentralized, elastic, fault-tolerant, tuneably consistent, highly available, and designed to massively scale on commodity servers spread across different data centers. It is in use at companies such as Digg, Facebook, Twitter, Cloudkick, Cisco, IBM, Reddit, Rackspace, SimpleGeo, Ooyala, and OpenX.

Cassandra was originally written at Facebook to solve their Inbox Search problem. The team was led by Jeff Hammerbacher, with Avinash Lakshman, Karthik Ranganathan, and Facebook engineer on the Search Team Prashant Malik as key engineers. The code was released as an open source Google Code project in July of 2008. In March of 2009, it was moved to an Apache Incubator project, and on February 17 of that year, it was voted into a top-level project.

A central paper on Cassandra by Facebook's Lakshman and Malik called "A Decentralized Structured Storage System" is available at *http://www.cs.cornell.edu/projects/ladis2009/papers/lakshman-ladis2009.pdf*.

A blog post from 2008 by Avinash Lakshman describes how they were using Cassandra at Facebook: *http://www.facebook.com/note.php?note_id=24413138919&id=9445547199&index=9*.

It is easy to see why the Cassandra database is aptly named: its community asserts that Cassandra and other related NoSQL databases are the future. Despite widespread use of eventually consistent databases at companies such as Amazon, Google, Facebook, and Twitter, there remain many skeptics ("nonbelievers") of such a model. It is further speculated that by naming the database Cassandra, after the Greek seer of the future, its creators are making a kind of joking reference to the Oracle database.

The Java client Hector by Ran Tavory is named for Cassandra's brother.

Chiton

In ancient Greece, a chiton was a cloth garment, typically sleeveless, worn by both men and women. It is the namesake for the open source project Chiton by Brandon Williams, which is a Python GTK-based browser for Apache Cassandra. It is currently hosted at *http://github.com/driftx/chiton*.

A related project is Telephus, a low-level client API for Cassandra written in Twisted Python. It is currently hosted at *http://github.com/driftx/Telephus*.

Cluster

A cluster is two or more Cassandra instances acting in concert. These instances communicate with one another using Gossip.

When you configure a new instance to introduce to your cluster, you'll need to do a few things. First, indicate a Seed Node. Next, indicate the ports on which Cassandra should listen for two things: Gossip and the Thrift interface. Once your cluster is configured, use the Node Tool to verify that it is set up correctly.

Column

A column is the most basic unit of representation in the Cassandra data model. A column is a triplet of a name (sometimes referred to as a "key"), a value, and a timestamp. A column's values, including the timestamp, are all supplied by the client. The data type for the name and value are Java byte arrays. The data type for the timestamp is a long primitive. Columns are immutable in order to prevent multithreading issues.

Columns are organized into column families.

The column is defined in Cassandra by the org.apache.cassandra.db.IColumn interface, which allows a variety of operations, including getting the value of the column as a byte[] or getting its subcolumns as a

`Collection<IColumn>`, and finding the time of the most recent change.

Columns are sorted by their type, which is one of `AsciiType`, `BytesType`, `LexicalUUID Type`, `LongType`, `TimeUUIDType`, `UTF8Type`.

See also Column Family.

Column Family

A column family is roughly analogous to a table in a relational model. It is a container for an ordered collection of columns.

Because each column family is stored in a separate file, be sure to define columns that you are likely to access together in the same column family.

You define your application's column families in the Cassandra configuration file. You can supply global (per-keyspace) values for the size of the row cache, the size of the key cache, and the "read repair chance." Column families can be one of two types: standard or super.

See also Column, Keyspace, Super Column.

Column Name

The name part of the name/value pair stored within a Row.

Column Value

The value part of the name/value pair stored within a Row. The size of a column value is limited by machine memory.

Commit Log

The commit log is responsible for all of the write operations in Cassandra. When you perform a write, it first enters the commit log so the data won't be lost in the event of failure; then the value is populated in the memtable so it's available in memory for performance. Once the Memtable fills up, the data is flushed to the SSTable.

It is represented by the `org.apache.cassandra.db.commitlog.CommitLog` class. On every write or delete, an entry in the form of a `RowMutation` object is serialized and appended to the commit log. These objects are organized into commit log segments. By default, commit logs roll once they reach a size threshold of 128MB; when a new commit log is created, it accepts writes in transit. This setting is configurable.

Compaction

Compaction is the process of freeing up space by merging large accumulated data-files. This is roughly analogous to rebuilding a table in the relational world. On compaction, the merged data is sorted, a new index is created over the sorted data, and the freshly merged, sorted, and indexed data is written to a single new file.

The operations that are performed during compaction to free up space include merging keys, combining columns, and deleting tombstones. This process is managed by the class `org.apache.cassandra.db.Compaction Manager`. `CompactionManager` implements an MBean interface so it can be introspected.

There are different types of compaction in Cassandra.

A *major* compaction is triggered in one of two ways: via a node probe or automatically. A node probe sends a TreeRequest message to the nodes that neighbor the target. When a node receives a TreeRequest, it immediately performs a *read-only compaction* in order to validate the column family.

A read-only compaction has the following steps:

1. Get the key distribution from the column family.

2. Once the rows have been added to the validator, if the column family needs to be validated, it will create the Merkle tree and broadcast it to the neighboring nodes.

3. The Merkle trees are brought together in a "rendezvous" as a list of `Differenc ers` (trees that need validating or comparison).

4. The comparison is executed by the `StageManager` class, which is responsible for handling concurrency issues in

executing jobs. In this case, the `Stage Manager` uses an anti-entropy stage. This uses the `org.apache.cassandra.concurrent.JMXEnabledThreadPoolExecutor` class, which executes the compaction within a single thread and makes the operation available as an MBean for inspection.

Compression

Data compression on return is on the road map for future versions, but as of 0.6 it is not yet supported.

Consistency

Consistency means that a transaction does not leave the database in an illegal state, and that no integrity constraints are violated. This is considered a crucial aspect of transactions in relational databases and is one of the ACID properties (Atomic, Consistent, Isolated, Durable). In Cassandra, the relative degree of consistency can be calculated by the following:

N = the number of nodes that store replicas of the data

W = the number of replicas that must acknowledge receipt of a write before it can be said to be successful

R = the number of replicas that are contacted when a data object is accessed in a read operation

W + R > N = strong consistency

W + R <= N = eventual consistency

Consistency Level

This configurable setting allows you to decide how many replicas in the cluster must acknowledge a write operation or respond to a read operation in order to be considered successful. The consistency level is set according to your stated Replication Factor, not the raw number of nodes in the cluster.

There are multiple levels of consistency that you can tune for performance. The best-performing level has the lowest consistency level. They mean different things for writing and reading. This is covered in Chapter 7.

For write operations:

- ZERO: Write operations will be handled in the background, asynchronously. This is the fastest way to write data, and the one that offers the least confidence that your operations will succeed.

- ANY: This level was introduced in Cassandra 0.6 and means that you can be assured that your write operation was successful on at least one node, even if the acknowledgment is only for a hint (see Hinted Handoff). This is a relatively weak level of consistency.

- ONE: Ensures that the write operation was written to at least one node, including its commit log and memtable. If a single node responds, the operation is considered successful.

- QUORUM: A quorum is a number of nodes that represents consensus on an operation. It is determined by `<ReplicationFactor>` / 2 + 1. So if you have a replication factor of 10, then 6 replicas would have to acknowledge the operation to gain a quorum.

- DCQUORUM: A version of quorum that prefers replicas in the *same* data center in order to balance the high consistency level of quorum with the lower latency of preferring to perform operations on replicas in the same data center.

- ALL: Every node as specified in your `<ReplicationFactor>` configuration entry must successfully acknowledge the write operation. If any nodes do not acknowledge the write operation, the write fails. This has the highest level of consistency and the lowest level of performance.

For read operations:

- ONE: This returns the value on the first node that responds. Performs a read repair in the background.

- QUORUM: Queries all nodes and returns the record with the most recent timestamp after a quorum of nodes have responded, where a "quorum" is $(n/2) + 1$.

- DCQUORUM: Ensures that only nodes in the same data center are queried. Applicable when using Rack-Aware placement strategy.

- ALL: Queries all nodes and returns the value with the most recent timestamp. This level waits for all nodes to respond, and if one doesn't, it fails the read operation.

Note that there is no such thing as READ ZERO, as it doesn't make sense to specify that you want to read some data and don't need any node to respond.

Data Center Shard Strategy
See Replication Strategy.

Decentralized
Cassandra is considered decentralized because it defines no master server, and instead uses a peer-to-peer approach in order to prevent bottlenecks and single points of failure. Decentralization is important in Cassandra because it is what allows it to scale up and also to scale down; peers can enter or exit the cluster as they like, with minimal disruption.

Denormalization
In relational databases, denormalization, or the creation of redundant data, is sometimes applied in order to improve performance of read-mostly applications, such as in online analytical processing (OLAP). In Cassandra, it is typical to see denormalized data, as this improves performance and helps account for the fact that data is structured according to the queries you'll need, in distinction to standard relational databases where the data is typically structured around the object model independently.

Durability
When a database is durable, it means that writes will permanently survive, even in the event of a server crash or sudden power failure.

Cassandra accomplishes durability by appending writes to the end of the commit log, allowing the server to avoid having to seek the location in the data file. Only the commit log needs to be synced with the file system, and this happens either periodically or in a specified batch window.

When working in a single server node, Cassandra does not immediately synchronize a file's in-core state with the storage device. That can mean that if the server is shut down immediately after a write is performed, the write may not be present on restart. Note that a single server node is not recommended for production.

See also Commit Log.

Dynamo
Created in 2006 by Amazon and, along with Google's Bigtable, a primary basis for Cassandra. From Dynamo, Cassandra gets the following: a key-value store, a symmetric peer-to-peer architecture, gossip-based discovery, eventual consistency, and tunability per operation.

You can read the complete paper "Dynamo: Amazon's Highly Available Key-Value Store" at *http://www.allthingsdistributed.com/2007/10/amazons_dynamo.html*.

Elastic
Read and write throughput can increase linearly as more machines are added to the cluster.

Eventual Consistency
Consistency is the property that describes the internal integrity of the data following an operation. In practical terms for a strongly consistent database, this means that once a client has performed a write operation, all readers will immediately see the new value. In eventual consistency, the

database will not generally be consistent immediately, but rather eventually (where "eventually" is typically a matter of the small number of milliseconds it takes to send the new value to all replicas, relative to the amount of data, the number of nodes, and the geographical distribution of those nodes). DNS is an example of a popular eventually consistent architecture. Eventual consistency is sometimes called "weak consistency."

Eventual consistency has become popular in the last few years because it offers the ability to support massive scalability. Although it is possible to achieve high scalability in traditional fully consistent databases, the management overhead can become a burden. Of course, eventual consistency presents certain disadvantages, such as additional complexity in the programming model.

Though the design of eventual consistency in Cassandra is based on how it is used in Amazon's Dynamo, Cassandra is probably better characterized as "tuneably" consistent, rather than eventually consistent. That is, Cassandra allows you to configure the Consistency Level across the spectrum—including ensuring that Cassandra blocks until all replicas are readable (which is equivalent to full consistency).

Riak, Voldemort, MongoDB, Yahoo!'s HBase, CouchDB, Microsoft's Dynomite, and Amazon's SimpleDB/Dynamo are other eventually consistent data stores.

Failure Detection

Failure detection is the process of determining which nodes in a distributed fault-tolerant system have failed. Cassandra's implementation is based on the idea of Accrual Failure Detection, first advanced by the Advanced Institute of Science and Technology in Japan in 2004. Accrual failure detection is based on two primary ideas: that failure detection should be flexible by being decoupled from the application being monitored, and outputting a continuous level of "suspicion" regarding how confident the monitor is that a node has failed. This is desirable because it can take into account fluctuations in the network environment. Suspicion offers a more fluid and proactive indication of the weaker or stronger possibility of failure based on interpretation (the sampling of heartbeats), as opposed to a simple binary assessment.

Failure detection is implemented in Cassandra by the `org.apache.cassandra.gms.FailureDetector` class.

You can read the original Phi Accrual Failure Detection paper at *http://ddg.jaist.ac.jp/pub/HDY+04.pdf*.

Fault Tolerance

Fault tolerance is the system's ability to continue operating in the event of a failure of one or more of its components. Fault tolerance is also referred to as graceful degradation, meaning that if the system operation degrades following a failure, the degraded performance is relative only to the failed component(s).

Gossip

The gossiper is responsible for ensuring that all of the nodes in a cluster are aware of the important state information in the other nodes. The gossiper runs every second to ensure that even nodes that have failed or are not yet online are able to receive node states. It is designed to perform predictably, even at sharply increased loads. The gossip protocol supports rebalancing of keys across the nodes and supports Failure Detection. Gossip is an important part of the anti-entropy strategy.

The state information that the gossiper shares is structured as key/value pairs. In Cassandra, the gossip protocol continues to gossip state information to other nodes until it is made obsolete by newer data.

When a server node is started, it registers itself with the gossiper. For more information, check out the `org.apache.cassandra.service.StorageService` class.

Also see the Amazon paper on gossip at *http://www.cs.cornell.edu/home/rvr/papers/flow gossip.pdf*.

Hector

An open source project created by Ran Tavory of Outbrain and hosted at GitHub, Hector is a Cassandra client written in Java. It wraps Thrift and offers JMX, connection pooling, and failover.

Hinted Handoff

This is a mechanism to ensure availability, fault tolerance, and graceful degradation. If a write operation occurs and a node that is intended to receive that write goes down, a note (the "hint") is given ("handed off") to a different live node to indicate that it should replay the write operation to the unavailable node when it comes back online. This does two things: it reduces the amount of time that it takes for a node to get all the data it missed once it comes back online, and it improves write performance in lower consistency levels. That is, a hinted handoff does not count as a sufficient acknowledgment for a write operation if the consistency level is set to ONE, QUORUM, or ALL. A hint does count as a write for consistency level ANY, however. Another way of putting this is that hinted writes are not readable in and of themselves.

The node that received the hint will know very quickly when the unavailable node comes back online again, because of Gossip. If, for some reason, the hinted handoff doesn't work, the system can still perform a read repair.

Key

See Row Key.

Keyspace

A keyspace is a container for column families. It is roughly analogous to the database in the relational model, used in Cassandra to separate applications. Where a relational database is a collection of tables, a keyspace is an ordered collection of column families. You define your application's keyspace in the Cassandra configuration file or by using the definition methods in the API. When you define a keyspace, you can also define its replication factor and its replica placement strategy. Within a given Cassandra cluster, you can have one or more keyspaces, typically one for each application.

See also Column Family.

Lexicographic Ordering

Lexicographic ordering is the natural (alphabetic) ordering of the product of two ordered Cartesian sets.

Memtable

An in-memory representation of data that has been recently written. Once the memtable is full, it is flushed to disk as an SSTable.

Merkle Tree

Perhaps better known as a "hash tree," a Merkle tree is a binary tree data structure that summarizes in short form the data in a larger dataset. In a hash tree, the leaves are the data blocks (typically files on a filesystem) to be summarized. Every parent node in the tree is a hash of its direct child node, which tightly compacts the summary.

In Cassandra, the Merkle tree is implemented in the `org.apache.cassandra.utils.MerkleTree` class.

Merkle trees are used in Cassandra to ensure that the peer-to-peer network of nodes receives data blocks unaltered and unharmed. They are used in cryptography as well to verify the contents of files and transmissions, and are used in the Google Wave product. They are named for their inventor, Ralph Merkle.

Multiget

Query by column name for a set of keys.

Multiget Slice

Query to get a subset of columns for a set of keys.

Node

An instance of Cassandra. Typically a Cassandra cluster will have many nodes, sometimes collectively called the node ring, or just "the ring." A node refers to any Cassandra server in a cluster, whereas "replica" refers to a node that specifically has a copy of some data from another node.

Node Tool

This is an executable file with the path *bin/ nodetool* that inspects a cluster to determine whether it is properly configured and performs a variety of maintenance operations. The commands available on `nodetool` are `cleanup`, `clearsnapshot`, `compact`, `cfstats`, `decommission`, `drain`, `flush`, `info`, `loadba lance`, `move`, `repair`, `ring`, `snapshot [snap shotname]`, `removetoken`, and `tpstats`.

For example, you can use `nodetool drain` to prevent the commit log from accepting any new writes.

NoSQL

"NoSQL" is a general name for the collection of databases that do not use Structured Query Language (SQL) or a relational data model. It is sometimes used to mean "Not *Only* SQL" to indicate that the proponents of various nonrelational databases do not suggest that relational databases are a bad choice—but rather that they are not the only choice for data storage. This term was coined by Cassandra committer Eric Evans of Rackspace, but he has since distanced himself from the term in preference of the term "Big Data" to highlight the fact that this family of nonrelational databases is defined not by what they're not (implementations of SQL), but rather by what they do (handle huge data loads). This term, in my view, has reached the end of its useful life, because it's confusing. It has proven too tempting to discuss a set of databases together that really have few goals, design decisions, or features in common. Let Cassandra be Cassandra, let CouchDB be CouchDB, and let Riak be Riak.

Order-Preserving Partitioner

This is a kind of **Partitioner** that stores rows by key order, aligning the physical structure of the data with your sort order. Configuring your column family to use order-preserving partitioning allows you to perform range slices, meaning that Cassandra knows which nodes have which keys.

This partitioner is somewhat the opposite of the **Random Partitioner**; it has the advantage of allowing for efficient range queries, but the disadvantage of unevenly distributing keys.

The order-preserving partitioner (OPP) is implemented by the `org.apache.cassandra .dht.OrderPreservingPartitioner`class.

There is a special kind of OPP called the *collating order-preserving partitioner* (COPP). This acts like a regular OPP, but sorts the data in a collated manner according to English/US lexicography instead of byte ordering. For this reason, it is useful for locale-aware applications. The COPP is implemented by the `org.apache.cassandra .dht.CollatingOrderPreservingParti tioner` class.

This is implemented in Cassandra by `org.apache.cassandra.dht.OrderPreser vingPartitioner`.

See also **Token**.

Partition

In general terms, a partition refers to a *network partition*, which is a break in the network that prevents one machine from interacting directly with another. A partition can be caused by failed switches, routers, or network interfaces. Consider a cluster of five machines {A, B, C, D, E} where {A, B} are on one subnet and {C, D, E} are on a second subnet. If the switch to which {C, D, E} are connected fails, then you have a network partition that isolates the two subclusters {A, B} and {C, D, E}.

Cassandra is a fault-tolerant database, and network partitions are one such fault. As such, it is able to continue operating in the face of a network partition and merge data in replication once the partition is healed again.

Partitioner

The partitioner controls how your data is distributed over your nodes. In order to find a set of keys, Cassandra must know what nodes have the range of values you're looking for. There are three types of partitioner: random partitioner, which is the default; order-preserving partitioner; and collating order-preserving partitioner. You configure this in *storage-conf.xml* or *cassandra.yaml* (for 0.7) using the `<Partitioner>` element: `<Partitioner>org.apache.cassandra.dht.RandomPartitioner</Partitioner>`. Note that partitioning applies to the sorting of row keys, not columns.

Once you have chosen a partitioner type, you cannot change it without destroying your data (because an SSTable is immutable).

See also Order-Preserving Partitioner and Random Partitioner.

Quorum

A majority of nodes that respond to an operation. This is a configurable consistency level. In a quorum read, the proxy waits for a majority of nodes to respond with the same value. This makes for a slower read operation, but also helps ensure that you don't get returned stale data.

Rack-Aware Strategy

See Replication Strategy.

Random Partitioner

This is a kind of Partitioner that uses a `BigIntegerToken` with an MD5 hash to determine where to place the keys on the node ring. This has the advantage of spreading your keys evenly across your cluster, but the disadvantage of causing inefficient range queries. This is the default partitioner.

See also Partitioner and Order-Preserving Partitioner.

Range Slice

Query to get a subset of columns for a range of keys.

Read Repair

This is another mechanism to ensure consistency throughout the node ring. In a read operation, if Cassandra detects that some nodes have responded with data that is inconsistent with the response of other, newer nodes, it makes a note to perform a read repair on the old nodes. The read repair means that Cassandra will send a write request to the nodes with stale data to get them up to date with the newer data returned from the original read operation. It does this by pulling all the data from the node, performing a merge, and writing the merged data back to the nodes that were out of sync. The detection of inconsistent data is made by comparing timestamps and checksums.

The method for reconciliation is the `org.apache.cassandra.streaming` package.

Replication

In general distributed systems terms, replication refers to storing multiple copies of data on multiple machines so that if one machine fails or becomes unavailable due to a Partition, the cluster can still make data available. Caching is a simple form of replication. In Cassandra, replication is a means of providing high performance and availability/fault-tolerance.

Replication Factor

Cassandra offers a configurable replication factor, which allows you essentially to decide how much you want to pay in performance to gain more consistency. That is, your consistency level for reading and writing data is based on the replication factor, as it refers to the number of nodes across which you have replicated data. The replication factor is set in the configuration file or the API.

See also Consistency Level.

Replication Strategy

The replication strategy, sometimes referred to as the placement strategy, determines how replicas will be distributed. The first replica is always placed in the node claiming the key range of its Token. All remaining replicas are distributed according to a configurable replication strategy.

The Gang of Four Strategy pattern is employed to allow a pluggable means of replication, but Cassandra comes with three out of the box. Choosing the right replication strategy is important because in determining which nodes are responsible for which key ranges, you're also determining which nodes should receive write operations; this has a big impact on efficiency in different scenarios. The variety of pluggable strategies allows you greater flexibility, so that you can tune Cassandra according to your network topology and needs.

Replication strategies are an extension of the `org.apache.cassandra.locator.AbstractReplicationStrategy` class. You can write your own replication strategy if you like by extending that class.

The replication placement strategy is configured per keyspace using the `<ReplicaPlacementStrategy>` element. They are discussed in depth in Chapter 6.

Row

In a column family, a row is a sorted map that matches column names to column values. In a super column, a row is a sorted map that matches super column names to maps matching column names to column values. The Row Key defines the individual row, and the row defines the name/value pairs of the columns. The size of a single row cannot exceed the amount of space on disk.

Rows are sorted by their Partitioner, which is one of these types: `RandomPartitioner`, `OrderPreservingPartitioner`, or `CollatingOrderPreservingPartitioner`.

Rows are defined by the class `org.apache.cassandra.db.Row`.

See also Row Key.

Row Key

Sometimes called simply "key," a row key is analogous to a primary key for an object in the relational model. It represents a way to identify a single row of columns and is an arbitrary length string.

In the Thrift interface, the Java client always assumes that row keys are encoded as UTF-8, but this is not the case for clients in other languages, where you may need to manually encode ASCII strings as UTF-8.

SEDA (Staged Event-Driven Architecture)

Cassandra employs a Staged Event-Driven Architecture to gain massive throughput under highly concurrent conditions. SEDA attempts to overcome the overhead associated with threads. This overhead is due to scheduling, lock contention, and cache misses. The effect of SEDA is that work is not started and completed by the same thread; this can make a more complex code base, but also yield better performance. Therefore, much of the key work in Cassandra—such as reading, mutation, gossiping, memtable flushing, and compaction—are performed as stages (the "S" in SEDA). A stage is essentially a separated event queue.

As events enter the incoming queue, the event handler supplied by the application is invoked. The controller is capable of dynamically tuning the number of threads allocated to each stage as demand dictates.

The advantages of SEDA are higher concurrency and better management of CPU, disk, and network resources.

You can read more about SEDA as it was originally proposed by Matt Welsh, David Culler, and Eric Brewer at *http://www.eecs.harvard.edu/~mdw/proj/seda*.

See also Stage.

Seed Node

A seed is a node that already exists in a Cassandra cluster and is used by newly added nodes to get up and running. The newly added node can start gossiping with the seed node to get state information and learn the topology of the node ring. There may be many seeds in a cluster.

Slice

This is a type of read query. Use `get_slice()` to query by a single column name or a range of column names. Use `get_range_slice()` to return a subset of columns for a range of keys.

Snitch

A *snitch* is Cassandra's way of mapping a node to a physical location in the network. It helps determine the location of a node relative to another node in order to assist with discovery and ensure efficient request routing. There are different kinds of snitches. The `EndpointSnitch` (or `RackInferringSnitch`), for instance, determines whether two nodes are in the same data center or the same rack. Its strategy for doing so is essentially to guess at the relative distance of two nodes in a data center and rack based on reading the second and third octets of their IP addresses.

The `DataCenterEndpointSnitch` allows you to specify IP subnets for racks, grouped by which data center the racks are in.

The `PropertyFileSnitch` allows you to map IP addresses to rack and data centers in a properties file called *cassandra-rack.properties*.

The snitch strategy classes can be found in the `org.apache.cassandra.locator` package.

Sparse

In the relational model, every data type (table) must have a value for every column, even if that value is sometimes `null`. Cassandra, on the other hand, represents a sparse or "schema-free" data model, which means that rows may have values for as many or as few of the defined columns as you like. This allows for a degree of efficiency. For example, consider a 1000 × 1000 cell spreadsheet, similar to a relational table. If many of the cells have empty values, the storage model is inefficient.

SSTable

SSTable stands for Sorted String Table. Inherited from Google's Bigtable, an SSTable is how data is stored on disk in Cassandra. It is a log that allows only appending. In-memory tables (memtables) are used in front of SSTables for buffering and sorting data. SSTables allow for high performance on writes and can be compacted.

SSTables are immutable. Once a memtable is flushed to disk as an SSTable, it cannot be changed by the application; Compaction changes only their on-disk representation.

To import or export data from JavaScript Object Notation (JSON), check out the classes `org.apache.cassandra.tools.SSTable Importer` and `SSTableExporter`.

Stage

Part of Cassandra's Staged Event-Driven Architecture (SEDA), a *stage* wraps a basic unit of work. A single operation can flow between various stages to complete, rather than getting completed in the same thread that started the work.

A stage consists of an incoming event queue, an event handler, and an associated thread pool. Stages are managed by a controller that determines scheduling and thread allocation; Cassandra implements this kind of concurrency model using the thread pool `java.util.concurrent.ExecutorService`. To see specifically how this works, check out the `org.apache.cassandra.concurrent.Stage Manager` class.

A few additional operations are implemented as stages too, including working with memtables in the `ColumnFamilyStore` class, and the consistency manager is a stage in the `StorageService`.

An operation may start with one thread, which then hands off the work to another thread, which may hand it off to other threads. This handing-off is not directly between threads, however; it occurs between stages.

See also SEDA (Staged Event-Driven Architecture).

Strong Consistency

For reads, strong consistency means that if it is detected that a repair needs to be made, first perform the read repair, then return the result.

Super Column

A super column is a column whose value is not a string, but instead a named list of other columns, which in this context are called subcolumns. The subcolumns are ordered, and the number of columns you can define is unbounded. Super columns also differ from regular columns in that they do not have an associated timestamp.

Super columns are not recursive; that is, they go only one level deep. A super column can hold a map only of other columns, and not a map of more super columns.

They are defined in *SuperColumn.java*, which implements both the `IColumn` and `IColumnContainer` interfaces. The interface allows you to perform a variety of operations, including the following: get all of the subcolumns in a super column, get a single subcolumn by name, add a subcolumn, remove a subcolumn, check the number of subcolumns in the super column, and check when a subcolumn was last modified.

super columns were one of the updates added by Facebook to the original data model of Google's Bigtable.

See also Column Family.

Thrift

Thrift is the name of the RPC client used to communicate with the Cassandra server. It statically generates an interface for serialization in a variety of languages, including C ++, Java, Python, PHP, Ruby, Erlang, Perl, Haskell, C#, Cocoa, Smalltalk, and OCaml. It is this mechanism that allows you to interact with Cassandra from any of these client languages.

It was created in April 2007 at Facebook and donated to Apache as an incubator project in May 2008. At the time of this writing, the Thrift interface is most likely being replaced by the newer and more active Apache project Avro. Another advantage of Avro is that it does not require static code generation.

You can read more about Thrift on its project page at *http://incubator.apache.org/ thrift*.

Timestamp

In Cassandra, timestamps for column values are supplied by the client, so it is important to synchronize client clocks. The timestamp is by convention the number of microseconds since the Unix epoch (midnight, January 1, 1970).

Token

Each node in the node ring has a single token that is used to claim a range of keys, based on the value of the token in the previous node in the ring. You can specify your own token or let Cassandra generate one for you. The representation of the token is dependent on the kind of partitioner used.

With a Random Partitioner, the token is an integer in the range $0-2^{127}$, generated by applying an MD5 hash on keys. This is represented by the `org.apache.cassandra.dht.BigIn tegerToken` class.

With an Order-Preserving Partitioner, the token is a UTF-8 string, based on the key. This is represented by the `org.apache.cassandra .dht.StringToken` class.

Tokens are represented in Cassandra by the `org.apache.cassandra.dht.Token` class.

Tombstone

Cassandra does not immediately delete data following a delete operation. Instead, it marks the data with a "tombstone," an indicator that the column has been deleted but not removed entirely yet. The tombstone can then be propagated to other replicas.

Tombstones are discarded on major Compaction.

Vector Clock

Vector clocks allow for partial, causal ordering of events in a distributed system. A vector clock maintains an array of logical clocks, one for each process, and each process contains a local copy of the clock.

In order to keep the entire set of processes in a consistent logical state, one process will send its clock to another process, which is then updated. In order to ensure consistency, some version of the following steps are typically followed.

All clocks start at 0. Each time a process experiences an event, its clock is incremented by 1. Each time a process prepares to send a message, this too counts as an event, so it increments its clock by 1 and then sends its entire vector to the external process along with the message. Each time a process receives a message, this too counts as an event, so it updates its own clock by 1 and then compares its vector to the vector wrapped in the incoming message from the external process. It updates its own clock with the maximum value from the comparison.

A vector clock event synchronization strategy will likely be introduced in a future version of Cassandra.

Weak Consistency

For reads, weak consistency improves performance by first returning results, and afterward performing any necessary **Read Repair**.

Index

We'd like to hear your suggestions for improving our indexes. Send email to *index@oreilly.com*.

About the Author

Eben Hewitt is the Director of Application Architecture for a global corporation, where he is responsible for system strategy and design. He has contributed documentation to the Apache Cassandra project and is the author of several technology books, including *Java SOA Cookbook* (O'Reilly). He contributed to *97 Things Every Software Architect Should Know* (O'Reilly) and has served as technical reviewer for several software books. Eben has been in IT for 12 years and has designed and implemented large-scale distributed systems across several domains, including retail, travel, government, and ISPs. He has been an invited speaker on Cassandra, SOA, REST, and event-driven architecture at many industry conferences in Asia and throughout the US and has been interviewed about these topics on leading industry sites. You can follow Eben on Twitter at @ebenhewitt.

Colophon

The bird on the cover of *Cassandra: The Definitive Guide* is a Paradise flycatcher. Part of the family of monarch flycatchers (*Monarchidae*), Paradise flycatchers are passerine (perching) insectivores. They're the most widely distributed of the monarch flycatchers and can be found from sub-Saharan Africa to Southeast Asia and on many Pacific islands. While most species are resident, others, including the Japanese Paradise flycatcher and the Satin flycatcher, are migratory.

Most species of Paradise flycatcher are sexually dimorphic, meaning that males and females look different. Females of most species tend to be less brilliantly colored than their male counterparts, which are also characterized by long tail feathers that vary in length according to species. For example, the male Asian Paradise flycatcher's tail streamers can be approximately 15 inches long. Female flycatchers are believed to select their mate based on tail length. Paradise flycatchers are monogamous, which makes their distinctive coloring and plumage unusual, as this form of sexual display is usually reserved for nonmonogamous species.

Because they're so widely distributed, Paradise flycatchers can be found in a variety of habitats, including savannas, bamboo groves, rain forests, deciduous forests, and even cultivated gardens. Most species catch their food on the wing, thanks in part to their quick reflexes and sharp eyesight.

The cover image is from *Cassell's Natural History, Vol. IV*. The cover font is Adobe ITC Garamond. The text font is Linotype Birka; the heading font is Adobe Myriad Condensed; and the code font is LucasFont's TheSansMonoCondensed.

Related Titles from O'Reilly

   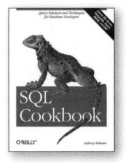

Database

The Art of SQL

Database in Depth

Essential SQLAlchemy

FileMaker Pro 9: The Missing Manual

Head First SQL

High Performance MySQL, *2nd Edition*

Learning MySQL

Learning PHP & MySQL, *2nd Edition*

Learning SQL

Managing & Using MySQL, *2nd Edition*

MySQL Cookbook, *2nd Edition*

MySQL in a Nutshell, *2nd Edition*

MySQL Pocket Reference, *2nd Edition*

MySQL Reference Manual

MySQL Stored Procedure Programming

Oracle Essentials, *4th Edition*

Oracle PL/SQL Best Practices, *2nd Edition*

Oracle PL/SQL Language Pocket Reference, *4th Edition*

Practical PostgreSQL

Programming SQL Server 2005

Refactoring SQL Applications

SQL and Relational Theory

SQL Cookbook

SQL in a Nutshell, *2nd Edition*

SQL Pocket Guide, *2nd Edition*

SQL Tuning

Understanding MySQL Internals

Get even more for your money.

Join the O'Reilly Community, and register the O'Reilly books you own. It's free, and you'll get:

- $4.99 ebook upgrade offer
- 40% upgrade offer on O'Reilly print books
- Membership discounts on books and events
- Free lifetime updates to ebooks and videos
- Multiple ebook formats, DRM FREE
- Participation in the O'Reilly community
- Newsletters
- Account management
- 100% Satisfaction Guarantee

Signing up is easy:

1. **Go to: oreilly.com/go/register**
2. **Create an O'Reilly login.**
3. **Provide your address.**
4. **Register your books.**

Note: English-language books only

To order books online:
oreilly.com/store

For questions about products or an order:
orders@oreilly.com

To sign up to get topic-specific email announcements and/or news about upcoming books, conferences, special offers, and new technologies:
elists@oreilly.com

For technical questions about book content:
booktech@oreilly.com

To submit new book proposals to our editors:
proposals@oreilly.com

O'Reilly books are available in multiple DRM-free ebook formats. For more information:
oreilly.com/ebooks

O'REILLY®

Spreading the knowledge of innovators   oreilly.com

Buy this book and get access to the online edition for 45 days—for free!

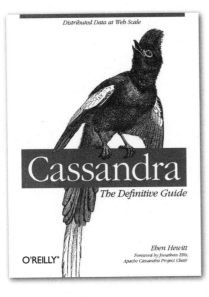

Distributed Data at Web Scale

Cassandra
The Definitive Guide

Eben Hewitt
Foreword by Jonathan Ellis,
Apache Cassandra Project Chair

O'REILLY®

Cassandra: The Definitive Guide
By Eben Hewitt
November 2010, $39.99
ISBN 9781449390419

With Safari Books Online, you can:

Access the contents of thousands of technology and business books

- Quickly search over 7000 books and certification guides
- Download whole books or chapters in PDF format, at no extra cost, to print or read on the go
- Copy and paste code
- Save up to 35% on O'Reilly print books
- **New!** Access mobile-friendly books directly from cell phones and mobile devices

Stay up-to-date on emerging topics before the books are published

- Get on-demand access to evolving manuscripts.
- Interact directly with authors of upcoming books

Explore thousands of hours of video on technology and design topics

- Learn from expert video tutorials
- Watch and replay recorded conference sessions

To try out Safari and the online edition of this book FREE for 45 days,
go to *www.oreilly.com/go/safarienabled* and enter the coupon code MSFOZBI.
To see the complete Safari Library, visit safari.oreilly.com.

O'REILLY®

Spreading the knowledge of innovators   safari.oreilly.com